C000277352

Tort

YOU'VE GOT IT
CRACKED

Nutshells – your essential revision and starter guides

* Presents you with the essentials of law in clear and straightforward language, explaining the basic principles

* Incorporates colour to help distinguish cases and legislation and aid ease of use

* Breaks the text down into bite-size chunks and includes bullets where appropriate to aid navigation, assimilation and retention of information

* Opens each chapter with a short introduction to outline the key concepts covered and condense complex and important information

* Closes each chapter with a checklist to enable you to check that all your learning needs have been met

* Provides a model question with answer plan at the end of each chapter to enable you to fully prepare for both exam and essay questions

* Includes diagrams throughout to illustrate difficult concepts

* Places important key definitions and statutory provisions in boxes to help highlight the key points to remember

* Contains a host of useful tools including tables of cases and statutes, a list of examination tips, and a list of useful web resources

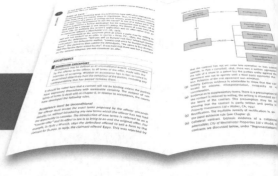

NUT**CASES**

Tort

SIXTH EDITION

VERA BERMINGHAM, MA, NTF
Director of Studies
Kingston Law School

SWEET & MAXWELL

THOMSON REUTERS

First Edition – 1996
Second Edition – 1999
Second Edition – 2002
Fourth Edition – 2005
Fifth Edition – 2008

Published in 2011 by Thomson Reuters (Professional UK) Limited (Registered in England & Wales, Company No 1679046. Registered Office and address for service: 100 Avenue Road, London NW3 3PF) trading as Sweet & Maxwell

For further information on our products and services, visit www.sweetandmaxwell.co.uk

Typeset by YHT Ltd, London
Printed in The Netherlands by Ten Brink, Meppel

*No natural forests were destroyed to make this product;
only farmed timber was used and re-planted.*

A CIP catalogue record for this book is available from the British Library.

ISBN 978-0-41404-485-2

Thomson Reuters and the Thomson Reuters logo are trademarks of Thomson Reuters. Sweet & Maxwell ® is a registered trademark of Thompson Reuters (Professional UK) Limited

Contents

Using this Book

Welcome to our new look NUTCASE revision series. We have revamped and improved the existing design and layout and added new features, according to student feedback.

NEW DETAILED TABLE OF CONTENTS for easy navigation.

REDESIGNED TABLES OF CASES AND LEGISLATION for easy reference.

NEW CHAPTER INTRODUCTIONS to outline
the key concepts covered and condense
complex and important information.

10

Protection of
in Land

INTRODUCTION

The estates and interests cap
Law of Property Act 1925. W'
law depends on its requi·
on the Formal and In'
Upon th

THINK POINT

Although an owner of land owns t.
to the heavens, there are statutory
the land. Think about what these ai
use of the land.

In addition, other third party ri
owner's use of the land. Consid
be.

NEW BOXED "THINK POINT"
throughout with further case
analysis and questions
to encourage critical thinking.

.ι tests for whethe·
ιe two tests set out in *Holland*
ιords in *Elitestone Ltd v Morris* [1997]
ecided that a bungalow erected on pillar:
These cases were also approved in *Che*
(2000) 22 E.G. 147, where it was held that a ho
ropes and connected to utilities was a chatte·
nature of the tenancy of a houseboat was
annexation. In *Cinderella Rockerfellas Ltd v Ruc*
decided that a vessel which was moored per
of the land for the purpose of assessing its ·
at it was nonetheless a chattel rather th
for rating purposes.
·ssex Reserve Forces & Cade·

NEW COLOUR CODING throughout
to help distinguish cases and
legislation from the narrative.
At the first mention, cases are
highlighted in colour and italicised
and legislation is highlighted in
colour and emboldened.

Table of Cases

Table of Statutes

Trespass to Person

INTRODUCTION

Trespass is one of the oldest torts which protects physical interests from direct and intentional harm. The tort takes three forms: trespass to the person, trespass to land, and trespass to goods which reflect the fact that one of the main functions of the tort of trespass was to protect interests in land, person, or property. Trespass requires an *intentional* and *direct* act and all forms of trespass are actionable per se (meaning that a claimant can succeed in an action in trespass even if no particular damage can be proved). An action in trespass can be used to protect civil rights, for example, modern cases of trespass to the person are sometimes taken against the police or other public officials to vindicate the claimant's rights rather than to obtain an award of damages in compensation. It should be noted at this point that the tort of negligence provide a remedies for *unintentional* or negligent loss or harm for which the claimant is likely to be seeking damages or compensation.

THE DISTINCTION BETWEEN TRESPASS AND NEGLIGENCE

Key Principle

In addition to the act of interference, trespass requires proof of either intention or negligence.

> **STANLEY V POWELL 1891**
> The defendant had inflicted the injury neither intentionally nor negligently when he fired a shot which ricocheted off a tree and hit the plaintiff.

Held

In confirming that trespass is a fault based tort, Denman J. further held that the burden of proof in negligence was on the plaintiff but in trespass the burden of disproving fault was on the defendant. [1891] 1 Q.B. 86.

Commentary

Whether there could be liability in trespass in the absence of negligence is a matter of some historical dispute. However, this case was interpreted to mean that if the defendant could show that he had not been negligent the plaintiff's claim would fail.

Key Principle

In trespass to the person the burden of proving negligence lies on the plaintiff.

FOWLER V LANNING 1959

Neither intention nor negligence was alleged by the plaintiff who was injured by a shot from the defendant's gun. He argued that in trespass the burden of disproving negligence lay on the plaintiff and his statement of claim merely recorded "the defendant shot the plaintiff".

Held

Since the claim lacked an allegation of intention or negligence, it was struck out as disclosing no cause of action. In this decision Diplock J. removed the supposed advantage of a trespass action, namely that the burden of disproving fault lay with the defendant. [1959] 1 Q.B. 426.

Key Principle

Today, the general principle is that direct intentional acts of interference are dealt with by the tort of trespass. Where acts are unintentional and indirect the action lies in negligence.

LETANG V COOPER 1965

The defendant negligently drove his car over the legs of the plaintiff who was sunbathing on an hotel car park. More than three years later the plaintiff sued the defendant. Personal injury actions for "negligence, nuisance or breach of duty" must be brought within three years under the Limitation Act 1980, but other tort actions are barred only after six years. The plaintiff relied on trespass in an effort to prevent her action from being statute barred.

Held

❖ (CA) Lord Denning, with whom Danckwerths L.J. agreed, held that actions for personal injuries should no longer be divided into trespass (where the harm is direct) and case (for indirect harm) but according to nature of the defendant's conduct. If the conduct was intentional it was trespass. Where the conduct was negligent, the case of action is in negligence and not trespass. [1965] 1 Q.B. 232.

Commentary

The views of Lord Denning and Danckwerths L.J. that where the contact between the plaintiff and defendant was unintentional the claim must be brought in negligence, was approved by the Court of Appeal in *Wilson v Pringle* (1987) (see p.5). Note also, Lord Denning's argument that the phrase "breach of duty" in the **Limitation Act 1980** covered any tort, including trespass, has been decisively rejected by the House of Lords in *Stubbings v Webb* [1993] 1 All E.R. 322.

ASSAULT AND BATTERY

ASSAULT

Key Principle

An assault requires no physical contact, it is essentially conduct which causes the reasonable apprehension of an immediate battery.

> STEPHENS V MYERS 1830
> The plaintiff was chairman of a parish meeting at which it was resolved, by a large majority, to expel the defendant. The defendant became vociferous and advanced towards the plaintiff saying that he would rather pull him out of the chair than be ejected. As he moved to unseat the plaintiff he was prevented by the churchwarden from doing so.

Held

The threat was sufficient to put the plaintiff in reasonable apprehension of an immediate battery. Lord Tindal C.J. stated that "though he was not near enough at the time to have struck him, yet if he was advancing with intent, I think it amounts to an assault in law." [1830] 4 C. & P. 349.

Key Principle

Where the plaintiff has no reasonable belief that the defendant has the intention or ability to carry out the threat immediately, no assault is committed.

> **TUBERVILLE V SAVAGE 1669**
> The defendant placed his hand on his sword and said: "If it were not Assize time, I would not take such language from you."

Held

By his own words the defendant had negated the possibility of a battery. (1669) 1 Mod. Rep. 3.

Commentary

This principle was applied in *Thomas v National Union of Mineworkers* [1986] Ch. 20 where picketing miners made violent gestures at working miners who were being taken into the colliery in buses. It was held that there was no danger of an immediate battery since the working miners were safely in vehicles behind police barricades.

BATTERY

Key Principle

Battery is the actual infliction of unlawful force on another person. Any physical contact, no matter how trivial, is sufficient "force".

> **COLLINS V WILCOCK 1984**
> A woman police officer tried to question a woman whom she suspected of soliciting contrary to the Street Offences Act 1959. When she took hold of the woman's arm in order to detain her and administer a caution, the officer was not exercising a power of arrest.

Held

The officer had gone beyond the scope of her duty in detaining the woman in circumstances short of arresting her and had therefore committed a battery. [1984] 3 All E.R. 374.

THINK POINT

Goff L.J. held the fundamental principle to be that every person's body is inviolate. However, he went on to state that bodily contact was not actionable if it was regarded as "falling within a general exception embracing all physical contact which is generally acceptable in the ordinary conduct of daily life."

Key Principle ....

Unless it is self evident from the act itself, the plaintiff must show the contact to be hostile.

> WILSON V PRINGLE 1987
>
> The defendant schoolboy admitted that as an act of ordinary horseplay in a school corridor he pulled the plaintiff's schoolbag from his shoulder. This caused the plaintiff to fall and suffer a hip injury and he applied for a summary judgment on the ground that the defendant's admission amounted to a clear case of battery to which there was no defence. The trial judge accepted this view and the defendant appealed.

Held ....

❖ (CA) The trial judge had been wrong to grant summary judgment. Croom-Johnson L.J. stated that

> "in battery there must be an intentional touching or contact in one form or another of the plaintiff by the defendant. That touching must be proved to be a hostile touching." [1987] Q.B. 237.

Commentary ....

(1) This decision has been criticised for failing to define what is meant by "hostile". The court gave a number of examples of what is not hostile, but only one example of what it is, but it seems to mean little more than that the defendant wilfully interferes with the plaintiff in a way to which he is known to object. The test has not been well received in the House of Lords, in *F (Mental Patient Sterilisation), Re* [1990] 2 A.C. 1, Lord Goff doubted whether it is correct to say that the touching must be hostile for the purpose of battery. He stated that:

> "A prank that gets out of hand, an over friendly slap on the back, surgical treatment by a surgeon who mistakenly thinks that the patient has consented to it, all these things may transcend the bound of lawfulness, without being characterised as hostile. Indeed, the suggested qualification is difficult to reconcile with the principle that any touching of another's body is, in the absence of lawful excuse, capable of amounting to a battery and a trespass."

(2) The intention required in battery is that the defendant must have intended to commit the act that constitutes the trespass. An intention to hurt the

plaintiff is not necessary. For example, in *Nash v Sheehan* [1953] C.L.R. 3726, the defendant hairdresser was liable in battery when a tone rinse was given to a plaintiff who had requested a permanent wave. *In Livingston v Ministry of Defence* [1984] N.I. 356 the defendant, a soldier, intended to hit someone other than the victim. He was found liable in battery when he fired a baton round at a rioter but missed and struck the plaintiff.

THINK POINT

As well as bodily integrity, the tort of battery protects the plaintiff's dignity. An action can be brought where there is indignity but no physical injury or where the plaintiff's rights have been infringed, for example, in relation to unlawful fingerprinting. In these cases, the plaintiff may only want to establish a principle, rather than to seek compensation and will therefore sue in trespass rather than negligence. Trespass is actionable per se (it is not necessary to prove damage) but in order to succeed in negligence the plaintiff must prove damage.

Key Principle
Where there is no contact or physical force used, liability can arise for any intentionally inflicted bodily harm.

WILKINSON V DOWNTON 1897
The defendant, as a practical joke, told the plaintiff that her husband had been seriously injured in an accident. As a result the plaintiff suffered a severe nervous disorder but the specific requirements of assault and battery, the application, or threat, of force, were not present.

Held
Where an act wilfully calculated to cause physical damage does actually cause such harm there will be liability in trespass. At the time of this case there was no liability in negligence for nervous shock. [1897] 2 Q.B. 57.

Commentary
(1) To amount to acts "calculated to cause harm" under the principle in *Wilkinson v Downton* [1897] 2 Q.B. 57 there must be both actual harm and an

intent to cause damage. In *Wong v Parkside Health NHS Trust* [2001] EWCA Civ 1721; [2003] 3 All E.R. 932, a campaign of rudeness and unfriendliness by colleagues was not regarded as the intentional infliction of harm. Although this decision restricts the principle in *Wilkinson v Downton*, the Protection from Harassment Act 1997 might now apply in circumstances such as the "course of conduct" to which the claimant in *Wong* was subjected (see *Majrowski v Guy's and St Thomas's NHS Trust* (2006) below).

(2) In *Khorasandjian v Bush* [1993] 3 All E.R. 669, a case involving intentional harassment by telephone calls, the Court of Appeal extended the principle in *Wilkinson v Downton*. The plaintiff succeeded because there was a risk that the cumulative effect of the unrestrained telephone calls would cause physical or psychiatric damage.

(3) Subsequently, in *Burris v Azadani* [1995] 4 All E.R. 802, the Court of Appeal recognised harassment as a cause of action.

(4) In *Hunter v Docklands Development Corp* [1997] A.C. 655 (see p.216) the House of Lords was prepared to preserve the rule in *Wilkinson v Downton* as a general cause of action. However, it anticipated that plaintiffs in these cases ought to rely on new statutory provisions contained in the Protection from Harassment Act 1997 rather than on the common law. Nevertheless, in cases where there is a single act of harassment (which is not covered by the act), rather than a Course of Conduct, it may still be open to the plaintiff to rely on *Wilkinson v Downton*.

THINK POINT

Harassment was not fully defined in the 1997 Act but in *Huntingdon Life Sciences v Curtin, The Times*, December 11, 1997, Eadie J. said that the Act was clearly not intended by Parliament to be used to clamp down on the discussion of matters of public interest or upon the rights of political protest and public demonstration. In *Majrowski v Guy's and St Thomas's NHS Trust* (2006) (see p.31) it was held that an employer could be vicariously liable under the Act for harassment committed by one of its employees in the course of employment.

Key Principle

Where no contact or physical force is used, emotional distress is not enough to establish liability for intentionally inflicted bodily harm. Nevertheless, if severe emotional distress causes bodily harm and the defendant either intended this or was reckless as to the consequences, there may be liability.

> WAINWRIGHT V HOME OFFICE 2003
> A mother and son wished to visit a family member who was in prison on remand. The prison governor suspected the prisoner of dealing in drugs in prison and gave instructions that anyone who wanted to visit him had to consent to be strip searched. Although the mother and son agreed to be strip searched, they subsequently alleged emotional distress and post-traumatic stress disorder as a result of the search. The strip search had been carried out in a manner which breached the Prison Service Rules and they both claimed for breach of privacy and the intentional infliction of harm which amounted to a trespass to person.

Held

In dismissing the appeal, the House of Lords:

(1) rejected a general right to of privacy in English common law and stated that the coming into force of the Human Rights Act 1998 weakens the argument for saying that a general tort of invasion of privacy is needed;

(2) stated that even if there was an intention to cause harm, *Wilkinson v Downton* was not authority for the proposition that damages for distress falling short of psychiatric injury were recoverable if there was an intention to cause it. In this case, the prison officers' deviation from the procedure laid down for strip searches was not calculated to cause harm. Their conduct showed no evidence of intention to cause distress or increase the humiliation necessarily involved but was merely the result of "sloppiness".

FALSE IMPRISONMENT

Key Principle

False imprisonment does not require incarceration or the use of force but the unlawful constraint on another's freedom of movement must be total.

Bird v Jones 1845

The defendants, in order to provide seating for spectators at a regatta, wrongfully cordoned off a footpath on Hammersmith Bridge. The plaintiff insisted on his right to use a part of the highway that had been cordoned off. He was prevented from doing so by the defendant and was told that he could go back the way he had come. [1845] 7 Q.B. 742.

Held

This was not false imprisonment. Since the plaintiff had a way out and decided not to take it there was no total restraint on his liberty.

Commentary

In *R. v Bournewood Community and Mental Health NHS Trust* [1998] 3 All E.R. 289, a majority of the House of Lords held that a patient in an open, unlocked ward was not in fact detained. This was the case, although the reality was that if the patient had attempted to leave, the medical staff would have prevented him from doing so by detaining him compulsorily under the Mental Health Act 1983.

Key Principle

Where the plaintiff consents to the confinement there is no false imprisonment.

Herd v Weardale Steel, Coal & Coke Co 1915

The plaintiff, a miner, refused to carry out what he believed to be dangerous work and demanded to be brought up to the mine surface. The employer refused to authorise the lift to be operated until the scheduled time at the end of the shift.

Held

❖ (HL) This was not false imprisonment because the plaintiff had voluntarily descended into the mine. [1915] A.C. 67.

Commentary

(1) An alternative explanation for this decision is that there was no positive act to restrain the plaintiff and trespass does not lie for a mere omission.

(2) *Herd* was applied in *Iqbal v Prison Officers Association* [2010] 2 W.L.R. 1055, where the claimant sued for false imprisonment because a sudden unannounced strike in breach of contract by prison officers meant that

prisoners spent an extra six hours of their day locked in their cell. The Court of Appeal held that as a general principle, a defendant was not to be held liable in tort for the result of his inaction unless there was a specific duty to act, arising out of the particular relationship between the claimant and defendant. Since the strike was a mere failure to act there was no liability in this case.

Key Principle

Where a plaintiff's liberty is subject to a reasonable condition it is not false imprisonment to restrain the plaintiff until that condition is fulfilled.

ROBINSON V BALMAIN FERRY CO LTD 1910

The plaintiff, a lawyer, decided that he could not wait 20 minutes for a ferry and decided to leave the wharf. When he refused to pay the 1 penny exit charge at the turnstile the defendant's employee refused to let him through.

Held

❖ (PC) There was no imprisonment because the condition of paying a penny to leave was a reasonable one in the circumstances. [1910] A.C. 295.

Key Principle

Knowledge of the restraint at the time is not necessary to succeed in an action for false imprisonment.

MEERING V GRAHAM WHITE AVIATION CO LTD 1920

The plaintiff was suspected of theft from his employers. He was taken by two of the work's police to the company's office for questioning. Unknown to the plaintiff, the police waited outside the office and, if the plaintiff had tried to leave, they would have prevented him from doing so.

Held

❖ (CA) Atkin L.J. said that there was no need for the plaintiff to have been aware of the imprisonment. However, knowledge of the detention might be relevant to the assessment of damages. [1919] 122 L.T. 44.

Commentary

(1) In this case the court failed to consider an earlier decision, *Herring v Boyle* (1834) 1 Cr. M. & R. 377, where, because of unpaid school fees, the

headmaster refused to allow a mother to take her son home for the Christmas holidays. It was held that, since the boy was unaware of the detention, there was no false imprisonment. However, the conflict of authority was resolved in *Murray v Ministry of Defence* [1988] 1 W.L.R. 692, where the House of Lords disapproved of *Herring* and approved *Meering*.

(2) In *R. v Bournewood Community and Mental Health NHS Trust* (1998) (p.9), the House of Lords held that although in cases of false imprisonment it is not necessary for the plaintiff to be aware of the detention, there must be an actual rather than a potential restraint on the plaintiff's liberty.

Key Principle

No action for false imprisonment lies where the detention is carried out under an order of the court and, until such an order is set aside, the detention is legally justified.

QUINLAND V GOVERNOR OF SWALESIDE PRISON 2003

The claimant had been convicted of certain offences for which a total sentence of two years and three months' imprisonment should have been imposed. The judge, however, made an arithmetical error in calculating the claimant's sentence and, due to administrative errors, his appeal against his sentence was not heard until after his release. The claimant claimed in false imprisonment for the period of his detention in excess of his sentence.

Held

The prison governor was not liable in false imprisonment. Until the court order was set aside the claimant's detention was legally justified as the prison governor had had no other option than to obey the warrant and could not legitimately have acted otherwise. [2002] EWCA Civ 174.

Key Principle

The relevant intention is the intention to detain the prisoner. Because false imprisonment is a tort of strict liability, where a prison governor has authority to release the prisoner without an order of the court to terminate the period of custody, there may be liability.

R. V GOVERNOR OF BROCKHILL PRISON EX P. EVANS (NO.2) 2001

The prison governor appealed from an award of £5,000 compensation for false imprisonment made on a majority decision by the Court of

Appeal in favour of the prisoner who had been detained at Brockhill Prison for 59 days beyond her release date. The prison governor had not been to blame for the miscalculation of the date of the prisoner's release which had been made according to the bad law that existed at the time of the calculation.

Held
House of Lords, dismissing the appeal, held that the prison governor's belief that the prisoner was lawfully detained was insufficient justification for the tort of false imprisonment even if based on court rulings. [2001] A.C. 19.

DEFENCES TO TRESPASS TO THE PERSON

A number of statutes authorise conduct that would, under different conditions, amount to trespass to the person: the Police and Criminal Evidence Act 1984 provides police with a defence to what might otherwise constitute false imprisonment or battery; the **Mental Health Act 1983** makes provision for the compulsory admission to hospital and treatment in relation to mental health; under the Children and Young Persons Act 1933 parents can justify an assault and battery by way of chastisement of their children. Disciplinary powers also remain for the captain of a ship: reasonable force may be exercised to preserve discipline for the safety of the ship, its crew, passengers and cargo. *Hook v Cunard Steamship Co* [1953] 1 W.L.R. 682.

SELF-DEFENCE

Key Principle
Self-defence will be a justification to an action in battery if the force used is reasonable.

> COCKROFT V SMITH 1705
> The plaintiff, Cockroft, was the clerk of the court. During a scuffle in court he ran his forefinger towards Smith's eyes. He sued Smith, who bit off his finger during the incident, and the question was whether self-defence was a proper defence. 11 Mod. 43.

Held
(1) A person may use reasonable force in self-defence. Holt L.J. said "... hitting a man a little blow with a little stick on the shoulder, is not a reason for him to draw a sword and cut and hew the other ...".

(2) The defendant has the burden of proving self-defence and the requirements for what the defendant needs to show to establish the defence in civil law is different to what is required in criminal law. In *Ashley v Chief Constable of Sussex Police* [2008] 2 W.L.R. 975 Mr Ashley was shot by the police during an armed drugs raid at his home in the early hours of the morning. The police admitted negligence but disputed liability for battery on the basis that the officer in question had acted in self-defence. The House of Lords held that a defendant who had mistakenly but honestly thought it was necessary to defend himself against an imminent risk could not rely on self-defence if his mistaken belief, although honestly held, had not been a reasonable one.

(3) See also *Revill v Newberry* (1996) (see p.203)

Commentary
Force may be used defensively under the Criminal Law Act 1967; s.3 provides that "a person may use such force as is reasonable in the circumstances in the prevention of crime ...". Although the defence is available to one who goes to assist another under attack, self-defence failed in the case of soldiers taking part in United Nations peacekeeping operations in Kosovo who were not being threatened with being shot when they fired their guns.

NECESSITY

Key Principle
The defence of necessity to trespass to the person may be invoked where the defendant acts for the purpose of protecting the plaintiff's own health or safety.

LEIGH V GLADSTONE 1909
The plaintiff, a suffragette prisoner on hunger strike, was forcibly fed by prison staff. When she claimed damages for trespass the defence was that that the acts were necessary to save her life and that the force used was the minimum necessary.

Held
Her action failed because the court held that it was lawful for prison officials to intervene because they had a duty to preserve the life and health of those in their custody. (1909) 26 T.L.R. 139.

Commentary

(1) However, in *Airedale NHS Trust v Bland* [1993] 1 All E.R. 821, the House of Lords said that an adult patient has the absolute right to refuse to consent to treatment, even if the consequence is that he will suffer serious injury or die. Lord Keith commented that the principle of sanctity of life is not an absolute one. It does not authorise force feeding of prisoners.

(2) In *R. v Bournewood Community and Mental Health NHS Trust* (see pp.9 & 11) the House of Lords applied the principle of necessity and confirmed that the test of what is necessary is the "best interests of the patient" and this is to be determined by the *Bolam* test (see pp.103 et seq.).

Key Principle

Where an adult permanently lacks the mental capacity to give a valid consent the defence of necessity, provided it is in the best interests of the patient, will protect a doctor who gives medical treatment.

> F v WEST BERKSHIRE HEALTH AUTHORITY 1990
> F, a 36-year-old woman, was said to have the mental capacity of a child about the age of five. She was cared for as a voluntary patient in a mental hospital and was thought by staff to have started a full sexual relationship with a male patient from the same hospital. It was proposed that she be sterilised and her mother applied to the court for a declaration that the operation would not be unlawful.

Held

❖ (HL) The operation would be lawful. Lord Goff stated that the doctor must act in the best interests of the patient and "... in accordance with a responsible and competent body of relevant professional opinion ... Bolam test" [1990] 2 A.C. 1.

Commentary

(1) Although Lord Goff said that any medical treatment of a competent adult patient will be unlawful unless the patient has consented to the treatment, in *S, Re* [1992] 4 All E.R. 671 the court declared it lawful to perform an operation on a competent pregnant woman who refused consent (on religious grounds) to a Caesarean section. The doctors were clear that the child could not survive without the operation and necessity was invoked in the vital interests of the patient and to protect the unborn child. However, in *MB (Medical Treatment), Re* (1997) 8 Med. L.R. 217, CA, where the Court of Appeal had to decide

whether to grant a declaration overriding a patient's refusal to consent to a Caesarian section, it was stated that *S, Re* was out of line with other authorities. The court restated the principle that a mentally competent patient had an absolute right to refuse to consent to medical treatment for any reason, rational or irrational, even where that reason might lead to his or her death. It was also confirmed that the only situation in which it was lawful for doctors to intervene was if the patient lacked the capacity to decide the treatment that was in the patient's best interests. In *MB, Re* the Court of Appeal authorised the surgical intervention on the basis that the patient's needle phobia put her in a state of such panic that she lacked the capacity to decide.

(2) *St George's Healthcare Trust v S* [1998] 3 All E.R. 673, involved a case where a pregnant mother rejected medical advice as to treatment necessary to protect her and her unborn child. The Court of Appeal held that there was no authority to detain a patient under the **Mental Health Act 1983** in order to perform a non-consensual Caesarian section.

Key Principle ....
A seriously physically disabled patient with the mental capacity to make decisions about treatment, even when a consequence of such decisions could be death, has the right to refuse treatment.

B v NHS Hospital Trust 2002

Ms B suffered an illness that had caused her to become tetraplegic, with complete paralysis from the neck down. She underwent surgery, but this improved her condition only slightly. At the beginning of 2001 her condition deteriorated, and she asked for the ventilator that was keeping her alive to be switched off. The doctors who were treating her, however, could not bring themselves to contemplate being a part of bringing Ms B's life to an end by the dramatic step of turning off the ventilator. The main issue to be determined in deciding the case was whether Ms B had the mental capacity to choose to accept or refuse medical treatment, in which circumstances refusal would lead almost inevitably to her death. If Ms B had the capacity to make this choice the question arose of whether she was entitled to a declaration that the NHS Trust had been treating her unlawfully and was therefore entitled to nominal damages in respect of trespass to person.

Held ....

A declaration that Ms B had the necessary mental capacity to give or refuse consent to medical treatment was granted. [2002] EWHC 429 (Fam).

Commentary ....

(1) The court was not asked directly to decide whether Ms B lived or died, but whether Ms B herself was legally competent to make that decision. Dame Elizabeth Butler-Sloss said that autonomy was a fundamental principle in English law (*F, Re,* above); sanctity of life was an equally fundamental principle (*Airedale NHS Trust v Bland*, below); there was a presumption of mental capacity (*MB, Re* above). The judicial approach to mental capacity was largely dependent upon assessments by the medical profession, and those considering competence were not to confuse the question of capacity with the nature of the decision, however grave the consequences.

THINK POINT

The case of *Airedale NHS Trust v Bland* [1993] A.C. 789 concerned the withdrawal of treatment from a patient in a persistent vegetative state (PVS) who was unable to make the vital decision for himself. In order to lawfully discontinue feeding him, the hospital was granted a declaration that the proposed action would be lawful. In the case of *R. v Director of Public Prosecutions (Respondent) Ex p. Dianne Pretty (Appellant)* [2001] UKHL 61, the appellant was mentally alert but terminally ill with an incurable degenerative illness. Already physically incapable of committing suicide without help, her request was for legal permission "to decide how and when I die". Her husband was prepared to help her to do this but he wanted to be sure that he would not be prosecuted for doing so. When immunity against prosecution was refused by the DPP, she appealed and attempted to enforce her rights under art.2 of the **European Convention on Human Rights 2002** which guarantees the "right to life". In a unanimous decision, the House of Lords held that the right to life was never intended to convey the right to be killed by someone else and that such an interpretation could not be given to art.2 of the **Convention 2002**.

CONSENT

Key Principle

There is implied consent to physical contact that occurs within the ordinary conduct of a game or sport.

> R. v BILLINGHURST 1978
>
> In the course of a rugby game the plaintiff, who did not have the ball at the time, was deliberately punched in the face by an opponent.

Held

There was a battery. Even though players are deemed to consent to force "of a kind which could reasonably be expected to happen during a game", this does not include foul play that goes beyond what a reasonable participant would expect. [1978] Crim. L.R. 553.

Commentary

(1) In *Condon v Basi* [1985] 2 All E.R. 453, the plaintiff suffered a broken leg as the result of a foul tackle in the course of a game of football. It was held that consent to reasonable contact is consent only to non-negligent behaviour and the defendant was found liable in negligence.

(2) In *Watson v British Boxing Board of Control* [2001] Q.B. 1134, it was held that although a boxer consents to injury caused by his opponent in the boxing ring, he does not consent to injury resulting from inadequate safety arrangements by the sport's governing body after being hit.

THINK POINT

There will be a trespass if there is a deviation from the procedure consented to. In *Nash v Sheehan* [1953] C.L.R. 3726 the application of a tone rinse to a plaintiff who requested a permanent wave was held to be trespass.

Key Principle

Participants who voluntarily involve themselves in fights are taken to have consented to the battery.

LANE V HOLLOWAY 1968

The plaintiff, a retired gardener aged 64, came back from the pub one night and provoked an argument by calling the defendant's wife "a monkey faced tart". The 23-year-old defendant struck the plaintiff a violent blow in the eye and inflicted a wound that needed 19 stitches.

Held

There is no action in battery available to those who take part in fights, especially "an ordinary fight with fists", because they would be taken to have consented to the battery. However, consent did not apply in this case because the plaintiff's conduct was trivial and the defendant gave a "savage blow out of all proportion to the occasion". [1968] 1 Q.B. 379.

Commentary

In *Barnes v Nayer*, *The Times*, December 19, 1986, provocation was again involved when the defendant killed the plaintiff's wife with a machete after he and his family were subjected to a prolonged course of abuse by their neighbours. The Court of Appeal held that contributory negligence, *volenti* and *ex turpi causa* (see Ch.7) could be a defence to trespass to the person. (The defences did not apply in this case because of the disparity between the deceased's acts and the defendant's deadly attack.)

Key Principle

Medical treatment involving the direct application of force administered without the patient's consent, or giving treatment different from that for which consent has been given, constitutes a battery.

CHATTERTON V GERSON 1981

The plaintiff was suffering from severe pain caused by a trapped nerve for which the defendant, a specialist in the treatment of chronic intractable pain, gave her spinal injections. This helped the pain for a while but it rendered her right leg numb. She claimed in trespass on the ground that her consent to the injection was invalid as she had not been warned of the risk or informed of the potential consequences.

Held

The defendant was not liable in trespass. Where a patient is informed in broad terms of the nature of the procedure and consent is obtained, failure to disclose the associated risks does not invalidate the consent. [1981] Q.B. 432.

Commentary ....

(1) Any action in respect of a doctor's failure to disclose sufficiently the risks inherent in medical treatment must be based in negligence. (See *Sidaway v Bethlem Royal Hospital Governors* (1985), p.106.)

(2) In *Chester v Ashfar* (2004) (p.113) a neurosurgeon who failed to warn a patient of a small inherent risk of injury was liable in damages because, the court held, unless that was done, the duty to warn would be a hollow one.

Vicarious Liability

2

INTRODUCTION

Before vicarious liability is imposed on a defendant there are three conditions which must be met. First, there must be a specific employer–employee relationship. This is distinguished from an employer's relationship with a self-employed independent contractor: employers are not usually liable for the torts of independent contractors. It can sometimes be difficult to define the status of an employment relationship, for example, in the case of casual workers or where the working relationship does not fall into a traditional pattern. One accepted distinction is that those working under "a contract of service" are employees and those working under "contract for services" are independent contractors. A further test which produces straightforward answers in some cases is that of control: the crucial factor being the degree of control exercised by the employer over the way in which the work is done. But in modern working conditions the control test is not sufficient. There are many contracts of service where the employer does not or cannot control the way in which the work is done, for example, a surgeon working for the National Health Service would not fit the control test. Therefore, the emphasis on the control test has been reduced and, instead of relying on a single test, the courts now consider a wide range of factors in each particular case.

The second condition which must exist before an employer will be held vicariously liable is that a tort (an actionable wrong) must be committed by the employee.

The third condition which must be met for vicarious liability is that the employee must be acting in the course of employment when the tort is committed. For example, in *Credit Lyonnais Bank Nederland NV v Export Credits Guarantee Department* [2000] 1 A.C. 486, the plaintiff claimed that the defendants were liable because one of their employees had assisted in a fraudster's deceit by underwriting guarantees. The House of Lords upheld the Court of Appeal decision that an employer had no liability in tort for his employee's acts, done in the course of employment to assist in the fraudulent scheme of a third person, unless the acts were within the employee's actual or ostensible authority. The mere fact that his employment provided the employee with the opportunity to facilitate fraud was not sufficient to render an employer vicariously liable.

The tort must be committed in the "course of employment" and the general rule is that if an employee committed the tort within the course of his employment the employer is liable; if the employee acted outside the scope of employment the employer is not liable. The question of whether an act is within or outside the course of employment is therefore crucial but there is no exhaustive definition of what falls within the scope of employment. The factors considered by the courts in determining the issue are outlined below but in cases involving an employee's intentional criminal conduct, the decision in *Lister v Hesley Hall Ltd* [2001] UKHL 22 (below) involving sexually abused claimants, reflects the role of policy in this area. The modern approach is to expand the definition of "course of his employment" as a means of enabling victims of an employee's tort to obtain compensation.

Key Principle

The express intentions of the parties as to the classification of their working relationship is an important factor, but it is not conclusive.

> FERGUSON V JOHN DAWSON & PARTNERS (CONTRACTORS) LTD 1976
> The plaintiff, a building worker, was injured when he fell off a roof at the defendant's construction site. Contrary to regulations there was no guard rail on the roof. If he had been an independent contractor he would have been responsible for his own safety and unable to sue the company. At the time of hiring the plaintiff was expressed to be a "labour only sub-contractor" although he was an unskilled labourer and subject to the control of the site agent.

Held

❖ (CA) The employers were liable. Despite the label that the parties had given to the relationship, in all other respects the plaintiff was treated as an employee working under a contract for service. [1976] 1 W.L.R. 1213.

Commentary

(1) In *Ready Mixed Concrete (SE) Ltd v Minister of Pensions* [1968] Q.B. 497 (see below) it was held that where the parties have specified that a person will be self-employed, and the other terms of the contract do not show otherwise, the contract will be regarded as a contract for services.

(2) In *Stevenson, Jordan & Harrison Ltd v Macdonald & Evans* (1952) 1 T.L.R. 101, the "integration test" was proposed by Lord Denning: an employee is someone whose work is an integral part of the business; an independent contractor is someone who would work for the business, but as an accessory rather than an integral part of it. This test has been applied in some

situations but it has failed as a universal test and the courts have now moved to a multiple approach.

Key Principle

In determining the nature of the employment relationship there are a number of relevant factors to be considered. The allocation of financial risk is one of these factors and this particular question should be addressed by asking: is the person in business on his or her own behalf?

> READY MIXED CONCRETE (SE) LTD V MINISTER OF PENSIONS 1968
> A concrete-manufacturing company introduced a scheme whereby its concrete would be transported by a team of "owner-drivers" who would be paid a fixed mileage rate for the service. The plaintiff driver's contract described him as an independent contractor, and he was obliged to maintain his vehicle in good order at his own expense. He had no fixed hours of work and could choose his own routes and he was also free to employ a competent driver when necessary. However, he undertook to make his lorry available whenever the company wanted it, to have it painted the company's colours, and to wear the company uniform. The issue was whether the owner-drivers were employees of the company: if so, the company was liable to pay national insurance contributions in respect of them.

Held

The driver was working under a contract for services. He owned the lorry, bore the financial risk and was, in fact, running his own business. [1968] 2 Q.B. 497.

Key Principle

Where an employee is lent out to another employer on a temporary basis the presumption is that the general (or original) employer remains vicariously liable.

> MERSEY DOCKS AND HARBOUR BOARD V COGGINS AND GRIFFITH (LIVERPOOL) LTD 1947
> A mobile crane and a driver had been hired out to a firm of stevedores under a contract which stipulated that the driver was to be the employee of the stevedores. In spite of this term his original employer, the Board, paid his wages and retained the right to dismiss him. The hirer directed the tasks which were to be performed by the driver but

not how he was to operate the crane. In the course of his work the driver negligently injured the plaintiff and the question to be determined was whether the stevedores or the Board were vicariously liable.

Held

❖ (HL) Several factors have to be considered but the decisive question to be asked was who bore the ultimate control over the manner in which the work was performed. On the facts of the case the Board remained liable. [1947] A.C. 1.

Commentary

(1) The burden of proof remains with the original employer to show that responsibility for the torts of the employee has shifted to the second employer.

(2) It was also held that an express term in the contract of hire stating that the workman is the employee of the hirer is not to be treated as conclusive.

Key Principle

Where dual vicarious liability provides a coherent solution to the problem of establishing liability for an employee's negligence it is possible for two separate employers to be vicariously liable for the tort of a single employee.

Viasystems Ltd v Thermal Transfer Ltd 2005

The claimants engaged the first defendants to install air conditioning at their factory. The first defendants sub-contracted ducting work to the second defendants who further contracted with the third defendants to provide fitters and fitter's mates on a labour-only basis. At the time of the accident, a fitter's mate negligently crawled through a duct causing damage to the fire protection sprinkler system. There was no question that the fitter's mate was negligent and the issue to be decided was which of the employers was vicariously liable for the extensive flood damage caused by his negligence.

Held

The Court of Appeal held that entire and absolute control of the employee was not a precondition of vicarious liability and there was no binding authority that dual vicarious liability was legally impossible. The inquiry should concentrate on the relevant negligent act and then ask whose responsibility it was to prevent it; the question in this case was to ask who was entitled to exercise control over the relevant act or operation of the fitter's mate. On the facts, both the second and third defendants had been entitled, and if they had the opportunity, obliged, to prevent the mate's negligence and accordingly both employers were vicariously liable. [2005] EWCA Civ 1151.

THINK POINT

In *Hawley v Luminar Leisure Ltd* [2006] IRLR the Court of Appeal said the decision as to whether an employee remains an employee of the general employer for the purposes of vicarious liability or whether he is deemed to be a temporary employee of the hirer, turns on the facts of the individual case. In this case Luminar had contracted with ASE Security Services Limited for the supply of doormen for their night-club. Mr Hawley sustained serious injuries as the result of the violence of one of the doormen and claimed that both Luminar and ASE were each responsible for failing to carry out a proper investigation into whether the doorman was a suitable person to be employed in that capacity and for failing to train or supervise him. The Court of Appeal considered a number of factors including who exercised control over the doormen, who paid them and to whom they were responsible while working at Luminar's clubs. The prima facie responsibility for the hired employee was held to have shifted from ASE the general employer to Luminar the temporary employer because Luminar had exercised considerable control over how the doorman carried out his duties.

COURSE OF EMPLOYMENT

Key Principle

Where an act which is authorised by an employer is performed by the employee in a wrongful and unauthorised manner, the employer remains liable.

WHATMAN V PEARSON 1868

The employees were allowed an hour for dinner but were forbidden to go home, or to leave their horses and carts unguarded. However, one of the employees went home for dinner anyway, making a deviation in his route of about a quarter of a mile. When he negligently left his horse out in the street it bolted and damaged the plaintiff's property.

Held

The employee's duties involved looking after the horse and cart all day and he was therefore acting within the scope of his employment. (1868) L.R. 3 C.P. 422.

Key Principle

A new and separate journey will take the employee outside the course of employment.

> STOREY V ASHTON 1869
> The employees were instructed to deliver some wine and on the return journey one of the employees persuaded the other that, since it was by then after hours, to set off in a different direction to visit some relatives. On the way there the plaintiff was injured by the employee's negligent driving.

Held

The driver was not acting in the course of employment, it was a new and independent journey which was entirely for his own business. (1869) L.R. 4 Q.B. 476.

Commentary

(1) This corresponds with *Joel v Morrison* (1834) 6 C. & P. 501 where the test was said to be whether the employee was engaged on the employer's business or "on a frolic of his own".

(2) Cockburn C.J. said it was a question of degree how far a deviation from the authorised route would be considered a separate journey.

(3) In *Harvey v RG O'Dell Ltd* [1958] 2 Q.B. 78, a five-mile journey to get a midday meal during working hours was held to be within the course of employment.

Key Principle

An employee travelling between home and work will not generally be in the course of employment. But an employee travelling in the employer's time from home to a workplace other than the regular workplace or between workplaces will be within the course of employment.

> **SMITH V STAGES 1989**
> A peripatetic lagger was working at a power station in the Midlands when his employer sent him and another employee to perform an urgent job in Wales. In addition to their hourly rate they were paid travelling expenses for the journeys there and back. They were using a private vehicle and had discretion as to how and when they would travel. Having worked without sleep they finished the job two days early and decided to drive straight home. As they were travelling back together in the car they were both injured when the employee driving the car crashed into a wall. The driver was uninsured and the plaintiff sued the employer on the basis of vicarious liability.

Held

❖ (HL) The employers were liable. Lord Goff said the fact that the men were travelling back early was immaterial since they were still being paid wages to travel there and back. Lord Lowry thought the crucial point was that the employees were "on duty" at the time of the accident. [1989] A.C. 928.

Key Principle

An act may be within the course of employment even though it has been expressly forbidden by the employer.

> **LIMPUS V LONDON GENERAL OMNIBUS CO 1862**
> A bus driver was instructed not to race with or obstruct the buses of rival companies. He disobeyed this instruction and caused an accident in which the plaintiff's horses were injured.

Held

Despite the prohibition the employers were liable since this was simply an improper method adopted by the employee in performing his duties. (1862) 1 H. & C. 526.

Commentary

It is outside the course of employment for an employee to do something which is not connected with what he is employed to do. In *Beard v London General Omnibus Co* [1900] 2 Q.B. 530, a bus conductor, in the driver's absence, decided to turn the bus around for the return journey. As a conductor, it was not his job to drive the bus and he was therefore acting outside the course of his employment.

Key Principle

Where a prohibited act is performed in furthering the employer's business it is usually within the course of employment.

> ROSE V PLENTY 1976
> A milkman employed a boy aged 13 to help him on his milk round despite his employer's express instruction not to do so. Due mainly to the milkman's negligent driving the boy was injured.

Held

❖ (CA) The employers were liable. Lord Denning said the driver was still within the course of employment despite the express prohibition because he was acting for the master's purposes, business, and benefit. [1976] 1 W.L.R. 141.

Commentary

In *Conway v George Wimpey & Co* [1951] 2 K.B. 266 a lorry driver, contrary to express instructions, who gave a lift to an employee of another firm of contractors was acting outside the course of his employment. Apart from the fact that the driver was held to be performing an act which he was not employed to perform at all, the unauthorised passenger must have known from the notices inside the vehicle that he was a trespasser.

Key Principle

When considering the scope of employment it is enough to show that the employee was generally doing his job at the time, and doing a job negligently does not take an employee outside the course of employment.

> CENTURY INSURANCE CO LTD V NORTHERN IRELAND ROAD TRANSPORT
> BOARD 1942
> The driver of a petrol lorry was transferring petrol from the lorry into a tank at a garage. He lit a cigarette and negligently threw down a lighted match. This caused an explosion and fire.

Held

❖ (HL) The defendants were liable. At the time of the act, even though the employee was plainly negligent, he was delivering petrol. This was the very purpose for which he was employed. [1942] A.C. 509.

Key Principle

Where a deliberate assault is involved the courts are reluctant to find that the employee was acting in the course of employment.

WARREN V HENLYS 1948

An employee engaged as petrol pump attendant by the defendant mistakenly thought that the plaintiff was attempting to drive away without paying for some petrol. He made this accusation to the plaintiff in violent language. The plaintiff paid his bill, called the police and when he threatened to report the pump attendant to his employers he was assaulted and injured by him. The plaintiff brought an action against the employers.

Held

The defendants were not liable, the assault was a mere act of personal vengeance and outside the course of employment. [1948] 2 All E.R. 935.

Commentary

Similarly in *Keppel Bus Co Ltd v Sa'ad bin Ahmad* [1974] 1 W.L.R. 1082 a passenger was not allowed to recover when a bus conductor blinded him with his ticket punch.

Key Principle

There are occasions when an employer will be vicariously responsible for deliberate criminal conduct of an employee.

LLOYD V GRACE SMITH & CO 1912

The defendants, a firm of solicitors, employed a clerk who fraudulently induced a client into transferring some cottages over to him. He then dishonestly disposed of the property and stole the proceeds.

Held

❖ (HL) Even though the fraud was not committed for the benefit of the employers and they were ignorant of his schemes they were liable because they had held the clerk out as having authority to perform the type of transaction in question. [1912] A.C. 716.

Commentary

Similarly in *Morris v Martin (CW) & Sons Ltd* [1996] 1 Q.B. 716, a firm of dry cleaners were found liable by the Court of Appeal when the plaintiff's fur coat was stolen by an employee.

Key Principle

The proper approach to the nature of employment is not to ask the simplistic question of whether the acts were modes of doing authorised acts but to adopt a broad assessment and to consider whether the torts committed were so *closely connected* with the employee's duties that it would be fair and just to hold the employers liable.

LISTER V HESLEY HALL LTD 2002

The defendants ran a school for boys with emotional and behavioural difficulties. The school, which had a boarding annex, had been managed by the defendants as a commercial enterprise. They had employed Mr Grain and his wife as warden and housekeeper to take care of the boys. The claimants attended the school and boarded in the annex where they were subjected to systematic acts of sexual abuse by Mr Grain.

Held

The test for the course of employment was restated by the House of Lords and directed to the connection between the employee's duties and his wrongdoing. The focus of the question in this case was whether the connection between the work that the warden was employed to do and the acts of abuse committed by him, was sufficiently close for those acts to have been committed in the course of employment. The fact that the employment provided him with the opportunity to commit the abuse was not enough to make the employer vicariously liable. The central question was whether the acts of abuse constituted a particular risk that was inextricably linked to and inherent in the performance of the warden's duties. The defendants had entrusted the care of the children to the warden and the acts of abuse committed by him had been inextricably interwoven with the carrying out of his duties. His torts had been so closely connected with his employment that it would be fair and just to hold the defendants vicariously liable. The decision of the Court of Appeal in *Trotman v North Yorkshire County Council* [1999] L.G.R. 584, where an employer was not vicariously liable on the grounds that a teacher was not acting in the course of employment when he used school trips to commit sexual assault, was held to be wrongly decided [2001] UKHL 22.

Commentary

(1) In *Dubai Aluminium v Salaam* [2002] UKHL 48, the House of Lords widened the principle in *Lister v Helsey Hall* to include, not just intentional torts, but also breaches of equitable duty which were so closely connected with the acts that the employee was authorised to do while acting in the course of the firm's business.

(2) *Lister v Hesley Hall* was applied by the Court of Appeal in *Mattis v Pollock* [2003] EWCA Civ 887; [2003] 1 W.L.R. 2158 where the owner of a nightclub was held vicariously liable to the claimant who suffered paraplegia following a stabbing by a doorman "bouncer" employed by the club. The doorman, who was involved in a fight with other customers in the nightclub, was forced to flee when the claimant intervened. The doorman went home to arm himself with a knife and, intent on revenge, he returned to the vicinity of the club where he stabbed the claimant. The assault on the claimant was held to be "so closely connected" with what Mr Pollock (the owner of the nightclub) authorised or expected of his employee in the performance of his employment that it would be fair and just to conclude that he was vicariously liable for the claimant's damage.

(3) The intense focus on the connection between the nature of employment and the tort committed was further emphasised by the Court of Appeal in *Gravil v Carroll* [2008] EWCA Civ 689 where the wrongful act of a rugby player during a match was so "closely connected" with his employment that his club was vicariously liable. In *Ministry of Defence v Radclyffe* [2009] EWCA Civ 635 the *Ministry of Defence* was vicariously liable for the negligence of an officer who urged Radclyffe to jump from a bridge during an adventure training exercise in Germany. The connection between the nature of his employment as an officer in the army and his breach of duty was held to be well within the *Lister v Hesley Hall* test.

THINK POINT

In *Maga v The Trustees of the Birmingham Archdiocese of the Roman Catholic Church* [2010] 1 W.L.R. 1441 the close connection test was considered in the case of a Catholic priest purporting to carry out his work as a priest when his true motive was to abuse the claimant (a non-Catholic boy who at no time had anything to do with the Church itself). The trial Judge had found the Catholic Church was not vicariously liable for the actions of the priest because he had not involved the claimant in the activities of the Church itself but instead had cultivated him for the purpose of sexual abuse. This decision was reversed by the Court of Appeal where Lord Neuberger said there was no doubt that the claimant's case was weaker than that of the claimant in *Lister* or of a Roman Catholic boy, such as M who was an altar server, however, he concluded:

> "I consider that, on the facts of this case, the test laid down by Lord Steyn in *Lister* ... is satisfied. Father Clonan's sexual abuse of the claimant was "so closely connected with his employment" as a priest at the Church "that it would be fair and just to hold the [Archdiocese] vicariously liable".

Key Principle

Vicarious liability is not restricted to common law claims. An employer may be vicariously liable under the **Protection from Harassment Act 1997** for breach of a statutory duty imposed on the employee, but not upon the employer directly, where it is fair and just to impose a duty and where there is a close connection between the breach of duty and the nature of the employment.

MAJROWSKI V GUY'S AND ST THOMAS'S NHS TRUST 2006

Mr Majrowski claimed that he had been bullied, intimidated and harassed by his departmental manager, acting in the course of her employment. He claimed for damages against the NHS for breach of statutory duty under the **Protection from Harassment Act 1997**. The judge below struck out his claim on the grounds that the Act did not create a statutory tort for which an employer could be vicariously liable. Mr Majrowski appealed against the decision and asked the court to consider whether an employer might be vicariously liable for breach of a statutory duty placed solely and personally on the employee for acts of harassment committed in the course of employment. The Court of Appeal allowed his appeal and held that, in general, an employer might be vicariously liable for a breach of statutory duty imposed on its employee, if in all the circumstances of the case, the test of fairness and justice was met and the connection between the employee's breach of duty and the nature of the employment was sufficient. The employer's appeal that the **Protection from Harassment Act 1997** was not intended to impose a burden on employers was rejected by their Lordships. [2006] UKHL 34.

Commentary

(1) It is important to note that in order to succeed under the **Protection from Harassment Act 1997** there is no need for the claimant to prove foreseeability of harm or personal injury.

(2) *Majrowski* was applied in *Green v DB Group Services Ltd* [2006] EWHC 1898 where a former employee claimed against her employer for damages arising from her psychiatric injury which she alleged was the result of workplace harassment and bullying by her fellow employees. The claimant had been the victim of a relentless campaign of mean and spiteful behaviour designed to cause her distress. This conduct was held to amount to a deliberate and concerted campaign of bullying within the ordinary meaning of that term, and constituted harassment within the meaning of the **Protection from Harassment Act 1997**. The connection between the nature of the employment of the women in question and their acts of harassment was so close that it was just and reasonable to hold the employer liable for it.

EMPLOYER'S INDEMNITY

Key Principle

An employer who has been held vicariously liable for an employee's negligence is entitled to seek an indemnity from the employee to recover any damages paid.

LISTER V ROMFORD ICE & COLD STORAGE CO 1957

Lister was employed as a lorry driver. In the course of his employment he was driving negligently when he injured his father, a fellow employee. The employers were vicariously liable and the father's damages were paid by the employers' insurers. Exercising their right of subrogation the insurers then brought an action against the son for an indemnity.

Held

❖ (HL) The son was liable to indemnify the employers, and hence the insurers. [1957] A.C. 555.

(1) It must be noted that the employer is liable as well as the employee. As joint tort-feasors they are each fully liable to the plaintiff.

(2) Because of the problems predicted for industrial relations following this decision the employers' liability insurers entered into a "gentleman's agreement" not to take advantage of this principle unless there was evidence of collusion or misconduct.

EMPLOYER'S LIABILITY FOR INDEPENDENT CONTRACTORS

Key Principle
Although employers are not generally liable for their contractor's torts, an employer will be responsible for the acts of independent contractors who carry out extra hazardous activities. Where the task is inherently dangerous the duty on an employer is so onerous that it cannot be delegated to anyone else.

> HONEYWILL & STEIN LTD v LARKIN BROS LTD 1934
> The plaintiffs did some work in a cinema and, having obtained the permission of the cinema owners, engaged the defendants as independent contractors to take photographs of their work. In those days this task involved igniting magnesium powder and, in doing so, the defendant's employee negligently set the curtains on fire. The plaintiffs paid the cinema owners for the damage caused by the fire and sought to recover from the defendants.

Held
❖ (CA) The plaintiffs had remained liable for the damage caused by the independent contractors because the task involved was extra hazardous. A duty is non-delegable where acts "in their very nature, involve ... special danger to others". [1934] 1 K.B. 191.

Commentary
(1) A further exception to the rule that an employer is not liable for the torts of an independent contractor is where the work is carried out on or adjoining the highway. In *Tarry v Ashton* (1876) 1 Q.B.D. 314 the occupier of a public house adjoining the highway was liable when a heavy lamp attached to the building injured a passer-by. Although the occupier argued that he had employed an independent contractor to keep the lamp in good repair, it was

held that the duty to maintain premises so close to the highway could not be delegated.

(2) In *Rowe v Herman* [1997] 1 W.L.R. 1390, the Court of Appeal restated the basic principle that an employer is not liable for an independent contractor's negligence. In this case there was no question of works on the highway involving extra hazardous acts and, on the facts of the case, the defendant occupiers were not responsible for the negligence of an independent contractor working on their land.

(3) Note also that an employer's duty for the safety of employees is non-delegable. *Wilsons & Clyde Coal Co Ltd v English* (1938) (see p.140).

Negligence: Duty of Care

. . . .

3

INTRODUCTION

As a tort, negligence consists of three elements: a legal duty to take care; breach of that duty; and damage suffered as a consequence of that breach. In this Chapter and in Ch.4 cases relating to the duty element will be outlined, Ch.5 will then focus on cases concerning breach of duty, and damage will be the subject of the cases in Ch.6. However, it might be useful at this point to note that these key concepts overlap and that the separate elements frequently fail to provide a clear answer as to whether a claim should be allowed. In *Lamb v Camden LBC* [1981] Q.B. 625 Lord Denning said: "it is not every consequence of a wrongful act which is the subject of compensation". Lines have to be drawn somewhere:

> "Sometimes it is done by limiting the range of persons to whom a duty is owed. Sometimes it is done by saying that there is a break in the chain of causation. At other times it is done by saying that the consequence is too remote to be a head of damage. All these devices are useful in their way. Ultimately, it is a question of policy for judges to decide".

In *Caparo Industries v Dickman* [1990] 2 A.C. 605 Lord Roskill commented that "it has now to be accepted that there is no simple formula or touchstone" in the formulation of the test for existence of a duty of care:

> "Phrases such as 'foreseeability', 'proximity', 'neighbourhood', 'just and reasonable' 'fairness', 'voluntary acceptance of risk' or 'voluntary assumption of responsibility' will be found used from time to time in the different cases. But ... such phrases are not precise definitions. At best they are but labels or phrases descriptive of the very different factual situations which can exist in particular cases and which must be carefully examined in each case before it can be pragmatically determined whether a duty of care exists and, if so, what is the scope of that duty."

Key Principle

Negligence is an independent tort for which the existence of a duty of care is a prerequisite of liability.

> ### DONOGHUE V STEVENSON 1932
>
> The plaintiff went to a café with a friend who ordered some drinks. When the drinks arrived the plaintiff drank some of the contents and she alleged that when her friend poured the remainder of the drink into her glass it contained the remnants of a decomposed snail. As a result she became seriously ill. She could not sue the retailer with whom she had no contract nor could she plausibly claim that he was negligent because the bottle was opaque and the snail could not be seen. Instead she sued the manufacturers of the drink in negligence. The manufacturers raised the defence of privity and claimed that since the plaintiff could not sue them in contract she could not sue them in tort either.

Held

❖ (HL) There could be a remedy in tort—a manufacturer had a duty of care in negligence to the ultimate consumer of his products. According to Lord Atkin:

> "You must take reasonable care to avoid acts or omissions which you can reasonably foresee would be likely to injure your neighbour."

"Neighbour", in the legal sense, he defined as

> "persons who are so closely and directly affected by my act that I ought reasonably to have them in contemplation as being so affected when I am directing my mind to the acts or omissions which are called in question." [1932] A.C. 562.

Commentary

(1) Liability for negligent conduct had previously been recognised only in certain carefully defined circumstances. The court allowed actions for damages in cases where the special circumstances gave rise to a duty of care such as, for example, doctor–patient, innkeeper–guest, or where fire damage resulted from negligence. Lord Atkin sought to unify these disparate duties of care in a single general theory and stated that the courts had previously been "engaged upon an elaborate classification of duties as they existed in various fact situations ...".

(2) In addition to the notion of foresight and reasonable contemplation of harm, Lord Atkin emphasised the need for a relationship of proximity between the parties, but this does not necessarily mean that the plaintiff must be in a close physical or spatial relationship to the defendant. Proximity is used as a convenient label to describe the relationship between the parties and the facts giving rise to a duty of care.

(3) In *Yuen Kun Yeu v Att.-Gen. of Hong Kong* (1988) (see p.40) Lord Keith held the expression "proximity or neighbourhood" to be a composite one importing the whole concept of necessary relationship between the plaintiff and defendant.

(4) In *Hedley Byrne v Heller* (1964) (see p.84), the House of Lords extended the neighbour principle to cover cases of pure economic loss not resulting from physical damage in circumstances where a "special relationship" arises between the parties.

Key Principle

In extending Lord Atkin's neighbour principle Lord Reid said that the test

> "... should be regarded as a statement of principle. It is not to be treated as if it were a statutory definition. It will require qualification in new circumstances. But I think that the time has come when we can and should say that it ought to apply unless there is some justification or valid explanation for its exclusion ...".

HOME OFFICE V DORSET YACHT CO LTD 1970

Some borstal trainees escaped from custody during the night when, it was alleged, the three officers in charge of them were asleep. The escapees went aboard a yacht and caused damage to the plaintiff's yacht which was moored close by. It was argued by the Home Office that it would be contrary to public policy to hold it (or its officers) liable to a member of the public for the acts of a third party (the borstal trainees) by failing to restrain them. In deciding whether the borstal officers owed a duty of care to the plaintiff, Lord Reid said the basic question for the court was: who should bear the loss caused by the carelessness of the officers, the innocent plaintiff or the Home Office?

Held

The majority of the House of Lords concluded that a duty of care was owed on the grounds that a "special relationship" existed. The relationship between the Home Office and the borstal boys and the relationship between the Home Office and the yacht owners was sufficiently proximate to give rise to a duty of care. The borstal boys were under the control of the officers and "control imports responsibility". It was also foreseeable that the boys would seek to escape and cause the damage suffered by the plaintiff.

THINK POINT

Lord Reid's suggestion that a duty of care based on reasonable foreseeability ought to apply in all cases unless there was some justification or valid explanation for its exclusion was seen as a liberating principle. This approach was confirmed in *Anns v Merton LBC* [1978] A.C. 728 (below).

THE TWO-STAGE TEST

Principle

The test for the existence of a duty of care is to be approached in two stages.

ANNS V MERTON LBC 1978
The plaintiffs were lessees of flats which they claimed suffered structural deterioration through being built on foundations of insufficient depth. They sued in negligence against the local authority on the basis that it had negligently failed to inspect the foundations or negligently carried out an inspection.

Held

❖ (HL) The local authority was liable: the exercise of statutory powers and statutory duties by public bodies could give rise to a duty of care to individuals. [1978] A.C. 728.

Commentary

(1) It should be noted that this case was overruled by the House of Lords in *Murphy v Brentwood District Council* (1990) (see p.40 below).

(2) In his speech Lord Wilberforce extended the neighbour principle based on

reasonable foresight and introduced a two-stage test. In summary, this test is approached by asking the following two questions: first, was the harm foreseeable and thereby bringing the plaintiff within the neighbour principle? If so, then, was there any valid policy reason to deny the existence of a duty of care in this case? The first stage of Lord Wilberforce's test presented no hurdle to litigants at all and it appeared possible that the plaintiff, having established foreseeability of harm, raised the presumption of the existence of a duty of care. This meant that, at the second stage of the test (the policy stage) the courts were left to restrict the scope of negligence liability by reference to policy considerations.

Anns was seen as a liberating principle; for example in *McLoughlin v O'Brian* (1983) (see p.75) the policy arguments, which were said to justify the restrictions on liability, were criticised. Lord Bridge dismissing the floodgates argument said: "I believe that the floodgates argument ... is, as it always has been, greatly exaggerated". This period of expansion of negligence liability reached its high-water mark in *Junior Books v Veitchi Co Ltd* (1983) (see p.82). The House of Lords went one step further than *Anns* and allowed a claim in negligence where there was no allegation that the factory floor in question was dangerously defective; the defect in question was one of quality.

(3) *Governors of the Peabody Donation Fund v Sir Lindsay Parkinson & Co Ltd* (1985) (see below) marked the beginning of a retreat from *Anns*. The House of Lords warned against the more liberal approach of the Wilberforce test, and in subsequent decisions the courts have sought to reassert limits on the scope of liability that had traditionally been recognised in the case law.

Key Principle
In the test for a duty of care it is now material to take into consideration whether it is "just and reasonable" that a duty should be imposed.

GOVERNORS OF THE PEABODY DONATION FUND V SIR LINDSAY PARKINSON & CO LTD 1985
The plaintiff development company was required by statute to provide an adequate drainage system for new dwellings under construction. The drainage system, which had been approved by the local authority, proved to be unsatisfactory and the plaintiff suffered economic loss. The plaintiff alleged that the local authority had been in breach of its duty to ensure that the system was suitable.

Held ....

❖ (HL) Lord Keith denied a remedy to the plaintiff. In retreating from the Wilberforce two-stage test he introduced a requirement that the plaintiff should identify policy grounds why a duty should arise; why the defendant should be made responsible for his welfare. He further stated:

> "... in determining whether or not a duty of care of particular scope was incumbent on a defendant it is material to take into consideration whether it is just and reasonable that it should be so ..." [1985] A.C. 210.

THINK POINT

Judicial criticism of *Anns* continued in *Yuen Kun Yeu v Att.-Gen. of Hong Kong* [1988] A.C. 175 where Lord Keith said:

> "In view of the direction in which the law has since been developing, their Lordships consider that for the future it should be recognised that the two-stage test in *Anns* is not to be regarded as in all circumstances a suitable guide to the existence of a duty of care."

Key Principle ....

A local authority is not liable in negligence to a building owner or occupier for losses arising from its failure to ensure that the building was designed or erected in accordance with building regulations.

MURPHY V BRENTWOOD DISTRICT COUNCIL 1990

The plaintiff had purchased a house which was constructed on a concrete raft foundation over an in-filled site. In 1981 he discovered cracks in the house threatening the whole fabric of the property. It was discovered that the concrete raft foundation had subsided and the plaintiff sued the local council for negligently approving plans for the foundations.

Held ....

The local authority was not liable. The house had only damaged itself and was therefore merely a defective house which was a bad bargain; unless and until actual physical damage had occurred the cost of making the house safe or any diminution in its value is purely economic loss. [1991] 1 A.C. 398.

Commentary ....

(1) A seven-member House of Lords found it necessary to overrule their own earlier decision in *Anns* (above). Of wider importance, the case marks a contraction in the scope of a duty of care in economic loss cases. See also *D & F Estates Ltd v Church Commissioners* [1989] A.C. 177.

(2) In *Caparo v Dickman* [1990] 2 A.C. 605 the House of Lords set down a tripartite test for establishing a duty of care: (i) the harm must have been reasonably foreseeable; (ii) there must have been a relationship of proximity between the parties; (iii) in all the circumstances of the case, it must be fair, just and reasonable to impose a duty of care. The court approved *Sutherland Shire Council v Heyman* [1985] 157 C.L.R. 424, in which Brennan J. rejected the broad principles approach taken by Lord Wilberforce in *Anns* and said that the law should develop "incrementally by analogy with established categories."

Key Principle ....

Reiteration of the *Caparo* principle—the relationship of proximity is not always enough to determine whether a defendant is under a duty of care; it is still necessary to consider the scope of that duty and the controlling principle that the imposition of a duty of care should be "fair, just and reasonable" in all the circumstances.

BHAMRA V DUBB (T/A LUCKY CATERERS) 2010

The defendant, a Sikh caterer, who was aware the Sikh religion forbids the consumption of meat, fish or eggs, provided the food to be served at a Sikh wedding celebration. A guest at the wedding, who had an egg allergy, died after eating ras malai supplied by the caterer, which did in fact contain eggs. The claimant contended that the defendant should have taken reasonable care to ensure that the food he was serving did not contain eggs, to both avoid offending Sikh principles and to pre-vent the injury of those allergic to eggs. The question was not about whether the defendant owed a duty of care to the deceased, it was accepted that he did, the issue for the court concerned the nature and scope of that duty. The trial judge had approached the issue of liability by asking: '... should the defendant have foreseen: (a) that food with egg in it might injure a guest who was allergic to egg; (b) that a guest or guests allergic to egg were reasonably to be anticipated, who would not be suspicious of there being egg in the food because it was being served at a Sikh temple; (c) if so, did the defendant take reasonable care to ensure that there was no egg in the food he served?' The judge answered yes to (a) and (b) and at (c) found that the defendant did not take reasonable care to ensure that there was no egg in the bought in ras malai. The caterer appealed against the decision that he was liable for personal injuries sustained by the deceased.

Held

In dismissing the appeal, the Court of Appeal said although there had obviously been a sufficient degree of proximity between the deceased and the caterer to support a duty of care in relation to the suitability of food served at the wedding, the critical question was whether the nature of the occasion was such as to extend the scope of the ordinary duty of care to encompass personal injury caused through the consumption of otherwise wholesome food containing eggs. Because in this case there was an additional requirement that the food at the wedding should not contain ingredients prohibited by Sikhism, the deceased had been entitled to rely on the defendant to ensure that he did not suffer harm as a result of eating food containing egg. [2010] EWCA Civ 13.

THINK POINT

The Court of Appeal reiterated the *Caparo* principle which had decisively rejected the proposition that the existence of a duty of care is to be determined merely by foreseeability of harm. The need for what is usually described as a sufficient degree of "proximity" between the claimant and the defendant and the controlling principle that the imposition of a duty of care should be "fair, just and reasonable" in all the circumstances was emphasised.

THE THREE-STAGE APPROACH

Key Principle

Whatever the nature of the harm suffered by the plaintiff, all three elements of the tripartite test, foreseeability, proximity and questions of justice and reasonableness, must be applied.

MARC RICH & CO V BISHOP ROCK MARINE CO LTD 1995

A vessel, *The Nicholas H*, developed a crack while carrying a cargo from South America to Italy. A surveyor employed by a marine classification society pronounced that, with temporary welding work, the vessel was fit to complete the voyage. A few days later the ship sank with a total loss of the cargo.

Held
❖ (HL) The House of Lords held that the classification society owed no duty of care to the cargo owners. Although the damage was physical harm (damage to property) rather than pure economic loss resulting from the surveyor's negligent statement that the vessel was seaworthy, this was insufficient to give rise to a duty of care. A number of policy factors pointed against a decision in favour of the owners. Classification societies were independent non-profit making entities, operating for the sole purpose of promoting the collective welfare, namely, the safety of ships and lives at sea. A finding of liability might lead to classification societies adopting a more "defensive position". If a duty of care was to be recognised it would enable cargo owners, or their insurers, to upset the balance of the international conventions governing shopowners' liability to cargo owners. In addition, another layer of insurance cover would be wastefully introduced into the structure. [1995] 3 All E.R. 307.

Commentary
In *Watson v British Boxing Board of Control* [2001] Q.B. 1134 (see p.61), a boxer who suffered brain damage following a boxing match alleged that the Board which regulates boxing had been negligent in not providing a better level of ringside medical care. Lord Phillips in the Court of Appeal described the case as a unique one because here, rather than preventing it, the causing of physical harm was the object of the activity. Taking account of the boxer's reliance on the Board to reduce the effects of injuries once they occurred the court concluded that in all the circumstances of the case it was fair, just and reasonable to impose a duty of care. It should be noted that the fact that the Board was a non-profit making organisation (like the defendant in the *Marc Rich* case, above) was not enough to deny the justice of finding liability.

Key Principle
In respect of claims for personal injury the question of whether a duty arises depends on the degree of control and responsibility which the defendant had over the situation which involved potential injury to the claimant.

PERRETT V COLLINS 1998
A passenger who was injured in an aircraft accident, allegedly caused by the unairworthy state of the aircraft, claimed in negligence against an inspector who had certified that it was fit to fly. In defending the claim in negligence the defendants sought to rely on *Marc Rich & Co.*

Held

A duty of care was owed in these circumstances. The defendants had assumed a degree of responsibility. The reasoning in *Marc Rich* was based upon broad policy considerations relating to the organisation of maritime trade which were peculiar to that situation. In the present case involving personal injury, the inspector had an independent and critical role because under the terms of the Air Navigation Order 1989 the aircraft could not lawfully fly unless such a certificate had been issued. On this ground the inspector owed a duty of care to potential passengers to use reasonable care in inspecting the aircraft and issuing the certificate. [1998] 2 Lloyd's Rep. 255.

Commentary

(1) *Perrett* was distinguished in *Sutradhar* (discussed below) where the defendant had no control whatever, whether in law or in practice, over the supply of drinking water in Bangladesh, nor was there any statute, contract or other arrangement which imposed upon it responsibility for ensuring that it was safe to drink. In *Perrett* the aircraft could not lawfully fly unless the certificate for fitness to fly had been issued.

(2) Unlike the comparatively narrow classes of potential claimants likely to be injured by the crashing aircraft in *Perrett*, the class of potential claimants in *Sutradhar* was the entire population of Bangladesh or, at the very least, that of the areas tested during the 1992 survey in question.

Key Principle

In circumstances where a defendant undertakes a duty under contract, the court may find any limitation on liability in the contract to be a good reason to limit the duty in tort as well. In these exceptional cases, mainly involving property damage rather than personal injury, allowing a claim would upset the prior allocation of risks between the parties.

NORWICH CITY COUNCIL v HARVEY 1989

The defendant sub-contractor's employee negligently used a blowtorch which resulted in the plaintiff building owner's swimming pool being destroyed by fire. A clause in the contract between the main contractor (who had sub-contracted work to Harvey) and the building owner excluded liability for fire damage and provided that loss or damage from fire would be at the sole risk of the plaintiff. Although the main contractor was clearly entitled to invoke the exclusion clause, there was no direct contract between the plaintiff and the defendant sub-contractor. The question before the court was whether the sub-contractor was entitled to take the benefit of the exclusion clause.

Held

Although this was a case of property damage and within the scope of the normal duty of care, the Court of Appeal held that the exclusion clause prevented any duty arising between the sub-contractor and the plaintiff. The allocation of risk formed part of the contractual context within which the sub-contractor had taken on the work and therefore neither the sub-contractor nor, consequently, his employee, was under a duty to the plaintiff with regard to fire damage. [1989] 1 All E.R. 1180.

Commentary

In *British Telecommunications Plc v James Thomson & Sons (Engineers) Ltd* [1999] 2 All E.R. 241, a duty of care was held to exist between British Telecommunications (BT) and the defendant sub-contractor who had allegedly caused damage by fire to BT's property. The conditions of contract entered into by BT and the main contractor provided that "nominated sub-contractors" were expressly entitled to cover under a policy of insurance against the risk of fire. Any sub-contractor other than a nominated sub-contractor was referred to as "domestic sub-contractor" and, by a letter dated January 8, 1990 the main contractor set out its terms of contract with Thomson under which Thomson became a domestic sub-contractor. When BT brought an action for damages Thomson argued that in light of the insurance provisions in the main contract it was not fair, just or reasonable to impose a duty of care upon them. In allowing BT's appeal, the House of Lords said that it was necessary to take full account of the contractual provisions and, in this case, the distinction between nominated sub-contractors and domestic sub-contractors was crucial. Since the insurance policy specifically covered nominated sub-contractors, it would not be fair to grant protection to domestic sub-contractors who were not covered under the policy.

POLICY AS A CRITERION OF DUTY: "NO DUTY" SITUATIONS

Key Principle

Public policy is capable of constituting a separate and independent ground for holding that liability in negligence should not be imposed.

> HILL V CHIEF CONSTABLE OF WEST YORKSHIRE POLICE 1988
> The plaintiff was the mother of the last victim of the mass murderer, the "Yorkshire Ripper" (Peter Sutcliffe). She claimed damages on the basis that the police had negligently failed to apprehend the murderer before her daughter was killed.

Held

❖ (HL) Notwithstanding that harm was reasonably foreseeable, there was insufficient proximity between the police and the victim. The requirement of foreseeability was fulfilled in the sense that the harm to victims such as Miss Hill was reasonably foreseeable if Sutcliffe were not apprehended. However, under the *Anns* test more was needed to establish a duty of care: either a relationship of control between the police and the killer (similar to that between the prison guards and the boys in *Dorset Yacht*) or a proximity of the police to the victim. As Sutcliffe could not be said to have been under their control and there was nothing to set Miss Hill apart as being more at risk than the rest of the female population, then this element of the *Anns* equation was not fulfilled and there been no duty of care. The House of Lords further stated that a general duty of care to protect all members of the public from the consequences of crime would be impracticable and, on grounds of public policy, deeply damaging to police operations. [1988] 2 All E.R. 238.

Commentary

In *Brooks v Commissioner of Police for the Metropolis* [2005] UKHL 24, Duwayne Brooks, a friend of Stephen Lawrence who witnessed Stephen's racist murder, suffered post-traumatic stress as the result of the way he was treated by the police following the murder, first as a suspect and later as a witness but not as the victim of crime. In rejecting a claim in negligence against the police the approach in *Hill* was applied by House of Lords. According to Lord Steyn:

> "[T]he core principle of *Hill* has remained unchallenged in our domestic jurisprudence and in European jurisprudence for many years. If a case such as the Yorkshire Ripper case, which was before the House in *Hill*, arose for decision today I have no doubt that it would be decided in the same way. It is, of course,

desirable that police officers should treat victims and witnesses properly and with respect … But to convert that ethical value into general legal duties of care on the police towards victims and witnesses would be going too far."

Key Principle
Even where a proximate relationship between the claimant and the police exists, the *Hill* immunity extends beyond the failure of police to apprehend criminals.

OSMAN V FERGUSON 1993
There were fatal consequences when police had failed to act on warnings that a teacher, who developed a disturbing infatuation with one of his students, was likely to commit serious offences. The teacher conducted a campaign of harassment against the Osman family, which culminated in his killing the father and injuring the son.

Held
Although the Court of Appeal was prepared to accept that this case was different from *Hill* in that there was a sufficient relationship of proximity between the plaintiff's family and the police, the *Hill* immunity was applied and the case failed on grounds of public policy. [1993] 4 All E.R. 344.

THINK POINT

Following the rejection of their claim, the applicants brought a case against the United Kingdom, alleging a violation of their rights under the **European Convention of Human Rights**. Subsequently, in *Osman v UK* (1998) 5 B.H.R.C. 293, the European Court of Human Rights held that there had been no violation of art.2 (right to life). It was held that the requirement that the police knew or ought to have known that there was a real and immediate threat to Osman family was not met since none of the incidents prior to the shootings were life threatening. However, a rule forbidding action against the police regardless of the circumstances and effectively granting a "blanket immunity" in negligence was found to be in breach of art.6 of the Convention (the right to a fair trial). Nevertheless, it was pointed out that the Convention does not prevent courts taking into account public policy issues: a public interest in protecting police from civil claims could be asserted but this must be balanced with other competing public interests.

Commentary

(1) In considering whether to exclude a duty of care on grounds of policy, effectively granting immunity to some defendants, the Human Rights Act 1998 (incorporating the **European Convention of Human Rights** into English law) will require the courts to balance whether granting such immunity to a defendant is proportionate to the interference with the claimant's human rights.

(2) *Van Colle* (below) also involved a claim under art.2 where a prosecution witness was shot dead shortly before he was due to give evidence in a criminal prosecution. The test in *Osman* was not met because it could not reasonably have been anticipated from the information available to the police at that time that there was a real and immediate risk to victim's life.

Key Principle

The policy reasons outlined in *Hill* and restated in *Brooks* (above) that the police owed no common law duty of care to protect individuals against harm caused by criminals are preserved. A duty of care in negligence would detrimentally affect the work of police by causing them to act defensively in order to avoid negligence claims and divert police resources away from their primary function of investigating and suppressing crime.

VAN COLLE V CHIEF CONSTABLE OF HERTFORDSHIRE AND SMITH V CHIEF CONSTABLE OF SUSSEX (2008)

In *Van Colle* the chief constable appealed against the finding that the police had been under a duty to take preventive measures to protect a witness who was being threatened and subsequently shot dead days before he was to give evidence. This claim relied on art.2 of the ECHR rather than common law negligence. In *Smith* the claimant, who had repeatedly informed the police that his former partner had threatened to kill him, brought an action under the common law. He claimed that the police had ample evidence of these threats and had no excuse for not preventing his partner from carrying out the threatened hammer attack which caused him serious injuries. The issue was whether the Court of Appeal had been correct to find that the police were not immune from negligence liability in these two cases.

Held ....

Both appeals against liability were allowed. In *Van Colle* the *Osman* test, that the police knew or ought to have known "at the time" of the shooting of "a real and immediate risk to the life" of an identified individual from the criminal acts of a third party was not met. In respect of Smith's claim, the balance of advantage in this difficult area lay in preserving the principle set out in *Hill* whereby, in the absence of special circumstances, the police owed no common law duty of care to protect individuals against harm caused by criminals. [2008] UKHL 50.

THINK POINT

It should be noted that in *Smith*, the Court of Appeal remarked that in cases involving the police the very proximity of the parties can not only create a duty of care, but can overcome the public policy considerations which would otherwise bar the claim (as in *Swinney* below) and said that whether under art.2 or at common law, it cannot be a valid ground of distinction that an informer is entitled to protection while a witness is not. This would indicate that the justification for the *Hill* immunity against police liability in negligence is becoming increasingly tenuous.

Key Principle ....

The immunity in negligence in respect of police activities in the investigation and suppression of crime may be displaced by other considerations of public policy.

SWINNEY V CHIEF CONSTABLE OF NORTHUMBRIA POLICE 1996
The plaintiff had supplied information to the police relating to serious crime. She and her husband had been subjected to threats of violence and arson when the defendant negligently allowed her name as a police informant to fall into the wrong hands. They suffered psychological injury and had to move house as the result of the threats and intimidation to which they were subjected and they sued the police in negligence on the basis that they had been a duty of care to keep her details confidential. The defence sought to have the case "struck out", arguing that, based on *Hill*, it disclosed no cause of action.

Held

The Court of Appeal found the required foreseeability and proximity. When it came to the policy stage of the test the plaintiff was found to have at least an arguable case on grounds of public policy because the fight against crime is daily dependent upon information fed to the police by members of the public. The immunity in respect of police activities in the investigation and suppression of crime could be displaced by other considerations of public policy. Therefore, in spite of *Hill*, the plaintiff had an arguable case in negligence: there was a sufficient degree of proximity as she was not merely a member of the public, but had a special relationship with the police which rendered her distinguishable from the general public. Moreover, the need to encourage informants to come forward without undue fear of their identities becoming known was vital to the suppression of crime, and this strong public policy argument had to be balanced against other public policy considerations. [1996] 3 All E.R. 449.

Commentary

Although the court refused to strike out the claim and a duty of care was imposed, the plaintiff's claim failed when the case proceeded to trial. On examination of the facts it was held that the police, in leaving the information in a locked briefcase in a locked car, had not been negligent. So, even though a duty of care was established there had been no breach of duty. *Swinney v Chief Constable of Northumbria (No.2)* [1999] 11 Admin. L.R. 811.

Key Principle

The public policy decision in *Rondel v Worsley* [1969] 1 A.C. 191 (below) that advocates enjoyed immunity from liability for the negligent conduct of a case in court is no longer justified. The abolition of this immunity applies whether the negligence alleged against the advocate relates to a civil action or to a criminal prosecution.

HALL (ARTHUR JS) & CO V SIMONS 2000

In three separate cases, clients brought proceedings against their solicitors in which they alleged that the solicitors had been negligent. The judge, at first instance, struck out claims in negligence on the grounds that the defendants were entitled to rely on the advocates' immunity recognised by the House of Lords in *Rondel v Worsley*. The Court of Appeal held that the claims should not have been struck out and the solicitors appealed against this decision.

Held

The seven-member House of Lords dismissed the appeals and held that because of the changes in society and in the law which have taken place since the decision in *Rondel v Worsley*, the propriety of maintaining such immunity could no longer be justified. The advantages which accrued to the public interest from advocates' immunity in negligence must be balanced with the normal right of an individual to be compensated for a legal wrong and there is no longer sufficient public interest to justify the maintenance of this immunity. Their Lordships were unanimous in their decision to abolish the immunity in civil proceedings and (by a majority) to abolish it in criminal proceedings. [2000] 3 W.L.R. 543.

Commentary

(1) *In Rondel v Worsley* [1969] 1 A.C. 191, the House of Lords had held that a barrister is immune from liability in negligence in respect of the manner in which a case is conducted in court on the following public policy grounds:

- (i) barristers should be able to carry out their duties independently and without fear;
- (ii) a barrister owes a duty to the court which transcends that owed to a client and potential liability might deflect from that duty;
- (iii) actions against barristers would in effect amount to a retrial in the cases where negligence was alleged;
- (iv) under the "cab rank" rule of the Bar, barristers are obliged to accept any client if a proper fee is paid.

(2) The court's response to (i) and (ii) was to dismiss the "divided loyalty" argument on the grounds that it was difficult to justify this in the case of advocates when other professionals—doctors, for example—enjoyed no such immunity. It was also pointed out that in Canada, where advocates have never enjoyed immunity in negligence, there is no evidence to suggest that their overriding duty to the court was compromised. The response to (iii) was that total immunity is now unnecessary because a separate doctrine of abuse of process exists to prevent undesirable retrials. With regard to (iv) it was thought that the significance of the cab rank rule in daily practice is not great and that barristers could use other means (e.g. higher fees) to deter unwanted clients.

Key Principle

The public interest in the abolition of an advocate's immunity in negligence must be balanced with the advocate's independence. The application of this principle should not stifle an advocate's independence of mind and action in the manner in which they conduct litigation and advise their clients.

MOY V PETTMAN SMITH 2005

The claimant underwent an operation which went wrong owing to the admitted negligence of the health authority concerned. A firm of solicitors and a barrister acted for him in his claim in negligence against the health authority. The health authority offered £150,000 in settlement and a waiver of the costs orders against the claimant but, on the barrister's advice, he rejected the offer. As the case subsequently progressed, the health authority's offer fell to £120,000 on the normal terms as to costs and, at this stage, the claimant was advised by the barrister to accept the offer as the best the health authority was willing to make. In an action in negligence against the barrister, the trial judge held that she had not been negligent in advising the claimant. However, the Court of Appeal held that although her assessment of the prospects of success in the case was not negligent, the barrister had been negligent in failing to give the claimant sufficiently detailed advice in order that he might make an informed decision as to whether to accept the offer in settlement. She appealed to the House of Lords.

Held

Her appeal was allowed. Taking account of all the circumstances, the advice given by the barrister was held to fall within the range of that to be expected of reasonably competent counsel of her seniority and experience. Given the need for urgent advice under a situation of some pressure, it could not be said that her advice to the claimant had fallen below that to be expected of a reasonable practitioner. The Court of Appeal was said to have judged her actions too harshly. [2005] UKHL 7.

POLICY AS A CRITERION OF DUTY: LIABILITY OF PUBLIC BODIES

Key Principle

There is no duty of care on local authorities in carrying out their discretionary statutory functions. Where, however, the conduct results from an improper exercise of that discretion there may be liability: the question then arises as to whether it is fair, just and reasonable to impose a duty of care in negligence upon a body exercising a public function.

Actions were taken by children against a number of local authorities for alleged breaches of the Children Act 1989. The cases against Bedfordshire and Newham concerned abuse: the local authorities had negligently failed to take abused children into care in one case, and in the other, identified the wrong person as the abuser and had wrongly taken the child into care. In the cases involving Dorset, Bromley and Hampshire, it was alleged that the authorities had failed to properly identify and provide for the special educational needs of the plaintiffs.

Held

The House of Lords ruled that it would not be fair, just and reasonable to subject the authorities to a common law duty to take care in carrying out their discretionary statutory functions. The impact of litigation could lead to that function being performed in a detrimentally defensive manner and contrary to the public interest. [1995] 3 W.L.R. 152.

Commentary

(1) In addition to their case in common law negligence, the children brought an action for breach of statutory duty, claiming that their injury resulted from breaches of the **Children Act 1989** by their local authority. Their Lordships held that in the light of the other range of remedies under the Act (e.g. the statutory appeals procedure in the education cases) it was inconceivable that Parliament intended an additional right of action for breach of statutory duty. A tortious duty of care was incompatible with these remedies and would also cut across a complex statutory framework (e.g. educational bodies, doctors, police, etc.) established by Parliament for the protection of children at risk.

(2) The imposition of a duty on a local authority in exercising its public function could lead to social services departments performing their duties in an "unduly defensive frame of mind". The resources directed towards the investigation and defence of spurious claims, together with awards of damages and costs, would diminish the limited funds available for other child protection activities.

Key Principle

A distinction is made between a statutory "duty" on a local authority which places it under a duty to provide a service, and a statutory "power" where a local authority has a power (but not a duty) to act.

STOVIN V WISE 1996

A road verge on which a bank of earth obstructed drivers' views had been responsible for several accidents. Norfolk County Council, which was aware of the problem, had a power (under the Highways Act 1980) to improve a road junction by removing the bank of earth which obstructed visibility on the highway. A decision to remove the hazard was taken but the authority then failed to exercise its statutory power to require the land owner to remove the obstruction. Wise negligently drove out from a side road and claimed that the dangerous junction had significantly contributed to the accident. The House of Lords (by a bare majority) held that the local authority owed no duty of care to road users for failure to exercise its powers: there was a statutory power to improve the dangerous road junction but the local authority was not under a duty to do so. This case was complicated by the fact that it involved an *omission* to act and in finding the local authority not liable for its *omission* to act, the court applied the principle that there is no liability where a breach consists of a pure omission and the defendant has not created the harm suffered. [1996] A.C. 923.

Commentary ....

(1) The significant factor in this case was that Parliament had chosen to give the council a *power* rather than a *duty* in respect of the removal of obstructions. According to Lord Hoffmann:

> "... the fact that Parliament has conferred a discretion must be some indication that the policy of the act conferring the power was not to create a right to compensation."

THINK POINT

In *Gorringe v Calderdale MBC* [2004] UKHL 15, the House of Lords applied *Stovin v Wise* and found that a highway authority's failure to place a marking or to install a road sign warning motorists that they were approaching a dangerous part of the road did not constitute a breach of statutory duty. The provision of road signs or markings was quite different from keeping the highway in repair and the existence of statutory powers and duties to promote and improve road safety under the **Road Traffic Act 1988** did not create a parallel common law duty.

Key Principle ....

In the light of *Osman* (above), the claimant is entitled to have his case tried and the facts found before excluding a duty simply because the actions of the local authority involved the exercise of discretion. Courts should be cautious about striking out a claim on the basis that it is not fair, just and reasonable to impose a duty of care without first hearing the evidence.

BARRETT V ENFIELD LBC 1999

A foster child, who had been in the care of the local authority between the ages of 10 months and 17 years, claimed that he suffered various psychiatric problems as a result of the authority's negligence in the way it made and supervised his foster placements during this time.

Held ....

The House of Lords reversed the Court of Appeal's decision to uphold the council's application to strike out the plaintiff's claim. [1999] 3 W.L.R. 79.

Commentary ....

(1) The decision in *X (Minors) v Bedfordshire County Council* was whether or not to take the plaintiff into local authority care (which involves exercising a statutory discretion). The factual distinction between this case and *X* is that here the alleged negligent treatment of the plaintiff took place after he had been taken into the local authority's care. Having taken the child into care, it was at least arguable that the local authority could be liable for negligence in its decisions concerning his foster placements and supervision.

(2) Lord Browne-Wilkinson was critical of the European Court of Human Rights' decision in *Osman*, and pointed out that art.6 of the **European Convention of Human Rights** appears to be concerned with a procedural right: the right to a fair trial. The duty of care in negligence is concerned with the substantive right of whether a claimant is ever entitled to bring an action for negligence in a given set of circumstances. Nevertheless, he thought that in the present, very unsatisfactory, state of affairs it was prudent not to use the striking-out procedure where it was not a clear and obvious case. (Since the enactment of the Human Rights Act 1998, the **European Convention of Human Rights** is now directly enforceable in domestic courts.)

THINK POINT

In *Z v United Kingdom* [2001] 2 F.C.R. 246, in a unanimous decision, the European Court of Human Rights held that failure by a UK local authority to provide children with appropriate protection against serious long-term neglect and abuse amounted to inhuman and degrading treatment in breach of art.3 of the **European Convention of Human Rights**. The court further held by 15 votes to 2 that the applicants had not been afforded an effective remedy in breach of art.13 of the Convention concerning the right to an effective remedy before a national authority. As to the alleged violations of the right to a fair trial guaranteed by art.6, the court held by 12 votes to 5 that the United Kingdom had not breached art.6 of the Convention. The majority thought that the House of Lords' decision in *X (Minors)* not to extend a duty of care to the claimants could not be characterised as either an exclusionary rule or an immunity which deprived them of access to court. Accepting that there was no simple exclusionary rule but an incremental development of the "fair, just and reasonable" filter on all negligence claims against public authorities which was compatible with art.6 suggests that a court can deny the existence of a duty of care as not fair, just and reasonable. This decision can be reached before holding a hearing to establish the facts and seems to mark a "retreat" by the European Court of Human Rights from its position in *Osman*.

Key Principle

X v Bedfordshire County Council did not lay down a principle that there should be a blanket immunity in respect of the liability of local authorities for the provision of educational services.

PHELPS V HILLINGDON LBC 2000
The Court of Appeal allowed an appeal against a first instance finding that an educational psychologist, employed by the local authority, was under a duty of care to the plaintiff for failing to diagnose her dyslexia. In the Court of Appeal, Stuart Smith L.J. expressed the view that it was most unsatisfactory that the local authority should be made liable in negligence by the "back door" of vicarious liability, unless that responsibility was clearly established.

Held ....

The House of Lords reversed the decision and held that the educational psychologist owed Miss Phelps a duty of care. The decision was based on the fact that an educational psychologist is specifically called in to advise in relation to the assessment and future provision for a specific child, and it is clear that parents and teachers will follow that advice. Educational psychologists assume a duty of care to pupils but according to Lord Slynn:

> "That phrase can be misleading in that it can suggest that the professional person must knowingly and deliberately accept responsibility. ... The phrase means simply that the law recognises that there is a duty of care. It is not so much that responsibility is assumed as that it is recognised or imposed by the law."

It was also held that Hillingdon LBC was vicariously liable for the educational psychologist's breaches of duty. [2000] 4 All E.R. 504.

Commentary ....

(1) This decision indicates a shift by the courts away from blanket immunity.

(2) In *Bradford-Smart v West Sussex County Council* [2002] EWCA 7, the Court of Appeal recognised that although, in general, a school was responsible for its pupils only when they were inside the school, in exceptional circumstances a school may be liable for failure to take reasonable steps to prevent bullying outside school (in this particular case the local authority was not in breach of its duty).

(3) *Phelps* was applied in *A v Essex CC* [2003] EWCA Civ 1848, a case involving two young children placed with the claimants for adoption. One of the children had severe behavioural problems and the adopting parents claimed that the defendant local authority was vicariously liable for the failure of its social workers to disclose relevant information known by them about the child's behaviour. Although it was not fair, just and reasonable to impose on professionals involved in compiling reports for adoption agencies a duty of care towards prospective parents, a local authority could be vicariously liable for social workers who failed to communicate to prospective adopters information about the child's health history and current state of health that the agency decided they should have.

Key Principle

The same action may give rise to a duty to one of the parties involved in a case but not to another.

> ### JD v East Berkshire Community Health Trust 2005
>
> In this case three different sets of parents sued for the psychological injuries they had suffered due to misdiagnosis of child abuse by social services or health authorities. In *JD* itself, a boy's allergic reaction was interpreted wrongly by the social service department as indicating mistreatment by his mother and he was put on the at-risk register for some months until the mistake was discovered. The mother contended that the health care professionals' duty to exercise due skill and care in the investigation of suspected abuse extended to the child's parents as primary carers as well as to the child.

Held

The House of Lords dismissed the parents' claims for damages for psychiatric injury. On public policy grounds, health professionals, acting in good faith in what they believed were the best interests of the child, should not be subject to potentially conflicting duties when deciding whether a child might have been abused. It was not fair, just and reasonable to impose such a duty, *Caparo Industries Plc v Dickman* (1990) applied. Apart from the policy reasons there could be a potential conflict of interest if a duty were owed to the mother as well as the child. [2005] UKHL 23.

Commentary

According to Lord Rodger:

> "The duty to the children is simply to exercise reasonable care and skill in diagnosing and treating any condition from which they may be suffering. In carrying out that duty the doctors have regard only to the interests of the children. Suppose, however, that they were also under a duty to the parents not to cause them psychiatric harm by concluding that they might have abused their child. Then, in deciding how to proceed, the doctors would always have to take account of the risk that they might harm the parents in this way. There would be not one but two sets of interests to be considered. Acting on, or persisting in, a suspicion of abuse might well be reasonable when only the child's interests were engaged, but unreasonable if the interests of the parents had also to be taken into account. Of its very nature,

therefore, this kind of duty of care to the parents would cut across the duty of care to the children."

JD v East Berkshire was distinguished in *Merthyr Tydfil CBC v C* [2010] EWHC 62 (QB) in a case involving children that had been sexually abused by a neighbour's child. The mother of the children claimed that she had suffered a psychiatric condition caused by the local authority's negligence in failing to properly deal with her reports of abuse. The local authority claimed that owing a duty of care to a parent would potentially conflict with the duty of care that it owed to the children and sought to rely on the decision in *JD*. The Court said that the decision in *JD* did not lay down any general principle that, where an authority owed a duty of care to a child, it could not as a matter of law at the same time owe a duty of care to parents of that child; a duty of care may be owed to parents as well as children, provided the parents are not suspected of abuse.

Key Principle

Fire brigades are not under a common law duty of care to answer an emergency call nor under a duty to take reasonable care to do so, because there is no proximity of relationship between the fire brigade and a building owner. Liability in negligence in the tackling of a fire would not arise unless the fire service negligently increased the damage or caused additional damage.

CAPITAL AND COUNTIES PLC V HAMPSHIRE COUNTY COUNCIL 1997
A number of consolidated appeals were heard in respect of claims in negligence against the fire brigade. In one case, the fire officer at the scene had ordered the sprinkler system in a burning building to be switched off. If the sprinkler had not been switched off the damage caused by the fire would have been far less extensive. In the second case, the fire brigade attended the fire and then left the scene believing that the fire was out. It failed, however, to notice smouldering debris which re-ignited and caused further damage. The third case involved the failure of the fire service to inspect and maintain hydrants and ensure that an adequate supply of water was available at the scene of the fire.

Held

The Court of Appeal held that there is no proximity of relationship between the fire brigade and a building owner in respect of negligence in the tackling of a fire, and the relevance of policy considerations including the possibility of defensive fire-fighting was confirmed. [1997] 2 All E.R. 865.

Commentary

In *Harris v Evans* [1998] 3 All E.R. 522, similar reasoning was applied. The plaintiff started to offer bungee jumps from his mobile telescopic crane. The specialist inspector from the Health and Safety Executive recommended that the plaintiff take further measures to ensure the safety of participants and spectators and a prohibition notice was served on the plaintiff. When it subsequently became clear that the inspector's advice had been out of line with the Health and Safety Executive's policy, the plaintiff sued for the economic losses that he had suffered as a result of the inspector's negligence. The Court of Appeal held that it was not fair, just and reasonable to impose a duty on the Health and Safety Executive. It was further held that the imposition of a duty of care would probably have a detrimental effect by producing an unduly cautious and defensive approach by inspectors to the use of their enforcement powers and undermine the framework public protection provided by statute.

Key Principle

Once an ambulance service accepts a call for assistance it assumes responsibility for the particular patient and a duty of care arises to those to whom it is summoned to assist.

KENT V GRIFFITHS 2000

In an emergency, a doctor called the ambulance service and requested that an ambulance be sent to the pregnant claimant's home as a matter of urgency. Despite a number of further calls, the ambulance did not finally arrive until 38 minutes after the original call. Although the claimant was given oxygen on the way to the hospital, she suffered respiratory arrest which resulted in brain damage and a miscarriage.

Held

The Court of Appeal held that in certain circumstances an ambulance service could be liable in negligence. Although no duty is owed to the public at large to respond to a call for help, once a 999 call in a serious emergency had been accepted, the ambulance service did have an obligation to provide the service for a named individual at a specified address. [2000] 2 W.L.R. 1158.

Key Principle

Where a body makes provision in its rules for medical precautions to be employed and makes compliance with the rules mandatory, there is a sufficient relationship of proximity between the body and its members so as to give rise to a duty of care.

WATSON V BRITISH BOXING BOARD OF CONTROL 2001

Michael Watson, a professional boxer, fought for a super-middleweight title according to the Board's rules. He suffered brain damage after the bout and claimed that the British Boxing Board of Control was under a duty to take reasonable care to ensure that personal injuries already sustained were properly treated. Watson alleged that the Board had negligently failed to impose rules which would ensure adequate medical facilities, and he contended that if he had received immediate attention at the ringside he would not have sustained permanent brain damage.

Held

As the sole organisation responsible for making rules and regulations governing the sport and in setting safety standards to be observed by those involved in professional boxing in the UK, in all the circumstances it was fair, just and reasonable to impose a duty of care on the Board. [2001] Q.B. 1134.

THINK POINT

In *Vowles v Evans* [2003] EWCA Civ 318, the Court of Appeal held that, as a matter of policy, a referee of a rugby match, acting in an amateur capacity, owed a duty of care to players. In applying the rules of the game, it was fair, just and reasonable that the players should be entitled to rely on the referee for their safety. It was further noted that it was possible for the referee or Welsh Rugby Union, the body who appointed him, to take out insurance cover against third party liability.

LIABILITY FOR THE UNBORN

Key Principle

A duty of care is owed to an unborn person which becomes actionable on the live birth of the child.

BURTON V ISLINGTON HEALTH AUTHORITY 1993

The plaintiff's mother was admitted for an operation to the defendant hospital. At the time, unknown to the hospital, the woman was pregnant. The plaintiff alleged that she had been born with abnormalities because of the operation the defendants had performed on her mother when she was an embryo in her mother's womb. The defendants applied to strike out the claim on the grounds, that, at the time of the alleged negligence, the plaintiff had no legal status.

Held

The plaintiff had a cause of action which is available to a child born alive for injuries sustained in the womb. [1993] Q.B. 204.

Commentary

The Congenital Disabilities (Civil Liability) Act 1976 was inapplicable in this case because the plaintiff was born before the Act came into force. The Act which provides that a child who is born alive but disabled as a result of an occurrence before its birth may have a cause of action in negligence has replaced the common law for births which occurred after July 22, 1976, the date upon which it came into force.

Key Principle

The common law recognises no claim for "wrongful life" whereby a child claims that s/he would not have been born at all, but for the defendant's negligence.

MCKAY V ESSEX AREA HEALTH AUTHORITY 1982

The plaintiff's mother had undergone tests during her pregnancy when she realised that she had been in contact with rubella (German measles). The mother would have opted for an abortion had the tests proved positive but she had been negligently told that her unborn child was not infected with rubella. The plaintiff was born with severe disabilities and claimed in respect of the harm caused to her by her birth encumbered by these disabilities.

Held ....

❖ (CA) The law recognised no claim for "wrongful life": to allow a child to recover damages for the pain and suffering of being alive at all was against public policy. [1982] Q.B. 1166.

Commentary ....

It was stated obiter that "wrongful life" claims could not be brought under the **Congenital Disabilities (Civil Liability) Act 1976** because of the wording of s.1(2)(b) which requires that when the negligence arises after conception that "the child is born with disabilities which would not otherwise have been present". It should be noted that in this case the claim was not for the disabilities, but only for failing to give the mother the chance to have an abortion. The plaintiff's disabilities were caused by the rubella, not by the negligence of the hospital.

Key Principle ....

Claims by parents for "wrongful birth" after the failure of negligently conducted sterilisations or abortions are recognised by the courts.

THAKE V MAURICE 1986

Mr Thake had a vasectomy operation which was carefully and competently performed by the defendant. The minute risk of natural reversal of the surgery materialised and three years later his wife conceived again. Believing her husband to be sterile she thought that she could not be pregnant and by the time the wife went to the doctor she was told that she was five months pregnant and too late for an abortion. The plaintiffs sued on the basis that the defendant had failed to warn them of the small chance that the vasectomy might reverse itself naturally.

Held ....

❖ (CA) The defendant was liable and the court rejected the contention that public policy would bar the award of damages to parents following the birth of a healthy child after the father had undergone a vasectomy which was alleged to have been negligently performed. [1986] Q.B. 644.

Commentary ....

(1) Initially, in *Udale v Bloomsbury Area Health Authority* [1983] 2 All E.R. 522, where the defendant health authority accepted responsibility for a surgeon's negligent performance of a sterilisation operation, Jupp J. refused the mother compensation towards the upkeep of the child. He said the birth of a child

was a blessing and the financial cost of such a blessing was irrecoverable. It offended society's notions of what is right and the value afforded to human life, and the knowledge that his parents had claimed damages in respect of his birth might distress and damage the child emotionally as he grows to maturity.

(2) Jupp J. was overruled on the policy issue by the Court of Appeal in *Emeh v Kensington Area Health Authority* [1985] Q.B. 1012, where their Lordships expressed a disinclination to place limits on the scope of the duty owed to the mother by reference to what was "socially unacceptable".

Key Principle
In claims for economic loss of earnings and for the costs of bringing up a child, the defendants must have known that their advice to the patient would be acted upon without further inquiry.

GOODWILL V BRITISH PREGNANCY ADVISORY SERVICE 1996
Some years after his vasectomy operation the patient began a sexual relationship with the plaintiff (who was not the doctor's patient) which resulted in her pregnancy and subsequent birth of the child. She claimed that she had relied on the doctor's negligent advice to her partner that his vasectomy had been successful and that he did not need to use contraception in the future.

Held
No duty of care was owed to the plaintiff because the defendants had not voluntarily assumed responsibility to her nor could they have known that their advice to the patient would be communicated to his future sexual partners. [1996] 2 All E.R. 161.

THINK POINT
The plaintiff was a member of a class of persons which was indeterminately large and she was not, therefore, foreseeable. The courts have been unwilling to extend the duty beyond the immediate doctor/patient relationship: the outcome in this case might have been different if, at the time, the plaintiff had been the patient's current sexual partner and the advice had been given directly to both of them.

Key Principle ....

Claims in respect of the financial costs of bringing up a healthy child following advice about, or performance of, negligent sterilisation are not recoverable.

> MCFARLANE V TAYSIDE HEALTH BOARD 1999
>
> The claimants, a married couple, sued the health authority for the negligent failure of a vasectomy performed on the husband and for negligent advice concerning his fertility following the operation. As a consequence of the alleged negligence, a healthy but unplanned child was born. Although the parents stated that they loved and cared for the child, they claimed for the financial costs of her upbringing until the age of 18.

Held ....

Their Lordships unanimously rejected the claim for the costs of the child's upbringing. According to Lord Slynn, claims in respect of the costs of bringing up a healthy child born as a consequence of a failed sterilisation fall into the category of economic loss. Although some potential costs (e.g. relating to the mother's pain and suffering during pregnancy) are recoverable, the economic cost of bringing up a healthy child is not recoverable: it would not be fair, just and reasonable to impose this duty on the doctor or the hospital. [2000] 2 A.C. 59.

Commentary ....

In *Parkinson v St James and Seacroft University NHS Trust* [2001] EWCA Civ 530, the Court of Appeal held that parents of a disabled child born as the result of a negligent sterilisation could claim the extra costs of bringing up the child.

Key Principle ....

For reasons of legal policy, the courts show an unwillingness to regard a child (even if unwanted) as a financial liability and nothing else. The *McFarlane* principle, that the financial costs of bringing up a healthy child could not be regarded as a loss that deserves compensation, cannot be departed from, even where the parent of the child is seriously disabled.

> REES V DARLINGTON MEMORIAL HOSPITAL NHS TRUST 2004
>
> The claimant, who was severely visually handicapped, did not want children because she felt that her eyesight would make it difficult for

her to look after a baby. She underwent a sterilisation operation (for which the defendant admitted negligence) and as a result of the failure of this operation the claimant gave birth to a healthy son. The issue was whether the decision in *McFarlane* (above) meant that none of the costs of bringing up a healthy child could ever be claimed whatever the circumstances. At first instance the trial judge held that the House of Lords decision in *McFarlane* precluded a disabled parent from recovering the economic costs of bringing up a healthy child born as the result of a negligently performed sterilisation. The Court of Appeal, however, said there was a crucial difference in the case of a seriously disabled parent who, unlike an able-bodied one, would be in need of assistance to discharge their basic parental responsibility of looking after a child properly and safely and held that it was fair, just and reasonable that the mother should recover the additional costs.

Held

The House of Lords allowed an appeal by a 4–3 majority on the ground that no exception to the principle in *McFarlane* was justified, even when the parent of the child was seriously disabled. In stating that the law must take the birth of a normal healthy baby to be a blessing and not a detriment, the House reaffirmed its unanimous decision in *McFarlane*. However, a conventional award of £15,000 over and above the award of damages for the pregnancy and birth was made to recognise that a legal wrong had been done and to mark the loss of the right to limit one's family. [2003] UKHL 52.

LIABILITY FOR ACTS OF THIRD PARTIES

Key Principle

There is no general duty of care to prevent third parties from harming others by their deliberate wrongdoing.

SMITH V LITTLEWOODS ORGANISATION LTD 1987

The defendants purchased a cinema which remained empty and unattended for over a month awaiting to be demolished and rebuilt as a supermarket. During this time it was regularly being broken into, mainly by child vandals. Contractors employed by Littlewoods knew about the vandals but neither the defendant nor the police were informed about this. Finally, a fire was deliberately started by the vandals which spread and caused serious damage to the plaintiff's property. Since the vandals would not be worth suing the plaintiffs sought compensation from Littlewoods claiming that the defendants should have prevented the vandals gaining access to the cinema.

Held

❖ (HL) The plaintiff's claim failed. Lord Goff dealt with the matter in terms of pure omission and held that there is no general duty of care to prevent a third party from causing damage. However, he expressed the view that liability would arise where:

> "the defender negligently causes or permits to be created a source of danger, and it is reasonably foreseeable that third parties may interfere with it . . .".

THINK POINT

In *Mitchell v Glasgow City Council* [2009] 1 A.C. 874 the House of Lords held that liability for the criminal act of a third party would arise only where the person who was said to be under that duty had by his words or conduct assumed responsibility for the safety of the person who was at risk. The question here was whether the local authority had assumed a responsibility to protect one of its social housing tenants who, following a long campaign of abuse and threats, was murdered by a fellow tenant. Although the local authority had been aware that the victim's neighbour might resort to violence after being informed that he risked being evicted the required element of a relationship of responsibility was absent, as it would not be "fair, just and reasonable" to impose this duty on a public authority coping with an onerous burden of anti-social behaviour among tenants.

Key Principle

Where there is an existing relationship with the wrongdoer that involves control, a duty of care for omissions may arise.

CARMARTHENSHIRE COUNTY COUNCIL V LEWIS 1955

This case concerned a young child who ran from his nursery school premises on to a nearby busy road. The claimant's husband swerved his car to avoid hitting the child and was himself killed when his car hit a tree.

Held

The House of Lords confirmed the responsibility of parents and teachers for the behaviour of children. The defendant County Council and the teachers at the school were held to have been jointly in control of the child. They were, therefore, under a duty to take reasonable steps to prevent him becoming a danger to others. [1955] A.C. 549.

Commentary

The courts are often reluctant to impose liability; for example, in *Topp v London Country Bus (South West) Ltd* [1993] 1 W.L.R. 976, the Court of Appeal found no liability for the wrongdoing of a third party when a minibus, which had been left parked in a lay-by near to a pub with the key in the ignition waiting for a relief driver who never arrived, was stolen by unknown persons. The plaintiff's wife was killed when the stolen minibus was being driven dangerously by the thief. When the plaintiff sued the defendant bus company it was held that the parked minibus did not fall within a special category of risk as a source of danger on the highway and the acts of the wrongdoer were regarded as a *novus actus interveniens* (see p.121).

Key Principle

Liability may arise in respect of the wrongdoing of others where the defendant is held to have undertaken a duty of care specifically to the plaintiff.

STANSBIE V TROMAN 1948
A decorator who was working in a house was warned by the householder to shut the front door if he left the premises. He carelessly left the house unlocked while he went to fetch more wallpaper. During his absence the house was burgled and some jewellery was stolen.

Held

The decorator was liable for the loss of the jewellery stolen by a third party. His duty to the householder arose from an implied term in his employment contract to keep the premises safe. [1948] 2 K.B. 48.

Key Principle

Where there is a sufficiently close proximity between the defendant and the claimant's harm the defendant may be held to assume a duty of care.

BARRETT V MINISTRY OF DEFENCE 1995

There had been a pattern of excessive drinking among soldiers at a remote Navy base, where drinks were very cheap. One night after a bout of heavy drinking a soldier became unconscious. The duty officer arranged for him to be taken to his room where he was left unchecked. He later died due to choking on vomit and his widow brought an action in negligence against the Ministry of Defence.

Held

The Navy was not liable for preventing the deceased from excessive drinking or for anything that happened prior to his collapse. However, when he collapsed the defendant assumed responsibility for him and the measures taken fell short of the standard reasonably to be expected. The defendant did not summon assistance and its supervision of the deceased was inadequate. [1995] 3 All E.R. 87.

Key Principle

A duty of care is not owed in all cases in which it is foreseeable that in the absence of care someone may suffer physical injury. There must be proximity in the sense of a measure of control over, and responsibility for, the potentially dangerous situation.

SUTRADHAR V NERC 2006

The claimant, a villager, was one of a large number of people in Bangladesh affected by arsenic contamination of his drinking water. Until about 1983 he drank pond water, then a well was sunk in his village and he drank its water instead. In 1991 he developed symptoms associated with arsenical poisoning which, over the years, had become worse. He alleged that the defendant caused or materially contributed to his illness, either by failing to draw attention to the presence of arsenic in the water or by issuing a report which represented that his water was safe to drink. The defendants had been commissioned by the Overseas Development Agency to test local water for minerals which might be harmful to fish. They had not been required to, nor did they ever consider, the testing of the water for arsenic. It was claimed that there was no arguable case that they were in a relationship of proximity with the population of Bangladesh which could make them liable on either of these grounds.

Held

The House of Lords (upholding the Court of Appeal decision) unanimously held there to be no relationship of proximity between the claimants and the defendant that would give rise to a positive duty to test for arsenic in the water. [2006] UKHL 33.

THINK POINT

According to Lord Hoffmann:

"There must be proximity in the sense of a measure of control over and responsibility for the potentially dangerous situation ... [The] principle is not that a duty of care is owed in all cases in which it is foreseeable that in the absence of care someone may suffer physical injury. There must be proximity in the sense of a measure of control over and responsibility for the potentially dangerous situation. Such a principle does not help the Claimant. ... The [defendant] had no control whatever, whether in law or in practice, over the supply of drinking water in Bangladesh, nor was there any statute, contract or other arrangement which imposed upon it responsibility for ensuring that it was safe to drink."

Special Duty Situations

Nervous Shock

. . . .

4

INTRODUCTION

Claims for psychiatric harm, which are not the result of physical injury to the claimant, are dealt with separately from claims for ordinary physical damage. Physical damage caused by negligence will be limited to those within the range of the harmful event, but psychiatric harm may affect a wide range of persons beyond the direct victim of negligent conduct. The courts have therefore adopted a cautious and restrictive approach to the imposition of liability. For example, in *Victorian Railway Commissioners v Coultas* (1888) 12 App. Cas. 222 it was held that harm through nervous shock was not compensatable at all (the use of the term "nervous shock" is no longer considered to be accurate and the term "psychiatric injury" is now preferred by the courts). Initially there was judicial scepticism about the existence of nervous shock as a medical condition and a fear of fraudulent claims. There was also the fear that if such actions were allowed to succeed the "floodgates" would open to allow a rush of claims. Changing judicial attitudes to claims for nervous shock, or psychiatric injury, which is the term now used, are reflected in the following cases. It will be seen that in such claims the courts have been reluctant to apply the foreseeability principle of negligence. A set of rules that place specific restrictions on those who can recover for psychiatric injury and which limit the circumstances in which a duty of care will be imposed has evolved.

Key Principle . . . .
Where psychiatric injury is sustained through fear for the plaintiff's own safety there is no need for physical impact to establish a claim for nervous shock.

> DULIEU V WHITE 1901
>
> The plaintiff, a pregnant woman, was working behind the bar of a public house when the defendant ran his van and horses through the window. She was not physically injured but was badly frightened and this resulted in the premature birth of her child.

Held ....

The plaintiff was entitled to recover because there was real and immediate fear of injury to herself. [1901] 2 K.B. 669.

Commentary ....

(1) The recovery of damages was limited to "shock which arises from a reasonable fear of immediate personal injury to oneself."

(2) A bystander who witnesses a particularly horrific event without fear of personal harm is not owed a duty of care. In *McFarlane v EE Caledonia Ltd* [1994] 2 All E.R. 1, the plaintiff suffered shock as a result of witnessing the fire on the Piper Alpha drilling platform in which 164 men were killed. His claim failed on the grounds that: he was a mere bystander and was not in fear for his own safety; he had no close relationship of love and affection with those in danger; nor was he actively involved in the rescue operations.

Key Principle ....

Shock which results from what is seen or perceived by a plaintiff's own unaided senses is recoverable: there is no action in respect of shock sustained as a result of what a plaintiff has been told by others.

> HAMBROOK V STOKES BROS 1925
> The plaintiff witnessed the defendant's lorry going out of control and round a bend just where she had left her children who were walking to school. Even though she did not see the collision which ensued, she feared for the safety of her children. She was subsequently told that a child fitting the description of her daughter might have been injured in the accident. The plaintiff eventually died from the shock.

Held ....

❖ (CA)

(1) The shock suffered by the plaintiff was induced by what she had seen by her own eyes rather than what she had been told and the defendants were liable. The limitation in *Dulieu v White*, that in order to succeed a plaintiff had to fear for his or her own safety, was rejected on the ground that to allow this would deny a remedy to a mother who feared for the safety of her children in circumstances where a plaintiff who thought only of her own safety could recover. [1925] 1 K.B. 141.

(2) The effect of this decision was to limit claims to plaintiffs who were in close physical proximity to the accident although it was not essential that

they had seen the accident itself. The "sight and sound" requirement was extended in *McLoughlin v O'Brian* (see below) to include the "aftermath" of the accident.

Key Principle

When applying the test of foreseeability of injury by shock, it has to be shown that the plaintiff is a person of reasonable fortitude and not particularly vulnerable to some form of psychiatric reaction.

BOURHILL V YOUNG 1943

The plaintiff, an Edinburgh fishwife, had just alighted from a tram when she heard the impact of an accident involving a tram and a motorcyclist. This occurred some 50 feet away on the other side of the tram and outside her line of vision. She approached the site of the accident and alleged that she suffered nervous shock and gave birth to a stillborn child about a month later.

Held

The House of Lords held that the plaintiff was owed no duty of care. She was so far from the accident that she was in no physical danger and was not within in the area of impact. The nature of the relationship between the primary accident victim and the plaintiff suffering the shock was relevant and Mrs Bourhill was a total stranger to the primary victim. Furthermore, the ordinary bystander can be expected to withstand the sight and sound of road accidents. As a pregnant woman the plaintiff was considered to be particularly vulnerable to mental trauma and therefore not of reasonable fortitude. [1943] A.C. 92.

Commentary

(1) Once some psychiatric harm is foreseeable to a person of reasonable fortitude, then the particularly vulnerable plaintiff can recover. (See *Brice v Brown* (1984), p.128.)

(2) Without evidence that a person of reasonable fortitude would become mentally ill through fear and anxiety about some harmful risk there is no cause of action. In *Rothwell v Chemical & Insulating Co Ltd* [2006] EWCA Civ 27 a former asbestos worker claimed that exposure to asbestos had led to anxiety and depression due to fear that he could in the future contract serious asbestos-related disease. The Court of Appeal found that there was no evidence that a person of reasonable fortitude would react so strongly to the risk as to become mentally ill and the employer was therefore not liable.

However, the situation would have been different if the exposure to the asbestos had damaged the worker's *physical* health.

Key Principle

In claims for nervous shock it is necessary to distinguish between primary and secondary victims. A "primary victim" is a person directly involved as a participant in the traumatic event and, if personal injury of some kind is foreseeable, it is not necessary to show that injury by shock was foreseeable. However, where the plaintiff is a "secondary victim" (such as a witness to the accident) the defendant will not be liable unless psychiatric injury is foreseeable in a person of reasonable fortitude.

> PAGE V SMITH 1996
> The plaintiff was driving with due care when a car driven by the defendant turned into his path. This caused an accident of moderate severity and although there was damage to the cars, the plaintiff was physically unharmed in the collision. However, he had suffered from myalgic encephalomyelitis (ME) for 20 years which at the time of the accident was in remission. He claimed that the accident resulted in the reactivation of this condition.

Held

Provided personal injury of some kind is foreseeable the defendant is liable for the psychiatric injury, irrespective of whether psychiatric injury was foreseeable. [1996] 1 A.C. 155.

Commentary

In the case of secondary victims, claimants will be required to satisfy the "proximity requirements" set out in *Alcock* (see below).

THINK POINT

In *Rothwell v Chemical & Insulating Co Ltd* (above) it was held that *Page v Smith* does not extend to a situation where the level of exposure was not sufficient to render the employee a primary victim. In the absence of a sufficient level of physical damage, anxiety itself could not constitute giving rise to liability. Fear of the "compensation culture" and the floodgates which could open were a factor in this decision; many people will react strongly to fear of future disease and the potential effects of liability would be incalculable.

Key Principle

Liability for nervous shock extends to rescuers and the relationship with any of the victims is not relevant to the claim.

CHADWICK V BRITISH RAILWAYS BOARD 1967

There was no danger to the plaintiff himself nor was he related to any of the victims of the train disaster for which the defendants were liable. In rescuing victims from the scene of the accident he witnessed horrific sights from which he suffered long-term psychiatric illness.

Held

A duty was owed to rescuers. Injury and danger to the passengers could have been forseen as could injury to someone who was trying to rescue them. (But see *White* (1998), below, p.92.) [1999] 1 W.L.R. 912.

Commentary

Permitting rescuers to recover for shock reflects judicial policy of accommodating such claims on the grounds that nothing should deter rescuers from acting in an emergency. However, no duty is owed to mere bystanders who are not actively taking part in the rescue operations. See *McFarlane v EE Caledonia* (p.72).

Key Principle

In addition to reasonable foreseeability the claimant must be: a close relative of the victim; witness the accident or the immediate aftermath with unaided senses; be proximate in both time and space.

McLOUGHLIN V O'BRIAN 1983

The defendant admitted liability for an accident in which the plaintiff's young daughter was killed and her husband and two other children suffered injuries. At the time of the accident the plaintiff was at home two miles away. She was informed of the accident an hour later and was driven to the hospital where her family had been taken. Upon arrival she was told of the death and saw the injuries to her family in distressing circumstances before they had been treated by medical staff. The plaintiff claimed for the nervous shock which she suffered as the result of these events.

Held

❖ (HL) The nervous shock had been the reasonably foreseeable result of injuries to her family and the defendants were liable. [1983] 1 A.C. 410.

Commentary

(1) This decision represented an extension of the existing law as the plaintiff was not at the scene of the accident and left the law in an uncertain state; it was arguable that the test for liability in nervous shock depended on foreseeability alone. Although the court unanimously agreed that the plaintiff's shock was readily foreseeable, the reasoning of their Lordships varied. Lord Bridge and Lord Scarman adopted a test based on foreseeability alone and considered the question of whether, as a matter of policy there should be some other limit on the duty of care, to be inappropriate for the court. But Lord Wilberforce, with whom Lord Edmund-Davies agreed, were of the opinion that it was open to the court to decide the issue on grounds of policy. They adopted an "aftermath test", in which foreseeability of shock was not sufficient and additional limits were required: close relationship with the victim; proximity in terms of time and space; shock from being told by a third party would not be compensated.

(2) In *Palmer v Tees Health Authority* [1999] Lloyd's Rep. Med. 351, a mother claimed for psychiatric injury following the abduction, sexual assault and murder of her four-year-old daughter by a psychiatric out-patient. In a unanimous decision, the Court of Appeal held no duty of care was owed to the mother in respect of psychiatric injury on learning of her daughter's injuries and death. Although she was involved in the search and in the vicinity at the time of the discovery of her daughter's body, she had not witnessed the events herself and did not therefore satisfy the immediate aftermath test. (The other reason for denying liability in this case was "lack of proximity" based on the decision in *Hill v Chief Constable of West Yorkshire Police* (1988) (see p.46) where it was held that the police do not owe a duty of care in negligence to the victims of crime.)

(3) In *AB v Thameside & Glossop Health Authority* [1997] 8 Med. L.R. 91, the defendant health authority discovered one of their health workers to be HIV-positive and wrote to inform patients whom he had treated that there was a small risk they might have been exposed to infection. The plaintiffs alleged that they suffered psychiatric illness as a result of the communication of bad news by letter rather than face-to-face. The Court of Appeal held that the

defendants had not been negligent in deciding to break the news in the way that they did.

In *Greatorex v Greatorex* [2000] 1 W.L.R. 1970, QBD, the defendant was seriously injured in a crash which was caused by his own careless driving. His father, a fire officer, was called to the accident in the course of employment and suffered post-traumatic stress disorder as the result of what he saw at the scene. The father's claim as a rescuer failed because he had not been exposed to physical danger. His claim as a "secondary victim" (being a direct witness of an injury to a person with whom he had a sufficiently close relationship of love and affection), also failed. The policy considerations against there being such a duty owed clearly outweighed the arguments in favour since to impose liability in such circumstances would have a potentially destructive impact upon family relationships.

Key Principle

In addition to reasonable foreseeability of nervous shock the following factors must be considered: the relationship between the primary victim and the plaintiff; the proximity of the plaintiff in time and space to the scene of the accident; the means by which the shock has been caused.

ALCOCK V CHIEF CONSTABLE OF SOUTH YORKSHIRE 1992

Actions for nervous shock were brought against the police arising from the Hillsborough football stadium disaster. As the result of overcrowding, 95 people were crushed to death and hundreds more were injured. The tragedy was witnessed by thousands of fans at the match and others witnessed the horrific events on live television broadcasts. Claims were brought by relatives and friends of the victims who suffered psychiatric illness as a result of their experiences. A number of them had been in other parts of the stadium from where they had witnessed the events and others had seen the disaster live on television. Some of the plaintiffs had identified bodies at the mortuary and others suffered solely from being told the news. The plaintiffs based their claim on the argument that the sole test for a duty in nervous shock was reasonable foreseeability.

Held

❖ (HL) This argument was rejected and the plaintiffs' actions were dismissed. The House of Lords applied Lord Wilberforce's "aftermath test" in *McLoughlin v O'Brian*. [1992] 1 A.C. 310.

Commentary

(1) The class of persons who would sue was not limited to spouse and parent–child relationships; the crucial factor was the existence of a sufficiently close tie of love and affection with the primary victim.

(2) Sight or sound of the accident will continue to satisfy the proximity test but their Lordships did not define immediate aftermath; in this case identifying a body in the mortuary eight hours after the incident was not within the immediate aftermath.

(3) The live television broadcast was found not to equate with the "sight or hearing of the event or its immediate aftermath" because the television authorities had followed the broadcasting code of ethics. Pictures of suffering by recognisable individuals had not been shown. However, the showing of such pictures could constitute a *novus actus interveniens* and break the chain of causation between the original breach of duty and the psychiatric illness.

Key Principle

In determining liability for psychiatric damage:
  (i) an employee is in no special position just because the incident was due to the negligence of the employer. Unless the employees were exposed to the risk of physical harm they remain "secondary victims" and therefore subject to the control mechanisms in *Alcock*;
  (ii) there are no special rules for rescuers engaged in rescuing others endangered by the defendant's negligence. Unless they had been exposed to personal danger, they also remain "secondary victims" subject to the control mechanisms in *Alcock*.

WHITE V CHIEF CONSTABLE OF SOUTH YORKSHIRE POLICE 1998
Four police officers who were actively helping to deal with the human consequences of the Hillsborough tragedy claimed for the post-traumatic stress disorder they suffered as the result of their experiences. They argued that there was no justification for regarding physical and psychiatric injury as different kinds of damage. It was also contended the employer was under the conventional employer's liability principles

to protect employees from harm through work. In addition, three of the officers claimed as rescuers and argued that as such they were not subject to the control mechanisms in *Alcock*.

Held

(1) Nowadays courts accepted that there was no rigid distinction between body and mind and in that sense there was no qualitative difference between physical and psychiatric harm. However, it would be an altogether different proposition to say that no distinction was made or ought to be made between principles governing the recovery of damages in tort for physical injury and psychiatric harm. Policy considerations had undoubtedly played a part in shaping the law in this area. To allow the claims of the police officers would substantially expand the existing categories in which compensation could be recovered for pure psychiatric harm. Moreover, the awarding of damages to them sat uneasily with the denial of the claims to bereaved relatives by the decision in *Alcock*.

(2) The rules to be applied to an action against an employer for harm suffered in the workplace were governed by the ordinary rules of the law of tort and which contained restrictions on the recovery of compensation for psychiatric harm. The rules governing such recovery do not at present include police officers who sustained such injuries while on duty. If such a category were to be created by a judicial decision, the new principle would be available in many different situations, for example, doctors and hospital workers who were exposed to grievous injuries and suffering. In addition, police officers who were traumatised by something in their work had the benefit of statutory schemes which permitted them to retire on pension. In that sense they were better off than the bereaved relatives in *Alcock*.

(3) None of the four police officers were at any time exposed to personal danger and none thought he was so exposed. In order to contain the concept of rescue in reasonable bounds the plaintiff must at least satisfy the threshold requirement that he objectively exposed himself to danger or reasonably believed that he was doing so. [1991] 1 All E.R. 1, HL.

THINK POINT

Although the majority held that in order to claim for psychiatric injury, rescuers must have been exposed to physical danger or would need to satisfy the *Alcock* criteria, *Chadwick* (above) was distinguished on its facts. By entering the wrecked train carriages Mr Chadwick had been objectively exposed to physical danger and he had therefore been within the range of foreseeable personal injury. In *Salter v UB Frozen & Chilled Foods Ltd* 2003 S.L.T. 1011 a forklift truck operator, not himself in danger, who suffered psychiatric injuries because he believed that he was the involuntary cause of a colleague's death, was held to fall within the class of victims identified in *Alcock*. The defendant argued that in nervous shock cases caused by witnessing the death of another, damages were only recoverable if the claimant was at risk of physical injury or reasonably believed he was, or if the secondary control mechanisms in *Alcock* were fulfilled. Although not in any danger himself, the claimant was a primary victim because he was actively involved in the accident which led to the death.

Key Principle

The category of those claiming to be secondary victims of psychiatric injury is a concept still to be developed in different factual situations.

W v Essex County Council 2000

The claimants, parents of four children of their own and also approved foster carers, had relied on the assurances of the local authority that a known or suspected sexual abuser would not be placed with them. Nevertheless, the authority placed a 15-year-old boy, a known sexual abuser, with the family without informing the parents of his full history. The boy perpetrated serious acts of sex abuse on the children of the family, and the parents claimed psychiatric injury which they alleged had been caused not only by the discovery of the abuse, but also by feelings of guilt that having brought the foster child into their home, they were indirectly responsible for the abuse of their children.

Held

The House of Lords held that the Court of Appeal had been wrong to strike out on grounds of policy the parents' claim in respect of the psychiatric harm they had suffered; it was not clear and obvious that the claim would fail and the parents had, at least, an arguable case.

Commentary

Since the enactment of the **Human Rights Act 1998,** the courts have shown a reluctance to grant "blanket immunity" and to exclude a duty of care on grounds of policy. [2000] 2 All E.R. 237.

In *JD v East Berkshire Community Health NHS Trust* [2005] UKHL 23 (see p.58) Lord Rodger said that, if in addition to the doctors' duty to the children, they also owed a duty to parents not to cause them psychiatric harm, two sets of interests would need to be taken into account. This would produce a conflict of interest in the diagnosis and treatment of children because doctors would always have to consider the risk that parents might suffer psychiatric injury.

PURE ECONOMIC LOSS

Key Principle

Pure financial loss unaccompanied by any physical loss to person or property is not recoverable in tort.

WELLER & CO LTD v FOOT AND MOUTH DISEASE RESEARCH INSTITUTE 1966

The plaintiffs, livestock auctioneers, were unable to continue their business because the defendants had negligently released a virus which caused an outbreak of foot and mouth disease in the area.

Held

Farmers whose cattle contracted the disease were held to be owed a duty of care in negligence; their loss was recoverable. However, local auctioneers, who had suffered loss indirectly through loss of business were denied a remedy; their loss was purely economic. [1966] 1 Q.B. 569.

Commentary

The "floodgates" argument is prevalent in the restriction on recovery for pure economic loss and is justified by the undesirability to expose defendants to a potential liability "in an indeterminate amount for an indeterminate time to an indeterminate class", per Cardozo C.J. in *Ultramares Corp v Touche* (1931) 174 N.E. 441.

SPECIAL DUTY SITUATIONS

Key Principle

There is a distinction between "pure economic loss" and economic loss which is consequent upon physical damage to person or property. Economic loss which results from physical damage is recoverable.

Spartan Steel & Alloys Ltd v Martin & Co (Contractors) Ltd 1973

The defendant contractor, in the course of digging the road, negligently cut a power cable causing the plaintiff's smelting works to be shut down. At the time of the power cut there was a "melt" in progress and to stop the steel solidifying it had to be drawn out of the furnace. This reduced its value by £368. The plaintiffs claimed for the reduced value of the melt and for the profit which would have been made had it been completed. They also claimed for the loss of profit from four further melts which would have been processed but for the 14-hour power cut.

Held

❖ (CA) The plaintiffs recovered the reduction in the value of the solidified melt and the profits they would have made from its sale. However, they obtained nothing for the loss of profits on the four further melts which could have been processed before the electricity was restored; that was pure economic loss independent of the physical damage. [1973] Q.B. 27.

Commentary

Lord Denning made clear the public policy justifications for this decision. He stated:

> "... the risk of economic loss should be suffered by the whole community who suffer the losses, usually many but comparatively small losses, rather than on the one pair of shoulders ...".

Key Principle

Where there is sufficient proximity between the parties there may be an exception to the rule that there is no recovery for loss which is not consequent upon physical loss.

Junior Books v Veitchi Co Ltd 1983

The plaintiff had employed the main contractors to construct a factory and they nominated the defendants, as specialist sub-contractors, to lay the floor. The plaintiff alleged that the floor was defective (though

not dangerous) and claimed the cost of replacing the floor plus con-
sequential financial loss.

Held

❖ (HL) The defendants were liable, the proximity of the relationship between
the parties was so close as to be as good as a contract and the building
owner had, to the sub-contractor's knowledge, relied on his skill and
experience. [1983] 1 A.C. 520.

It was also held that there was no question of indeterminate liability in
this situation because the plaintiff was plainly foreseeable as an
identified individual. However, this decision has not subsequently
been followed and has been distinguished to the extent that it can be
said to be unique to its own facts. In *Simaan General Contracting v
Pilkington Glass Ltd (No.2)* [1988] Q.B. 758 Dillon L.J. stated: "I find it
difficult to see that future citation from Junior Books can ever serve
any useful purpose."

Key Principle

There is insufficient proximity between an ordinary purchaser and the manufacturer of defective products to impose a duty of care in respect of pure
economic loss.

MUIRHEAD V INDUSTRIAL TANK SPECIALITIES LTD 1986

The plaintiff planned to buy lobsters when they were cheap, store them
in tanks, and to supply them when they were scarce and in high
demand. The pumps in the tanks failed to function properly and the
plaintiff's lobsters died. In attempting to repair the pumps the plaintiff
also suffered economic loss.

Held

The manufacturer of the pumps was liable for the loss of the lobsters
(property damage) but not for the money spent on the pumps or the cost of
attempting to repair them (pure economic loss). Notwithstanding the imposition of liability in the absence of a contract in *Junior Books* the Court of
Appeal held that liability for economic loss arising from defective products
falls within the scope of contract law. [1986] Q.B. 507.

Commentary ....
The above cases have considered pure economic loss resulting from negligent acts but it is important to note that that pure economic loss resulting from negligent misstatements is recoverable under the principle in *Hedley Byrne v Heller* (1964) (see below) and is the subject of the next section.

NEGLIGENT MISSTATEMENT

Where negligent words cause direct physical harm the plaintiff need only prove that such harm was foreseeable, as was the case with the workman in *Clayton v Woodman & Son (Builders)* [1962] 2 Q.B. 533, who was injured when an architect negligently instructed a bricklayer to remove the keystone of an archway. More recently, this finding has been approved by Lord Oliver in *Caparo Industries Plc v Dickman* (1990). But where negligent words cause pure economic loss the courts take a much more restrictive approach. This restriction is justified by Lord Pearce in *Hedley Byrne* on the basis that "... words are more volatile than deeds, they travel fast and far afield, they are used without being expended."

Key Principle ....
Liability for pure economic loss without injury to person or property can arise in the making of negligent misstatements. However, once a statement is put into circulation it may be broadcast and relied on in different ways by many different people; therefore the criterion of reasonable foreseeability of the loss was rejected as giving rise to potentially too wide a liability. In order to establish a duty of care, additional requirements must be met in the context of a "special relationship" between the parties.

HEDLEY BYRNE V HELLER 1964
The appellants, advertising agents, became doubtful about the financial status of one of their clients, Easipower Ltd. They made enquiries of the defendant bankers with whom Easipower had an account. The defendants replied, first orally and then in writing, that Easipower was financially sound. The appellants relied on this advice and suffered financial loss when Easipower went into liquidation.

Held ....
A duty of care would arise in relation to statements where there is a "special relationship" between the giver and the recipient of the advice. [1964] A.C. 465.

Commentary ....

(1) The nature of a "special relationship" was not fully defined by the court but the requirements for its existence appeared to be:

(i) a reliance by the plaintiff on the defendant's special skill and judgment;

(ii) knowledge, or reasonable expectation of knowledge on the part of the defendant, that the plaintiff was relying on the statement;

(iii) it was reasonable in the circumstances for the plaintiff to rely on the defendant.

(2) The duty of care under *Hedley Byrne* has been restated in more restricted terms by the House of Lords in *Caparo Industries v Dickman*.

THINK POINT

....

The concept of "a voluntary assumption of responsibility" has subsequently been used to establish proximity in determining the existence of a duty of care. This arises from an undertaking either expressed or implied that the defendant will exercise care in giving information or advice. However doubt has been expressed as to whether this criterion was necessary or useful. In *Smith v Bush* [1990] 1 A.C. 831 (see p.89) Lord Griffiths suggested that it is not a helpful or realistic test for liability, but in *Henderson v Merrett Syndicates Ltd* [1995] 2 A.C. 145 Lord Goff said that the criticism of the concept of a voluntary assumption of responsibility in *Smith v Bush* is misplaced.

....

Key Principle ....

Assumption of responsibility can be the basis of recovery where the defendant undertakes a professional task.

HENDERSON V MERRETT SYNDICATES 1995
A number of claims arising out of the near-collapse of the Lloyd's of London insurance market were taken by Lloyd's syndicates (known as "names") alleging negligence on the part of the underwriting agents. The underwriting agents argued that the position with the names should be governed by the terms of the contracts between the parties and not by the law of tort which favoured some of the names because of the more advantageous limitation period in tort. [1995] 2 A.C. 145.

Held

The managing agents had assumed a direct responsibility to the names and a prima facie duty of care arose. Accordingly, sub-agents acting on behalf of indirect Lloyd's names owed a duty of care to the names because they had assumed such responsibility. This was so notwithstanding that the parties were not in a contractual relationship.

Commentary

In *Williams v Natural Life Health Foods Ltd* [1998] 2 All E.R. 577 the plaintiffs entered a contract with a company to franchise a health food store. The plaintiff's business was not a success and they sought to prove that the defendant had personally assumed responsibility for the negligent advice provided by the company (which had subsequently been wound up). Although it was held in this case that the defendants had not personally assumed responsibility to the plaintiff, Lord Steyn said that the extended *Hedley Byrne* principle established in *Henderson* does not merely apply to negligent statements, but also covers the negligent performance of services and can even found a tort duty concurrently with contract.

THINK POINT

Henderson was applied in *West Bromwich Albion Football Club v El-Safty* [2006] EWCA Civ 1299 where a duty of care to the patient was not accompanied by an assumption of a duty to a third party not to cause financial loss. Here the football club brought an action against a consultant surgeon for the financial losses suffered by the club when one of its valuable players was negligently prescribed treatment by the defendant. Although a degree of foreseeability and proximity was found to exist between the consultant and club (which had paid for the treatment) the *Caparo* test was applied. The Court of Appeal said that it would not be fair, just and reasonable to impose a duty to the club on the ground that such a duty could conflict with the doctor's primary duty to care for his patient.

Key Principle

If the "voluntary assumption of responsibility" is present then it may suffice to impose a duty without separate consideration of policy issues. In circumstances where the voluntary assumption of responsibility test does not provide a clear statement of duty then the *Caparo* three-stage test may be applied and policy issues considered.

CUSTOMS AND EXCISE COMMISSIONERS V BARCLAYS BANK PLC 2006

The claimants had obtained a "freezing order" against the assets of two companies in order to protect VAT payments which were owed to the claimants. The orders should have alerted the bank not to allow the companies to withdraw money from their accounts. Nevertheless, the companies managed to withdraw large sums which the Commissioners were unable to recover back from the money that was owed. The judge at first instance held that the defendant bank had not owed a duty of care to the Commissioners but the Court of Appeal held that they were owed a duty of care on the basis of an assumption of responsibility by the bank as soon as the freezing order was served and by the application of the *Caparo* "fair, just and reasonable" test. [2006] UKHL 28.

Held

The House of Lords reversed the Court of Appeal finding of liability and restored the trial judge's original decision. No common law duty of care could be said to arise out of the freezing order itself. The *Hedley Byrne* special relationship was not easily established on the basis of reliance because the Commissioners did not rely on the defendants to comply with the order. The Commissioners relied on the courts to enforce the order. A degree of voluntariness is essential to an "assumption" of responsibility but in this case the defendants had the freezing order "thrust upon them" by the court. Lord Bingham said:

> "I think it is correct to regard an assumption of responsibility as a sufficient but not a necessary condition of liability, a first test which, if answered positively, may obviate the need for further enquiry. If answered negatively, further consideration is called for."

Then, as was done in the *West Bromwich Albion* case (above), the *Caparo* three-part test was applied. Foreseeability of possible loss by the claimants was present, but proximity between the parties was doubtful. Most importantly, it would not be fair, just and reasonable to impose a duty of care. Such a duty would make banks liable for potentially huge sums in response to minor mistakes on their part; additionally there are better means than the law of tort for maintaining strict standards of propriety in banking.

Key Principle ....

Liability under the *Hedley Byrne* principle should be restricted to defendants where the prominent purpose of the business was giving the advice in question, or who claimed that they had the requisite expertise.

> MUTUAL LIFE AND CITIZENS ASSURANCE CO LTD V EVATT 1971
> The plaintiff sought advice from his insurance company about the financial soundness of an associated company. On the basis of the information he was given not only did he keep his investment in the company but he invested more money. The insurance company had given him false information and he suffered financial loss.

Held ....

The Privy Council took a narrow approach to the requirement for special skill on the part of the defendant. The majority held that the insurance company was not in the business of giving advice about investments and that the duty only arose when the defendant was in the business of giving the advice in question or had held himself out as competent to do so. [1971] A.C. 793.

THINK POINT
....

Lords Reid and Morris, dissenting, expressed the opinion that it was sufficient that considered advice was sought from a businessman in the course of his business. In subsequent decisions the minority view, that the "special relationship" could include any business or professional relationship, has gained acceptance. For example, in *Esso Petroleum Ltd v Mardon* [1976] 1 Q.B. 801, the Court of Appeal held that although the defendants were not in the business of giving advice they had special knowledge and skill in estimating the petrol throughput at a filling station, whereas the plaintiff did not.
....

Key Principle ....

A gratuitous agent might owe a duty of care where the circumstances make it clear that considered advice is being sought.

> CHAUDHRY V PRABHAKAR 1989
> The plaintiff asked a friend who had some knowledge of cars, though not a mechanic, to find a suitable car that had not been involved in an accident. The defendant found her a car which he recommended but

which was subsequently discovered to have been involved in a serious accident, poorly repaired and unroadworthy. [1989] 1 W.L.R. 29.

Held

The Court of Appeal imposed liability on the defendant but Stocker L.J. stated that:

> "in the absence of other factors giving rise to such a duty, the giving of advice sought in the context of family, domestic or social relationships will not in itself give rise to any duty in respect of such advice."

In such situations there would not be reasonable reliance.

Key Principle

Liability will arise where the defendant has known, or has been in such a position to reasonably be expected to have known, that the plaintiff would rely on the statement, and the plaintiff's reliance on the statement must have been reasonable.

SMITH V BUSH 1990

The plaintiff purchaser was required to pay for a surveyor's valuation for the purpose of a mortgage application. The defendant surveyor was acting for the building society mortgagees to enable them to decide if the property provided adequate security for the loan. The plaintiff, to her detriment, relied on the valuation.

Held

The plaintiff succeeded. The surveyor, acting for the building society, owed a duty of care to the intending purchaser who, as he knew, would rely upon his skill without obtaining an independent survey. [1990] 1 A.C. 831.

Commentary

(1) In this case the fact that the size of the house price was relatively small when compared with the cost of commissioning an independent survey was an important factor in categorising the plaintiff's reliance as reasonable. However, it may not be reasonable for all purchasers to rely on the mortgagee's valuer (e.g. very expensive houses or commercial property).

(2) The impact of the Unfair Contract Terms Act 1977 can be seen in both this case, and in *Harris v Wyre Forest District Council* [1990] 1 A.C. 831, concerning a survey which had been carried out by a local authority surveyor. In both

cases disclaimer clauses which had been inserted in the valuations were struck down by the House of Lords as unreasonable under the Act.

Key Principle

For liability to arise:

(i)   the loss must be reasonably foreseeable;

(ii) there must be a relationship of proximity between the parties; and

(iii) it must be fair, just and reasonable that the law should impose a duty.

CAPARO INDUSTRIES PLC V DICKMAN 1990

The plaintiffs owned shares in a public company whose accounts were audited by the defendants for the purposes of the annual statutory audit. The plaintiffs purchased further shares and made a successful takeover bid for the company. They subsequently suffered a substantial loss and brought an action against the auditors. It was alleged that the shares had been purchased in reliance on the audit which was negligently prepared and gave a misleading impression of the company's financial position.

Held

❖ (HL) The plaintiff's claim failed. The auditors owed no duty of care in respect of the accuracy of the accounts to either members of the public or existing shareholders when they rely on such an audit to invest in the company; there was not sufficient proximity between the plaintiffs and the defendants. Also, the audit was prepared for the purpose of enabling the shareholders as a body to exercise control over the company; it was not prepared for the purpose of providing information for investors. [1990] 2 A.C. 605.

Commentary

In this case the statement was placed into general circulation as opposed to the "one to one" situations in *Hedley Byrne* and *Smith v Bush*. Lord Bridge said that an essential ingredient of the required proximity in situations where a statement is put into more or less general circulation is to prove that:

> "the defendant knew that his statement would be communicated to the plaintiff, either as an individual or as a member of an identifiable class, specifically in connection with a particular transaction or transactions of a particular kind ... and that the plaintiff would be very likely to rely on it ...".

This restricted approach to liability was applied in *Al-Nakib Investments (Jersey) Ltd v Longcroft* [1990] 3 All E.R. 321, where directors issued a prospectus inviting shareholders to subscribe for additional shares in the company. The purpose of the prospectus was specifically to invite existing shareholders to apply and a claim brought by purchasers in the market was struck out.

Key Principle

Where express representations are made on a business occasion the form in which the information is given may negative the existence of a duty of care.

JAMES MCNAUGHTON PAPER GROUP LTD V HICKS ANDERSON & CO 1991
The defendant accountants became aware that the plaintiffs were considering a takeover of their clients, M.K. At a meeting between the two companies the defendants were asked to confirm the accuracy of the draft accounts which they had prepared for M.K.'s chairman to be used in the negotiations. They responded in a general way that M.K. was breaking even or doing marginally worse. After the takeover the plaintiffs discovered discrepancies in the accounts and sued the defendant accountants.

Held

❖ (CA) The defendants owed no duty of care to the plaintiffs because the accounts were prepared for M.K. and not the plaintiffs. The plaintiff as buyers were aware of the poor state of M.K.'s affairs and could be expected to consult their own accountants. [1991] 2 Q.B. 113.

Commentary

(1) Neil L.J., accepting that there could be considerable overlap, made an analysis of the relevant cases and identified criteria which might be applied in determining the existence of a duty of care following *Caparo*:
 (i)   the purpose for which the statement was made;
 (ii) the purpose for which the statement was communicated;
 (iii) the relationship between the adviser, advisee and any third party;
 (iv) the size of any class to which the advisee belongs;
 (v)   the state of knowledge of the adviser; and
 (vi) reliance by the advisee.

(2) In *Morgan Crucible Co Plc v Hill Samuel Bank Ltd* [1991] 1 All E.R. 148, the defendants who had prepared profit forecasts expressly designed to induce the plaintiffs to bid for a company in a contested takeover were found to owe a duty of care. *Caparo* was distinguished on the ground that the representations were made after, not before the identified bidder had emerged and the representations were made in the knowledge and with the intention that they should be relied on.

VARIATIONS ON HEDLEY BYRNE

Key Principle
Reliance on the statement by the plaintiff is not essential to establish a duty of care; the assumption of responsibility by a solicitor towards a client extends to the intended beneficiary.

> WHITE V JONES 1995
> The plaintiffs were disinherited by their father in his will after a family row in 1986. Six months later a reconciliation took place and in July 1986 the father gave his solicitors instructions to draw up a new will giving his daughters £9,000 each. The solicitors delayed in carrying out the father's request and after a month he renewed his instructions. The solicitors still failed to act by the time the father, who was 78, died in September 1986.

Held
A remedy under the *Hedley Byrne* principle was extended and the sisters were entitled to recover damages from the defendants in negligence. [1995] 1 All E.R. 691.

Commentary
The House stated that by accepting instructions to draw up a will, a solicitor came into a "special relationship with those intended to benefit under it" and this, in consequence, imposed a duty on the solicitor to "act with due expedition and care" on behalf of the beneficiaries. This decision reaffirmed *Ross v Caunters* [1980] Ch. 297, a first instance decision, where the defendant solicitor had failed to warn the testator that the will should not be witnessed by the husband of the intended beneficiary. When the disappointed beneficiary under the ineffective will sued the solicitors they admitted negligence but argued that the only duty they owed was to the testator. But Megarry V.C. held that a duty of care was owed to the plaintiff as a sufficient relationship of neighbourhood or proximity existed between the parties.

In *Gorham v British Telecommunications Plc* [2000] 1 W.L.R. 2129, the Court of Appeal confirmed that *White v Jones* is not confined to claims relating to wills. In this case, Mr Gorham was sold a personal pension without being advised that BT's occupational pension might be better for him. Although, even if he had joined the BT scheme when he was informed that it might be better, his family would not have been entitled to a pension because he would not have been a member of the scheme for two years before his death. They would, however, have been entitled to a lump sum and it was clear that Mr Gorham had intended to create a benefit for his dependant wife and family and therefore a duty of care was owed to them by the insurance company.

Key Principle

A party who negligently supplies a defamatory reference about a person in response to a request from a potential employer may be liable in negligence to the subject of the reference.

SPRING V GUARDIAN ASSURANCE 1994

The plaintiff was dismissed from his job by the defendant and attempted to set up his own business selling life assurance policies on behalf of other companies. Before he could start work, regulations relating to the financial services industry required the defendant to provide a reference. The defendant supplied a damning reference which mistakenly alleged that the plaintiff was dishonest. As a consequence the plaintiff's business failed. Even though the reference was defamatory the plaintiff would not have succeeded in an action for defamation since, in the absence of malice, the defendant would have been able to establish a defence of qualified privilege. The plaintiff instead sued in negligence. The defendant argued:

(i) to give a cause of action in negligence would distort and subvert the tort of defamation; and

(ii) if the plaintiff won employers fearful of liability would be reluctant to write references or supply only bland references that conveyed no relevant information.

Held ....

In holding the defendant liable, the majority in the House of Lords agreed that the preservation of the law of defamation would not be sufficient to deny the plaintiff a remedy. [1994] 3 All E.R. 129.

Commentary ....

The majority (Lord Keith dissenting) decided that the two torts were different. Defamation exists to protect reputation but a negligent reference can do harm without affecting a person's reputation. This decision approves *Lawton v BOC Transhield Ltd* [1987] 2 All E.R. 608 where it was held that a duty could be owed, at least to check the facts upon which the statement was made were accurate, by an employer who gives a negligent reference about an employee. Both this case and *White v Jones* (above), endorsing the wider interpretation of *Hedley Byrne*, mark a reversal of the trend to restrict the development of negligence.

THINK POINT

....

In *Patchett v Swimming Pool & Allied Trades Assn Ltd* [2009] EWCA Civ 717 the question was whether a website owner owed a duty of care to users for statements on its website. The Patchetts contracted for a swimming pool to be built in their garden with an installer they found on the Swimming Pool & Allied Trades Association Limited's (SPATA) website on the Internet. It transpired that the installer (who became insolvent before the pool was completed) was not a full member of SPATA and therefore not subject to the vetting procedure or subject to the Association's bond and warranty scheme. The Patchetts sought recovery for their financial loss from SPATA alleging negligent mis-statement on the grounds the statements on its website were inaccurate and misleading. The Court of Appeal found there was no assumption of responsibility, because the degree of reliance by its customers which SPATA intended, or should reasonably have expected, was limited by its advice in a statement to customers to obtain an information pack. The Court held that the statements on the website had to be taken as a whole and it was reasonable to expect potential customers to have regard to all the information available on the website. The website referred customers to information packs supplied by SPATA and if the Patchetts had obtained one they would have discovered that the installer was not a full SPATA member and not covered by its warranty scheme. According to Lord Clarke M.R. in these circumstances, it would not be fair, just and reasonable to hold that SPATA owed the Patchetts a duty of care and that to find such a duty would be an unwarranted extension of existing case law.

Negligence: Breach of Duty   5

INTRODUCTION

The standard of care required by the common law is that of the reasonable man. This was defined in *Blyth v Birmingham Waterworks Co* (1856) 11 Ex. 781 as the omission to do something that a reasonable man would do or doing something which a reasonable and prudent man would not do. In *Glasgow Corp v Muir* [1943] A.C. 448 Lord Macmillan stated that this objective standard does not take account of the idiosyncrasies or weaknesses of the particular person whose conduct is in question. The question for the court is not did the defendant act reasonably, but in all the circumstances, would a reasonable person behave as the defendant did. It must then be proved by the plaintiff that, on the facts, the defendant's conduct fell below the appropriate standard. It is for the judge to decide what is reasonable or what could have been foreseen and the cases below will illustrate a number of guiding principles which are considered by the court.

There is increasing concern about the danger in setting too high a standard of care in negligence as it could lead to inhibiting consequences, for example the reduction in or prohibition of traditional activities on village greens. In *Cole v Davis-Gilbert* 2007 EWCA Civ 396 the claimant brought an action against the owners of a green and the Royal British Legion, who had organised a May Day fête which had been held on the green. As part of the fête, a maypole was placed into a hole on the green that had been dug for that purpose. At the end of the fête the hole was filled with soil and stones and subsequently with a bung. Two years later, the hole had become exposed and while walking across the green the claimant had stepped into it suffered injury to her leg. The judge held that the British Legion had breached its duty of care to the claimant as it had not taken adequate steps to ensure that the hole had been filled in properly. However, the Court of Appeal found for the defendants on the grounds that it was the unexplained removal of the infill, not the infill itself, that was the primary cause of the accident. It was not possible to establish that the accident was caused by any negligence on the part of the British Legion as it appeared that the hole only became exposed shortly before the accident. Although there was no evidence as to how the hole became exposed it was most likely to have been the actions of children playing on the green.

This case was subsequent to the introduction of the **Compensation Act 2006** (below) and the approach of the Court of Appeal can be seen in the following statement by Scott Baker L.J.:

> "Accidents happen and sometimes they are what can only be described as 'proper accidents', in the sense that the victim cannot recover damages because fault cannot be established … If the law courts were to set a higher standard of care than what is reasonable, the consequences would quickly be felt. There would be no fetes, no maypole dancing and no activities that have come to be a part of the English village green for fear of what might go wrong."

A perception that society is becoming "risk averse" and concerns about the emergence of a "compensation culture" led to a fear that many worthwhile activities would be curtailed because of the deterrent effect of potential liability. One of the aims of the **Compensation Act 2006** is to address this concern and to serve as a reminder to judges to consider carefully the impact which decisions about potential negligence liability might have in deterring the organisation and pursuit of worthwhile activities. Section 1 of the Act deals with the deterrent effect of potential liability and provides:

> "A court considering a claim in negligence or breach of statutory may, in determining whether the defendant should have taken particular steps to meet a standard of care (whether by taking precautions against a risk or otherwise), have regard to whether a requirement to take those steps might—
>
> (a) prevent a desirable activity from being undertaken at all, to a particular extent or in a particular way, or
>
> (b) discourage persons from undertaking functions in connection with a desirable activity."

In *Hopps v Mott MacDonald Ltd* [2009] (p.143) s.1 of the Act was applied on the ground that a finding of liability on the employer would prevent the desirable activity of reconstructing the infrastructure of Iraq being undertaken. Although Section 1 was not specifically referred to in *Harris v Perry* [2008] EWCA Civ 907, the reluctance of courts to perpetuate a culture which is excessively risk-averse is nevertheless reflected in the decision of the Court of Appeal. The question here was whether parents who hired a bouncy castle for a child's birthday party owed a duty of care to watch the children playing in the castle continuously to prevent injury occurring. In allowing the parents' appeal against liability the Court of Appeal held that trial judge had imposed too high a standard of care in finding that the bouncy castle required uninterrupted supervision.

Key Principle

Where some precautions are required the standard of care that can reasonably be expected will vary according to the magnitude of the risk, the purpose of the defendant's activity and the practicability of precautions.

> BOLTON V STONE 1951
> The plaintiff was standing in a quiet road when she was struck by a cricket ball which had been driven from the defendants' cricket ground. It was rare for balls to be hit out of the ground; only on about six occasions in 28 years had balls been hit out and no injury had resulted. Even though the risk of such an accident was foreseeable the chance that it would actually occur was very small.

Held

❖ (HL) The defendants were not liable because in the circumstances it was reasonable to ignore such a small risk. [1951] A.C. 850.

Commentary

(1) In *Miller v Jackson* [1977] Q.B. 966 by a majority the Court of Appeal held that the risk of harm was so great that the defendants were liable where cricket balls were hit out of their ground eight or nine times a season and, on numerous occasions, had damaged the plaintiff's property.

(2) In *Haley v London Electricity Board* [1965] A.C. 778, HL, the defendant's servants who had been excavating a hole in the street took precautions for the protection of passers-by. The precautions which were taken were adequate for sighted persons but not for the plaintiff who was blind and fell into the hole. The defendants were held liable because the presence of blind persons on the pavement was foreseeable and adequate precautions would have been simple to take.

Key Principle

The obligations of a potential defendant may increase where the risk to a plaintiff is of greater damage than normal.

> ### PARIS V STEPNEY BOROUGH COUNCIL 1951
>
> The defendants knew that the plaintiff was blind in one eye. He was working in conditions which involved some risk of eye injury but the likelihood of this injury was not sufficient to call upon the defendants to provide goggles to a normal two-eyed workman. The plaintiff was rendered totally blind when a chip of metal entered his good eye.

Held

❖ (HL) The duty of employers was owed to each particular employee and they were negligent in failing to provide goggles to the plaintiff. In this case the risk to a two-eyed workman was the loss of one eye but the plaintiff risked the much greater injury of total blindness. [1951] A.C. 367.

Commentary

In *Watson v British Boxing Board of Control* (2001) (p.61), a sporting body was held to be under a specific duty to inform itself adequately about the risks inherent in a blow to the head and to provide resuscitation facilities at the ringside with persons capable of operating them.

Key Principle

A referee is under a duty of care towards the players in an amateur rugby match to implement the rules of the game designed to minimise the inherent risks.

> ### VOWLES V EVANS 2003
>
> A rugby player confined to a wheelchair as a result of the injury he sustained during an amateur match claimed that the referee had been negligent in carrying out his refereeing duties and that the second defendant, the Welsh Rugby Union, was vicariously liable. The match was being played under the rules of the game issued by the Council of the International Rugby Football Board and the referee had failed to comply with the rules in allowing a player who had lacked suitable training and experience to play in the front row.

Held ....
The Court of Appeal upheld the finding of the judge below and said that because of the dangers inherent in the game of rugby, players were dependant for their safety on the enforcement of the rules by the referee. [2003] EWCA Civ 318.

Commentary ....
One of the issues in this case was whether it was "fair, just and reasonable" that a duty of care towards the players be imposed on an amateur referee. It was argued that amateur referees receive no remuneration for their service and potential liability in negligence for injuries to players would discourage volunteers from acting as referees. However, the court said that the sporting bodies who appointed referees could be expected to take out insurance against the negligence of their referees.

Key Principle ....
The risk has to be balanced against the end to be achieved and, if sufficiently important, justifies the assumption of abnormal risk.

WATT V HERTFORDSHIRE COUNTY COUNCIL 1954
The plaintiff was a fireman called out to an emergency where a woman was trapped under a lorry. A heavy lifting jack was urgently required but, since a vehicle designed to carry this was not available, it was loaded on to a lorry which was not equipped to secure it. On the way to the scene of the accident the lorry had to brake suddenly and the plaintiff was injured when the jack slipped.

Held ....
❖ (CA) The fire authorities had not been negligent. The risk had to be balanced against the end to be achieved and the saving of life or limb justifies taking considerable risk. [1954] 1 W.L.R. 835; [1954] 2 All E.R. 368.

THINK POINT

Lord Denning took the view that if the accident had happened in a commercial venture without any emergency the plaintiff would have succeeded, but "the commercial end to make profit is very different from the human end to save life or limb."

Key Principle

The risk has to be weighed against the measures necessary to eliminate it.

> **SMITH V LITTLEWOODS LTD 1987**
> The defendants were the owners of a cinema which was left unoccupied and unguarded during the time it was awaiting redevelopment. When youths entered the premises and deliberately started a fire which spread to, and seriously damaged the plaintiffs' buildings next door, it was alleged that the defendants should have prevented access to the cinema. The defendants were not aware of the presence of the vandals and had no reason to assume that they constituted a significant threat.

Held

The defendants were not liable. Short of posting a 24-hour guard over the property they would not have been in a position to prevent the vandals getting in. To require such a measure would impose an intolerable burden. [1987] A.C. 241.

Commentary

See also *Latimer v AEC Ltd* (1953) (see p.141).

Key Principle

Where a person undertakes a task which requires a particular skill he will be judged by the standards of a person who is reasonably competent in the exercise of that skill.

> **WELLS V COOPER 1958**
> The plaintiff, who went to deliver fish to the defendant's house, was invited to stay for a cup of tea. After drinking the tea he was leaving the house by the back door when the door-handle came away in his hand. He fell to the ground from the back steps. The handle had been fitted a few months earlier by the defendant who had some experience as an amateur carpenter and who frequently did such jobs around the house.

Held

❖ (CA) The defendant had exercised such care as was required of him and was not liable. A householder who does some small repair about his house is not expected to show the skill of a professional carpenter working for reward; he need only do his work with the skill of a reasonably competent carpenter doing the work in question. [1958] 2 Q.B. 265.

Commentary

The degree of skill was not to be measured by the skill which the defendant personally happened to possess, but by reference to the degree of care and skill which a reasonably competent carpenter might apply to the work in question.

Key Principle

The test for competence is objective: there is no variable standard for different levels of experience, competence or temperament.

> NETTLESHIP V WESTON 1971
>
> The plaintiff was teaching the defendant to drive. During the course of the defendant's third lesson, she panicked and steered the car into a lamp-post and the plaintiff suffered a broken knee cap. At first instance the trial judge decided that the plaintiff had not been at fault because she had been doing her best to control the car.

Held

❖ (CA) The Court of Appeal disagreed with the trial judge and held that the standard of care required of a learner-driver is the same as that of the ordinary qualified driver. The defendant's driving had fallen below this standard and it was irrelevant that this was because of her inexperience. According to Lord Denning: "A learner driver may be doing his best but his incompetent best is not good enough". [1971] 2 Q.B. 691.

Commentary

(1) In *Roberts v Ramsbottom* [1980] 1 W.L.R. 823 the defendant, who suffered a stroke which severely impaired his consciousness, continued to drive for some distance and collided with two vehicles in succession. He was found liable because he had retained some control and a prudent person would have stopped driving under such circumstances. His illness would only have provided a defence if it had rendered his actions wholly beyond his control so as to amount to automatism.

(2) In *Wilsher v Essex Area Health Authority* [1988] 1 All E.R. 871 (see p.115) the Court of Appeal rejected the argument that a inexperienced junior doctor owed a lower duty of care. Glidewell L.J. commented:

> "the law requires the trainee or learner to be judged by the same standard as his more experienced colleagues. If it did not,

inexperience would frequently be urged as a defence to an action for professional negligence."

(This point was not raised on appeal to the House of Lords [1988] 2 W.L.R. 557.)

Key Principle

The appropriate test for judging the standard of professional behaviour is not that of the ordinary man; the defendant is judged by the standard of the ordinary skilled person exercising and professing to have that special skill.

BOLAM V FRIERN HOSPITAL MANAGEMENT COMMITTEE 1957

The plaintiff agreed to undergo electro-convulsive therapy (ECT) during which he suffered a fracture to the pelvis. The issue was whether the doctor was negligent in failing to give a relaxant drug before the treatment, or in failing to provide means of restraint during the procedure. Evidence was given of the practices of various doctors in the use of relaxant drugs before ECT treatment. One body of medical opinion favoured the use of relaxant drugs, but another body of opinion took the view that they should not be used because of the risk of fractures.

Held

The action failed. A defendant is not negligent if he acts in accordance with a practice accepted at the time as proper by a responsible body of professional opinion skilled in the particular form of treatment. [1957] 2 All E.R. 118.

Commentary

(1) In *Bolitho v City and Hackney HA* (1997) (see p.112), although the issue was one of causation, the medical experts had disagreed as to whether a doctor ought to have intubated the plaintiff. The court said that whether it would have been a breach of duty not to intubate had to be decided by applying the *Bolam* test. However, the House of Lords emphasised that ultimately it was for the court, and not for medical opinion, to decide what was the standard of care required in each case. The court had to be satisfied that the opinion had a logical basis, which would involve the weighing of risks against benefits, in order to reach a defensible conclusion.

(2) This test, set down in a High Court decision and approved by the House of Lords (see below), is of general application and not limited to doctors. In

Luxmoore-May v Messenger May Baverstock [1990] 1 All E.R. 1067, the test was applied to a firm of provincial auctioneers valuing a painting for a client prior to sale. The defendant auctioneers were "general practitioners" and were not liable for failing to identify a valuable painting in circumstances where a specialist London firm would have been held negligent.

THINK POINT

The test is not conclusive. A common professional practice will sometimes be condemned as unreasonable. The courts take the view that neglect of duty does not cease by repetition to be neglect of duty: in *The Herald of Free Enterprise, Re, Independent*, December 18, 1987, there was ample evidence that most ferries set sail with their bow doors open. The Divisional Court held that this was not evidence of the required standard of care but rather of a general and culpable complacency in respect of elementary safety precautions.

Key Principle

The *Bolam* test applies to treatment and clinical judgment.

WHITEHOUSE V JORDAN 1981

The defendant, a senior registrar, had delivered the plaintiff's baby. The birth was a difficult one and it was alleged that the defendant had pulled too long and too hard in attempting a forceps delivery before eventually performing a Caesarean section. This had resulted in severe brain damage to the plaintiff for which the trial judge held the doctor liable.

Held

❖ (HL) The defendant was not negligent as the evidence did not establish that the doctor had departed from accepted practice. [1981] 1 All E.R. 267.

Commentary

The House of Lords emphatically restated the *Bolam* test and rejected the argument that there was a difference between an error of judgment and negligence. In the Court of Appeal Lord Denning had argued: "When I give a judgment and it is afterwards reversed by the House of Lords, is it to be said that I was negligent?" According to Lord Edmund-Davies:

"To say that a surgeon committed an error of clinical judgment is wholly ambiguous, for while some such errors may be completely consistent with the due exercise of professional skill, other acts or omissions in the course of exercising 'clinical judgment' may be so glaringly below proper standards as to make a finding of negligence inevitable."

Key Principle

The *Bolam* test applies to making a diagnosis and where there is conflicting medical opinion a doctor is not negligent merely because there is a body of opinion that takes a contrary view.

MAYNARD V WEST MIDLANDS REGIONAL HEALTH AUTHORITY 1984

A consultant physician and a surgeon were uncertain whether the plaintiff was suffering from tuberculosis or from Hodgkin's disease. Hodgkin's disease can be fatal unless treated early so they carried out an operation before obtaining test results which would have determined her illness. The operation carries an inherent risk of damage to the vocal cords and this risk materialised in the plaintiff. She claimed that the consultants were negligent in carrying out the operation before the test results were available.

Held

❖ (HL) The defendants were held not to be negligent. Although there was a body of competent opinion which said that the consultants' decision was wrong there was an equally competent body which supported their approach. [1984] 1 W.L.R. 634.

THINK POINT

Lord Scarman stated the justification for the *Bolam* test in the following terms:

"... a judge's 'preference' for one body of distinguished professional opinion over another, also professionally distinguished is not sufficient to establish negligence."

NEGLIGENCE: BREACH OF DUTY

Key Principle

A defendant is not expected to have anticipated future developments in knowledge or practice but will be judged by reference to the state of knowledge at the time of the event.

> ROE V MINISTRY OF HEALTH 1954
> The two plaintiffs entered hospital for minor surgery and emerged permanently paralysed from the waist down. Anaesthetic which was injected spinally during the course of the operation had become contaminated by seepage through invisible cracks in the glass. At the time of the accident in 1947 the risk of this seepage occurring was not known.

Held

❖ (CA) It was not negligent for the defendant not to have known of the danger. Lord Denning warned that it is so easy to be wise after the event and said: "We must not look at the 1947 accident with 1954 spectacles." [1954] 2 Q.B. 66.

Key Principle

The *Bolam* test applies to the disclosure of information by doctors to patients about risks of proposed procedures.

> SIDAWAY V BETHLEM ROYAL HOSPITAL GOVERNORS 1985
> The plaintiff agreed to undergo an operation to her spine in order to relieve pain in her right arm and shoulder. She was not informed that the operation carried a risk (of less than 1 per cent) that she would suffer damage to the spine. The operation was performed without negligence but unfortunately the risk materialised and the plaintiff became severely disabled. She sued the defendants on the ground that the surgeon had failed to inform her of the risk.

Held

❖ (HL) The defendants were not liable. The surgeon had followed approved practice of neurosurgeons in not disclosing the risk of damage to the spinal cord and was not negligent. [1985] 1 All E.R. 643.

Commentary

The contention that the standard of care ought to be what the reasonable patient would want to know, rather than what the reasonable doctor was prepared to tell, was rejected by the court. In failing to adopt the doctrine of "informed consent" which operates in other jurisdictions and allows the patient access to full and frank information about treatment and prognoses, the English courts leave discretion to the professional judgment of the doctor regarding the disclosure of information.

THINK POINT

A doctor who fails to give proper warning to his patient about a risk inherent in surgery may be held to have caused the injury if the risk materialises, even where the surgery is performed without negligence: see *Chester v Afshar* (2004) (p.113).

Key Principle

Children are to be judged against the standard of the ordinary child of the same age.

> MCHALE V WATSON 1966
>
> The defendant, a boy of 12, threw a pointed steel rod at a wooden post. It glanced off the post and struck the plaintiff in the eye.

Held

The defendant was not liable in negligence. The standard of care is adjusted for the child's age and is therefore such a standard as can reasonably be expected of an ordinary child of the same age as the defendant. [1966] A.L.R. 513.

Commentary

(1) This is an Australian case; there was little authority in English law dealing with the position until *Mullin v Richards* [1998] 1 W.L.R. 1304, a case where two 15-year-old schoolgirls were "fencing" with plastic rulers when one of the rulers snapped and caused a serious eye injury in one of the girls. The Court of Appeal adopted the approach taken in *McHale v Watson* and held that in the circumstances (such games were common at the school and were not prohibited) the risk of injury was not reasonably foreseeable by a 15-year-old.

(2) Parents are generally not liable for the torts of their children. However, in circumstances where failure of the parent to supervise a child adequately results in injury to the child or a third party, the parent may be personally liable in negligence. Similarly, teachers may be responsible for failure to supervise children. In *Carmarthenshire County Council v Lewis* [1955] A.C. 549

(see p.67) the House of Lords held a school authority liable where a four-year-old child, left unattended in a classroom, wandered on to a road. A lorry driver was killed trying to avoid him, and it was held that under the circumstances it was reasonably foreseeable that the child would cause an accident.

RES IPSA LOQUITUR

There has been disagreement in the courts about the exact effect of the maxim *res ipsa loquitur* and it had been argued that it shifted the burden of proof to the defendant. However, in *Ng Chun Pui v Lee Chuen Tat* (1988) R.T.R. 298, the Privy Council stated that the burden of proof does not shift to the defendant and that the doctrine

> "... is no more than the use of a Latin maxim to describe the state of the evidence from which it is proper to draw an inference of negligence."

Key Principle

The facts of the accident itself may give rise to a *res ipsa loquitur* inference if the following three conditions are met:
(i)   the defendant must have had sole control of the thing that caused the damage;
(ii) the accident could not have occurred without lack of proper care;
(iii) there is no other direct evidence of what caused the accident.

> SCOTT V LONDON AND ST KATHERINE DOCKS CO 1865
> The plaintiff, who was standing near the doorway of the defendant's warehouse, was struck when several bags of sugar fell from a hoist. The defendant's employees had been using a hoist nearby to load sugar.

Held

The plaintiff succeeded. In establishing liability on the part of the defendants there must be reasonable evidence of negligence, but if the three conditions above apply,

> "... it affords reasonable evidence, in the absence of explanation by the defendant, that the accident arose from want of care."
> (1865) 3 H. & C. 596.

Commentary ··

The Civil Evidence Act 1968 provides that, unless the contrary is proved, the burden of proof in negligence shall be reversed where a person is proved to have been convicted of an offence.

Key Principle ··

To establish if the defendant has control of the situation which caused the damage, the test is whether outside interference was likely.

> **EASSON V LONDON AND NORTH EASTERN RAILWAY CO 1944**
> The plaintiff, a four-year-old boy, fell through a door of a corridor train during the journey from Edinburgh to London.

Held ··

The defendant did not have sufficient control over the door for the doctrine of *res ipsa loquitur* to apply. It was impossible to say that the doors of an express train were continuously under the control of the railway company; passengers could have interfered with the doors. [1944] K.B. 421.

Commentary ··

If it is improbable that some unauthorised person could have interfered with the thing that caused the damage, the defendant has sufficient control. In *Gee v Metropolitan Railway* (1873) L.R. 8 Q.B. 161, the plaintiff fell from a local train when the door flew open a few minutes after it had left the station. This was held to be evidence of negligence on the part of the railway company.

Key Principle ··

For *res ipsa loquitur* to apply it must be shown that the accident could not have occurred without negligence.

> **CASSIDY V MINISTRY OF HEALTH 1951**
> The plaintiff went into hospital to have treatment for two stiff fingers. On leaving hospital he had four stiff fingers and a useless hand.

Held ··

❖ (CA) This should not have happened if due care had been used and the doctrine applied. [1951] 2 K.B. 343.

Key Principle

For *res ipsa loquitur* to apply there must be no evidence of the actual cause of the accident.

> BARKWAY V SOUTH WALES TRANSPORT CO LTD 1950
>
> The plaintiff was travelling as a passenger in the defendants' bus. He was killed when a tyre burst and the bus veered across the road and went over an embankment. It was established that the cause of the accident was a defect in one of the tyres which might have been discovered beforehand.

Held

❖ (HL) As the cause of the accident was known *res ipsa loquitur* did not apply. (However, the defendant's negligence was established on the facts of the case.) [1950] 1 All E.R. 392.

THINK POINT

In *George v Eagle Air Services Ltd* [2009] UKPC 21 the Court of Appeal in Saint Lucia held that there was no evidence of negligence for a plane crash in which appellant's husband was killed. However, the Privy Council said that aircraft was airworthy when it took off and held that the doctrine of *res ipsa loquitur* applied to her claim. Owing to the difficulty of proving of negligence in plane crashes the Privy Council noted that the maxim of *res ipsa loquitur* was potentially of great importance in these cases.

Negligence: Damage

6

INTRODUCTION

The principles of causation and remoteness of damage are common to all torts. However, they are dealt with in this Chapter because most of the cases on the subject have involved the tort of negligence. In order to prove damage the plaintiff must first show that the harm suffered was as a matter of fact caused by the defendant's breach of duty. This element is known as causation in fact and if "but for" the defendant's negligent conduct the damage would not have happened then that negligence is the cause of the damage. Where causation is in fact established the question of remoteness of damage then arises. This is known as causation in law and liability may still be avoided if the defendant can show that the damage suffered was too remote a consequence of the breach of duty.

Key Principle

If the harm to the plaintiff would not have occurred "but for" the defendant's breach of duty then that negligence is a cause of the harm.

BARNETT V CHELSEA AND KENSINGTON HOSPITAL MANAGEMENT COMMITTEE 1969

The plaintiff's husband was one of three night watchmen who went to the defendant's hospital complaining of vomiting after drinking some tea. The nurse on duty consulted the casualty doctor by telephone and was instructed by him to tell the three men to go home to bed and to call their own doctors. Soon afterwards the plaintiff's husband died of arsenical poisoning. It was discovered that arsenic had been put into the tea of the workmen by persons unknown. There was no dispute that in failing to examine the plaintiff the doctor was negligent. The issue to be decided was whether the doctor's breach of duty had caused the man's death.

Held

The claim failed. The hospital was able to produce evidence to show that even if the deceased had been examined and treated with proper care he would still have died. Since the death would have occurred in any event the defendant's breach of duty was not a factual cause. [1969] 1 Q.B. 428.

Commentary

(1) This case established what is known as the "but for" test. Even though the test is widely applied it is not always adequate as, for example, where there are multiple causes of the plaintiff's damage.

(2) The "but for" test was applied in *Robinson v Post Office* [1974] 2 All E.R. 737. The plaintiff sought medical treatment following a leg injury sustained through the defendant's negligence. During the treatment he suffered a serious reaction to an anti-tetanus vaccination which was administered by a doctor who omitted to test for the allergy. The defendant was held liable for this injury also; the doctor was not liable for his omission to test for an allergic reaction because the vaccination was urgently needed and the test would not have revealed the allergy in time.

Key Principle

In a case of breach of duty by omission, such as the failure of a doctor to attend a patient, it is necessary to decide what would have happened had the defendant's duty been discharged. Whether the doctor's failure to attend causes the plaintiff's damage depends on what the doctor would have done had s/he turned up.

BOLITHO V CITY AND HACKNEY HEALTH AUTHORITY 1997

The plaintiff, a two-year-old patient in the defendant's hospital, suffered respiratory failure and cardiac arrest from which he subsequently died. It was accepted that, having been called on more than one occasion by a nursing sister, one of the doctors was in breach of her duty to attend the child. The issue before the court was causation; did this breach of duty cause the plaintiff's injuries? Whether the doctor's failure to attend caused the plaintiff's damage depended on what she would have done had she turned up. If the plaintiff had been intubated (to provide an airway) the respiratory difficulties would not have resulted in cardiac arrest. However, the doctor who failed to respond said that even if she had attended she would not have intubated, and therefore the cardiac arrest would have occurred in any event (no "but for" causation). Both the plaintiff and the defendant called distinguished medical experts in determining whether the professional standard of care required any doctor who attended the plaintiff to intubate.

Held
The action failed on the ground of causation. The House of Lords accepted that if the doctor had attended, her failure to intubate would not have been negligent because it was supported by a responsible body of professional opinion. [1997] 3 W.L.R. 1151.

THINK POINT

In assessing the whether the treatment has been negligent the court has to be satisfied that the professional opinion is capable of logical analysis. However, in a rare case where professional medical opinion does not withstand logical analysis it is open to the court to hold that it cannot be relied on to assess the doctor's conduct.

Key Principle
Where a risk that eventuates falls within the scope of a duty to warn, the "but for" test of causation may be satisfied on grounds if policy. In such circumstances the injury may be regarded as having been caused, in the legal sense, by the breach of that duty.

CHESTER V AFSHAR 2005
Following an elective surgical procedure on her spine, the claimant suffered paralysis and brought an action against the defendant neurosurgeon in negligence. The operation had not been negligently performed, the issue was one of causation as the claimant argued that she had not been given adequate warning of a 1–2 per cent risk of paralysis. Had she been aware of the risks of the proposed surgery she would not have consented to the operation taking place so soon and also, before deciding what to do, she would have sought a second or possibly even a third opinion.

Held
There was a sufficient causal link between the defendant's failure to warn of the risk in the surgical procedure and the damage sustained by the claimant and that link was not broken by the possibility that the claimant might have consented to surgery in the future. [2004] UKHL 41.

THINK POINT

The majority House of Lords decision in favour of the claimant could not be based on conventional causation principles because the risk of which she should have been warned was not created or increased by the failure to warn. Nevertheless, the "but for" test was satisfied on the ground that the claimant would not have had the operation when she did if the warning had been given. The approach in this case is to enable rights to be vindicated and to provide a remedy when the duty to warn patients of risks associated with procedures has been breached. However, despite the fact that the claimant might well have gone on to have the surgery in the future when the risk would still have existed, a majority ruled in her favour on grounds of policy. According to Lord Steyn:

> "Standing back from the detailed arguments, I have come to the conclusion that, as a result of the surgeon's failure to warn the patient, she cannot be said to have given informed consent to the surgery in the full legal sense. Her right of autonomy and dignity can and ought to be vindicated by a narrow and modest departure from traditional causation principles."

Key Principle

If the plaintiff cannot positively prove that the defendant's breach of duty caused the damage it is sufficient to show that the defendant's negligent conduct made the injury more probable.

MCGHEE V NATIONAL COAL BOARD 1973

The plaintiff worked at the defendant's brick kilns where the conditions were hot and dusty. The brick dust adhered to his sweaty skin and because his employer failed to provide washing facilities the plaintiff had to cycle home with his body still caked in brick dust. He contracted dermatitis and alleged that if washing facilities had been provided he would not have developed the disease. The medical evidence was unable to show that had washing facilities been provided the plaintiff would have escaped the disease. However, the evidence did show that the provision of showers would have materially reduced the risk of dermatitis.

Held ....

❖ (HL) The defendants were liable on the ground that it was sufficient for a plaintiff to show that the defendants' breach of duty made the risk of injury more probable even though it was uncertain whether it was the actual cause. [1973] 1 W.L.R. 1.

Commentary ....

(1) This case was distinguished in *Wilsher v Essex Area Health Authority* [1988] 1 All E.R. 871, where a premature baby was negligently given excessive oxygen. It is known that excessive oxygen given to premature babies can lead to blindness and the plaintiff alleged that this was the cause of his blindness. But there were up to five possible causes of the plaintiff's injury, any one of which might have caused his blindness. The House of Lords held that the burden of proof remained with the plaintiff who must establish that the defendant's breach of duty was at least a material contributory cause of the harm. Showing the defendant's negligence to be one out of five possible causes of the plaintiff's blindness was not evidence that it was the cause. In *McGhee* the plaintiff had established his disease was caused by the brick dust; the only question was whether the additional period of exposure to the brick dust had contributed to his dermatitis.

(2) In *Bonnington Castings Ltd v Wardlaw* [1956] A.C. 613 a steel worker who was exposed to noxious dust over a period of years as the result of his employer's negligence, contracted a progressive disease. However, some of the exposure to which he was exposed was from a "non-negligent" source and there was no evidence of the proportions of negligent and non-negligent exposure to the dust, so the "but for" test could not be satisfied. The House of Lords held that in these circumstances causation could be established because the employer's act or omission made a "material contribution" to the harm which constituted an application of, or an exception to, the but-for test.

Key Principle ....

Where cumulative causation is not present the plaintiff must prove on the balance of probabilities that the damage was caused by the defendant's breach of duty.

HOTSON V EAST BERKSHIRE AREA HEALTH AUTHORITY 1987
The plaintiff was rushed to hospital when he suffered a hip injury following a fall from a tree. The damage to his hip created a 75 per cent

chance that he would develop a permanent disability. The defendants negligently failed to correctly diagnose the plaintiff's hip condition and it went untreated for five days. By the time the mistake was discovered permanent disability was inevitable. The trial judge found that the delayed treatment had deprived the plaintiff of a 25 per cent chance of recovery and he awarded 25 per cent of the full compensation.

Held

❖ (HL) In reversing the decision it was held that there was no basis in tort for the judge's decision to award damages for loss of "chance" of complete recovery. If the plaintiff could prove, on the balance of probabilities, that he would have recovered if given proper treatment, he was entitled to full compensation. Otherwise he was entitled to nothing. [1987] A.C. 750.

Commentary

(1) In *Gregg v Scott* [2005] UKHL 2, the misdiagnosis of the appellant's medical condition by a medical practitioner had reduced his chances of surviving for more than 10 years from 42 per cent to 25 per cent. The judge dismissed his claim because the delay had not deprived him of the prospect of a cure; at the time of his misdiagnosis, the appellant had less than a 50 per cent chance of surviving more than 10 years anyway. This decision was upheld in the Court of Appeal and the House of Lords where it was held that liability for loss of chance of a more favourable outcome should not be introduced into personal injury claims.

(2) In *Allied Maples Group Ltd v Simmons & Simmons* [1995] 1 W.L.R. 1602 the Court of Appeal confirmed a first instance decision that a plaintiff can succeed if a real and substantial rather than speculative chance can be shown; the principle of the contract case *Chaplin v Hicks* [1911] 2 K.B. 786 was applied.

Key Principle

Where medical science cannot establish the probability that "but for" the defendant's negligence the damage would not have happened but the claimant can establish, on the balance of probabilities, that the negligence made a "material contribution" to the damage the but for test is modified and the claimant will succeed.

The claimant, a patient in a hospital managed by the MoD who had undergone an unsuccessful medical procedure, became very weak because of a negligent lack of post operative care. She suffered a cardiac arrest due to aspiration of vomit and which caused her brain damage and claimed that this would not have happened had she not been in a weakened state due to the defendant's earlier failures in her care. Breach of duty was not disputed; the issue was causation. The question was whether the damage was the result of the claimant's state of weakness because of the negligence in her post-operative care at the MoD's hospital or a non-negligent cause, each of which had made a material contribution to her overall weakness.

Held

The MoD's appeal against liability was rejected. The Court of Appeal held that it was enough for a patient to establish that, on the balance of probabilities, a lack of post-operative care and what flowed from that made a material contribution, namely something greater than negligible, to the overall weakness of her condition and the resulting brain damage. [2008] EWCA Civ 883.

Commentary

In considering *Hotson* (above) the Court noted that if the evidence demonstrated on a balance of probabilities that the injury would have occurred as a result of a non-negligent cause, the claimant would have failed to establish causation.

Key Principle

Where the evidence shows more than one employer to have contributed to the claimant's inhalation of asbestos dust causing mesothelioma (a form of cancer) the claimant does not need to satisfy the "but for" test. If a claimant is unable to prove, on the balance of probabilities, that the defendant's breach of duty was the cause of the disease, it is sufficient to show that the asbestos exposure for which any one defendant is responsible has contributed materially to the risk which has in fact materialised.

FAIRCHILD V GLENHAVEN FUNERAL SERVICES LTD 2002

The claimants had suffered asbestos-induced mesothelioma after being exposed to asbestos dust during the course of employment with several different employers, some of whom had gone out of business and could not now be sued. Because of the current limits of human science, it could not be proved which of the employers' breach of duty was the cause of the disease. The claimants appealed from the Court of Appeal's decision applying the "but for" test that they had failed to prove on the balance of probabilities which period of employment had caused or materially contributed to the cause of the mesothelioma.

Held

On the balance of probabilities each defendant's wrong-doing had materially increased the risk of the claimant's contracting the disease and this was to be treated as proof that each defendant had materially contributed to it. The decision in *McGhee* was applied; it varied the ordinary "but for" approach to causation. [2002] UKHL 22.

THINK POINT

These appeals raised conflicting policy considerations but their Lordships found the injustice of denying a remedy to employees who had suffered grave harm to outweigh the potential unfairness in imposing liability on successive employers who could not be proved to have caused the harm. According to Lord Nicholls:

> "The present appeals are another example of such circumstances, where good policy reasons exist for departing from the usual threshold 'but for' test of causal connection. Inhalation of asbestos dust carries a risk of mesothelioma. That is one of the very risks from which an employer's duty of care is intended to protect employees. Tragically, each claimant acquired this fatal disease from wrongful exposure to asbestos dust in the course of his employment. A former employee's inability to identify which particular period of wrongful exposure brought about the onset of his disease ought not, in all justice, to preclude recovery of compensation".

Key Principle

In cases where there is more than one defendant, a defendant can still be liable without proof of causation but his liability only extends to the relative proportion to which he could have contributed to the chance of the harm (several liability).

Several liability is where the defendant is only liable up to the extent of the damage he caused. *Joint* liability is where the claimant can sue one defendant for the whole of the damage leaving the defendant to seek compensation from the other defendants.

BARKER V CORUS UK 2006

This case concerned exposure to asbestos on three separate occasions. One of these exposures was for six weeks with an employer who was insolvent and uninsured and the second exposure was for six months with a different employer. The negligence for third exposure was that of the claimant himself during short periods when he worked as a self-employed plasterer. The facts here differed from those in *Fairchild* in that one of the periods of the claimant's exposure to asbestos was when he was self-employed. The question arose as to whether the *Fairchild* approach to proof of causation could apply in these circumstances and whether the defendants were liable for all the damage suffered or only for its contribution to the risk that materialised.

Held

The House of Lords partially reversed the ruling in *Fairchild* to the extent that it held that liability was several rather than joint. As a consequence, although a defendant could still be liable without proof of causation, his liability could only extend to the relative proportion to which he could have contributed to the chance of the outcome. The defendant's liability was therefore limited to the extent that its negligence exposed the claimant to the risk of contracting the disease. There was a 20 per cent discount on the overall amount of damages to reflect the claimant's contributory negligence. [2006] UKHL 20.

Commentary

This decision was seen as a victory for insurers but it met with strong resistance from trade unions and victim support groups. The adverse publicity surrounding claimants who were sick and dying being required to spend much of their remaining time trying to establish the relative extent of liability of former employers led to the introduction of emergency legislation to restore the *Fairchild* position of joint and several liability in cases of mesothelioma. The **Compensation Act 2006** (s.3) provides that where the employee has contracted mesothelioma as a result of exposure to asbestos causation can be established by showing that the exposure made "a material contribution to the risk".

Key Principle ....
In cases where there was a tortious as well as an environmental exposure to asbestos, it is not necessary for a claimant to show that the risk arising from the tortious exposure was more than twice the risk arising from the non-tortious causes. It is sufficient to show that the tortious exposure materially increased the *risk* of contracting mesothelioma.

Sienkiewicz v Grief (UK) Ltd. 2009
An office employee, who had been exposed to asbestos dust in the factory where she worked for 18 years, died of mesothelioma. In this case there was only one employer, but the woman had also been exposed to asbestos dust in the environment of the town where she lived. Her estate could not therefore prove that the disease had probably been caused by the workplace exposure, because there was another potential cause which did not arise from the tort of the employer. The trial judge said that since there was only one employer the claimant should have to prove causation on the normal balance of probabilities test and he found that she failed to discharge this test.

Held ....
The Court of Appeal allowed the claimant's appeal and said that in meso-thelioma cases a claimant could establish causation by showing that the workplace exposure to asbestos had materially increased the *risk* of the employee developing the disease. Interpreting s.3(1) of the **Compensation Act 2006**, the Court said the intention of Parliament was to reflect the common law requirements of causation in mesothelioma cases, which required proof of causation in by reference to a material increase in risk. [2009] EWCA Civ 1159.

Key Principle ....
Where two independent events cause the damage, and the second defen-dant's breach produces the same damage as that caused by the first defendant, the first event should be treated as the cause.

Baker v Willoughby 1970
In a road accident caused by the defendant's negligence the plaintiff suffered an injury to his left leg. Before the trial of his negligence action the plaintiff was the victim of an armed robbery at his place of work. He suffered gunshot wounds to his left leg and as a result of his injuries his leg had to be amputated. The defendant admitted negligence but argued that his responsibility ended when the plaintiff was shot and

therefore all losses from the date of the shooting flowed from the robbery.

Held

❖ (HL) The court rejected the defendant's argument on the ground that it produced a manifest injustice and held that he remained liable for the full extent of the plaintiff's damage. [1970] A.C. 467.

Commentary

Similar facts arose in *Jobling v Associated Dairies Ltd* [1981] 2 All E.R. 752 where the defendants were liable in negligence when the plaintiff sustained a back injury at his place of work. This injury led to a 50 per cent reduction in his earning capacity. Three years later, and before his negligence action, the onset of a disease of the spine rendered the plaintiff totally unfit for work. But in this case the second event was brought about by natural causes and the House of Lords held that the defendants were only liable for the reduced earning capacity up to the time of the onset of the disease.

INTERVENING CAUSE

NOVUS ACTUS INTERVENIENS

Key Principle

Where it can be established that an intervening act, a *novus actus interveniens*, has caused the damage, it may break the causal link between the defendant's breach of duty and the damage.

> MCKEW V HOLLAND & HANNEN & CUBITTS 1969
> Through the defendants' negligence the plaintiff suffered an injury and for a short time afterwards he occasionally lost control of his leg. He went to inspect a flat and, without asking for assistance, he attempted to descend a steep flight of stairs with no handrail. When his leg gave way without warning he fell and sustained further injuries.

Held

❖ (HL) The defendants were not liable for his additional injury because the plaintiff's own act broke the chain of causation. By placing himself in a position which might involve such a risk his own conduct had been unreasonable. [1969] 3 All E.R. 1621.

Commentary ....

(1) Similar facts arose in *Weiland v Cyril Lord Carpets* [1969] 3 All E.R. 1006 where the plaintiff had been negligently injured and forced to wear a surgical collar. This restricted her ability to focus her bifocal glasses and as a result she sustained further injuries when she fell down some steps. But here the defendants were found liable because the plaintiff had not acted unreasonably in attempting to descend the steps.

(2) In *Pigney v Pointers Transport* [1957] 1 W.L.R. 1121, a depressive mental illness which resulted from a negligently inflicted head injury had affected the deceased's capacity for rational judgment and his suicide was therefore held not to break the chain of causation. In *Corr v IBC Vehicles* [2008] UKHL 13 it was held that in these circumstances the suicide is merely the culmination of the depression. Here, following a near-fatal accident at work as a result of the defendant's negligence the claimant's husband suffered ongoing physical and psychological problems. The House of Lords upheld a Court of Appeal decision allowing an appeal against the judge's finding that his subsequent suicide was not reasonably foreseeable. Depression as a result of the accident was within the compensable damage flowing from the injury and the chain of causation had not been broken by the intentional act of suicide.

THINK POINT

In *Spencer v Wincanton Holdings Ltd (Wincanton Logistics Ltd)* [2009] EWCA Civ 1404 the appellant employer admitted liability for the injury which resulted in an above the knee amputation requiring a prosthesis to be fitted. When the respondent pulled into a petrol station to fill his car with petrol without wearing his prosthesis or using his sticks, he had a second accident which resulted in him becoming wheelchair dependent. The employer sought to rely on *McKew* arguing there was no liability to pay damages for the second accident because it had been caused by the respondent's unreasonable conduct and that the damage was too remote. The Court of Appeal noted the that the line between a set of facts which results in a finding of contributory negligence and a set of facts which results in a finding that the claimant's unreasonable conduct constitutes a *novus actus interveniens* is not capable of precise definition. The required threshold is high and involves judgments about whether it is "fair" to hold the defendant liable. The fact that the claimant's conduct could be described as unreasonable would not necessarily be sufficient to break the chain of causation. Here, the employer's appeal against liability was dismissed because the employee's conduct towards the second accident had been below the standard of unreasonableness required to break the chain and contributory negligence was available to deal with the sharing of responsibility.

Key Principle

A deliberate and informed act of suicide while of sound mind can amount to a *novus actus interveniens*. Where the defendant is under a specific legal duty to guard against the commission of that very act, suicide does not break the chain of causation.

REEVES V COMMISSIONER OF POLICE OF THE METROPOLIS 1999

The deceased, who was in police custody, had made two previous attempts to kill himself while in custody. Although the doctor who examined the deceased upon his arrival at the police station found no evidence of psychiatric illness, the doctor gave instructions that he was a suicide risk and should be frequently observed. The deceased was checked by an officer who inadvertently left the wicket hatch in his cell door open, and shortly afterwards the deceased was found to have hanged himself by tying his shirt through the open wicket. The defendants conceded that they owed the deceased a duty of care but denied liability on the basis that his own suicide was a *novus actus interveniens* breaking the chain of causation.

Held

The House of Lords held that because the defendants knew that the deceased was a suicide risk, his suicide was not a new act but the very harm they were under a duty to try to prevent. However, their Lordships also found that the deceased bore at least partial responsibility for his death, and damages were consequently reduced by 50 per cent. [1999] 3 All E.R. 897.

Key Principle

Where the subsequent event is the intervening act of a third party, negligent conduct is more likely to break the chain of causation than conduct which is not.

KNIGHTLEY V JOHNS 1982

The defendant's negligent driving caused the blocking of a busy road tunnel. A police inspector sent the plaintiff police constable to drive back against the traffic flow to close the tunnel entrance. As he was driving back into the tunnel the plaintiff was injured by a car being driven the other way.

Held

❖ (CA) The defendant was not liable. While it might be natural, probable and foreseeable that police would come to deal with the accident and that there might be risk-taking, there were so many errors before the plaintiff was sent back into the tunnel that the police inspector's negligent behaviour was the cause of the plaintiff's injuries. [1982] 1 W.L.R. 349.

Commentary

When a tort occurs first a subsequent act of nature may supervene and break the chain of causation. In *Carslogie Steamship Co Ltd v Royal Norwegian Government* [1952] A.C. 292 the plaintiff's ship was damaged in a collision caused by the defendant's negligence. Having set out on a voyage she would not have made had the collision not occurred, she suffered extensive damage due to heavy weather conditions. The defendants were not liable for the weather damage which was held to be an intervening event in the ordinary course of the voyage. The tort was merely part of the history of events which placed the ship in that place at that time.

REMOTENESS OF DAMAGE/CAUSATION IN LAW

Key Principle

Where a duty of care is owed, a defendant is liable for all the direct consequences of negligent conduct, no matter how unusual or unexpected.

POLEMIS AND FURNESS, WITHY & CO, RE 1921
Stevedores unloading a ship at Casablanca negligently let a plank fall into the hold in which a cargo of cans containing petrol was stored. A spark ignited petrol vapour and caused an explosion in which the ship was destroyed.

Held

❖ (CA) The defendants were liable for the loss of the ship because it was a direct, although not a foreseeable, consequence of their negligence. Scrutton L.J. observed that, "once the act is negligent, the fact that its exact operation was not foreseen is immaterial." [1921] 3 K.B. 560.

Commentary

Polemis, Re was strongly criticised by the Privy Council who refused to follow it in *The Wagon Mound* (see below). Foreseeability of damage has been adopted by subsequent courts as the test of remoteness of damage in negligence.

Key Principle

The defendant is not liable for all the direct losses; the kind of harm sustained by the plaintiff must be reasonably foreseeable.

OVERSEAS TANKSHIP (UK) LTD V MORTS DOCK AND ENGINEERING CO LTD, THE WAGON MOUND, 1961

Owing to the carelessness of the defendants a large quantity of fuel oil was discharged from their ship into Sydney Harbour. The oil was carried by wind and tide to the plaintiff's wharf about 600 feet away where welding on another ship was being carried out. After making enquiries the plaintiffs were advised that it was safe to continue with the welding operations on their wharf. Two days later the oil caught fire and the wharf and the ships being repaired were damaged in the blaze. The oil also congealed on the slipways and interfered with the plaintiff's use of the slips. Because there was a breach of duty and direct damage, at trial and at appeal, following *Polemis, Re*, judgment was given for the plaintiff.

Held

The Privy Council reversed the decision. The fact that some of the damage suffered (the damage to the slipways) was foreseeable did not make the defendants liable for the fire damage which was unforeseeable. The test for remoteness of damage was whether the kind of damage sustained was reasonably foreseeable. The court also stated that *Polemis* should no longer be regarded as good law. [1961] A.C. 388.

Commentary

In *Jebson v Ministry of Defence* [2000] 1 W.L.R. 2055, the claimant, who was one of a group of soldiers returning in a drunken state from a night out, fell when he tried to climb on to the roof of the army truck. It was held at first instance that, although the defendant was in breach of a duty to supervise the soldiers, the damage was too remote because it was not reasonably foreseeable that the soldier would have tried to climb on to the roof [of the truck]. The Court of Appeal allowed the claimant's appeal and held that under the circumstances rowdy behaviour was foreseeable and therefore the damage was not too remote.

Key Principle

If the kind of damage suffered is reasonably foreseeable, the precise manner in which it occurred need not have been.

HUGHES V LORD ADVOCATE 1963

Employees of the Post Office negligently left an open manhole unattended in the street. It was covered by a canvas tent and surrounded by paraffin warning lamps. Out of curiosity two young boys entered the tent and the plaintiff, a boy aged eight, took one of the lamps in with him. The lamp was knocked into the hole and caused a violent explosion in which the plaintiff suffered severe burns.

Held

❖ (HL) The defendants were held liable. Even though in the circumstances the explosion was unforeseeable the kind of damage which occurred, burns, was of a type which was foreseeable. [1963] A.C. 837.

Commentary

This case was distinguished by the Court of Appeal in *Doughty v Turner Manufacturing Co Ltd* [1964] 1 Q.B. 518 where an asbestos cover was knocked into a cauldron of molten liquid. A minute or two later, due to a chemical reaction which was unforeseeable at the time, the liquid erupted and the plaintiff suffered burns. The plaintiff failed on the ground that a splash causing burns was foreseeable but the damage which occurred was of an entirely different kind.

Key Principle

Provided that the type of harm and its occurrence are reasonably foreseeable it is irrelevant that the damage is more extensive than could have been foreseen.

VACWELL ENGINEERING CO LTD V BDH CHEMICALS LTD 1971

The defendants negligently failed to warn the plaintiffs that a chemical which they supplied was liable to cause an explosion if mixed with water. The plaintiff's employee allowed the chemical to come into contact with water and the reaction led to an explosion of unforesee-able violence which destroyed much of the plaintiff's premises.

Held

❖ (CA) The defendants were liable; it was no defence that an explosion much greater in magnitude than was foreseeable had resulted. [1971] 1 Q.B. 111.

Key Principle

The amount of damage that a victim suffers as the result of negligence depends upon the individual's characteristics and constitution. This is known as the "egg-shell skull" principle; tort-feasors must take their victims as they find them.

SMITH V LEECH BRAIN & CO 1962

The plaintiff employee suffered a burn to his lip as a result of inade-quate safety measures in the defendant employer's factory. The plaintiff's lip was in a pre-malignant condition and the burn caused him to develop cancer which ultimately led to his death. The defendants argued that it was not reasonably foreseeable that the plaintiff would suffer cancer from being burned.

Held

The defendants were liable, even though the only foreseeable injury was a splash causing a burn the "egg-shell skull" rule applied. The question to be asked was whether the burn could be foreseen; not whether the cancer was foreseeable. [1962] 2 Q.B. 405.

Commentary

(1) In *Robinson v Post Office* [1974] 1 W.L.R. 1176 the plaintiff's damage was a combination of the defendant's negligence and the administration of medical treatment to which he was allergic. Applying the "egg-shell skull" rule the defendant was held liable for both the original injury and the allergic reaction to the injection.

(2) The rule was also applied in *Pigney v Pointers Transport Services Ltd* [1957] 1 W.L.R. 1121 (see p.122) where the defendant's negligence caused a severe head injury which induced a depressive mental illness in the plain-tiff's husband. It was the victim's reaction to this illness which led to his suicide and the defendants were liable.

Key Principle

The "egg-shell skull principle" applies to cases of "nervous shock" as it does to any other type of injury.

> ### BRICE V BROWN 1984
>
> A plaintiff and her nine-year-old daughter were passengers in a taxi which was involved in a collision with a bus. The daughter suffered minor injuries. Even though the physical injuries sustained by the mother were trivial, owing to a pre-existing personality disorder, she suffered a hysterical reaction and lasting nervous shock resulting from the injuries suffered by her daughter.

Held

The test is whether it is foreseeable that a person of normal disposition and phlegm might suffer nervous shock through the risk created by the defendant's negligence. The plaintiff was allowed to succeed on the basis that a person of customary phlegm would have suffered nervous shock in these circumstances and the defendant's argument, that the plaintiff's unusual and exceptional reaction to the accident was unforeseeable, was rejected. [1984] 1 All E.R. 997.

THINK POINT

In *Page v Smith* [1995] 2 W.L.R. 644, the House of Lords held that in claims for nervous shock it is necessary to distinguish between primary and secondary victims. Where the plaintiff is a primary victim, personal injury of some kind must be foreseeable, but it is not necessary to show that injury by shock was foreseeable. Where the plaintiff is a secondary victim the defendant will not be liable unless psychiatric injury is foreseeable in a person of normal fortitude.

Defences to Negligence

7

INTRODUCTION

Not all possible defences in tort actions are discussed here. Some defences are specific to particular torts, for example, justification in defamation, and are considered with those torts. This Chapter is concerned with defences which have a particular relevance to claims in negligence. The first of these, contributory negligence, operates where the plaintiff's own fault has contributed to the damage suffered and the damages payable are reduced in proportion to the degree of fault. The second defence is *volenti non fit injuria*, i.e. no wrong is done to one who consents. This means that a plaintiff who voluntarily agrees to undertake the risk of harm is not permitted to sue for the consequent damage. It is a complete defence and if it succeeds the plaintiff gets nothing. The third defence of *ex turpi causa non oritur action*, no right of action arises from a bad cause, means that a defendant is not liable for damage in circumstances where the plaintiff was participating in an unlawful act.

CONTRIBUTORY NEGLIGENCE

Before the **Law Reform (Contributory Negligence) Act 1945**, contributory negligence was a complete defence and no damages were recoverable where injuries were caused partly by the plaintiff's own fault. Under the Act, s.1(1) the court has power to apportion the damage and, where a plaintiff's own conduct has contributed to the accident or harm, to reduce the damages awarded. In *Pitts v Hunt* [1991] 1 Q.B. 24 the Court of Appeal announced that for the Act to come into operation there must be fault on the part of both parties. A finding that the plaintiff was 100 per cent contributory negligent was not allowed on the basis that holding the plaintiff entirely at fault would effectively defeat his claim.

Key Principle
The plaintiff's carelessness need not be a cause of the accident but it is essential to show that it contributed to the damage suffered.

FROOM V BUTCHER 1976

The plaintiff was involved in a collision caused by the defendant's negligence. He was not wearing a seat belt but if he had been wearing a belt the head and chest injuries which he sustained in the accident would have been avoided.

Held

❖ (CA) The standard of care is objective. In failing to wear a seat belt the plaintiff failed to take reasonable precautions for his own safety and his damages were reduced accordingly. Lord Denning set out two broad categories of typical cases where the evidence showed that a seatbelt would have prevented the damage altogether if it had been worn and a general proposition that, absent something exceptional, there should be no reduction in a case where the injury would not have been reduced "to a considerable extent" by the seat belt. He suggested that in cases where the injury would have been reduced to a considerable extent the damages should be reduced by 25 percent. He pointed out that some injuries to the head for instance, would have been a good deal less severe if a seat belt had been worn, but there would still have been some injury to the head. In such cases he suggested that the damages attributable to the failure to wear the seat belt should be reduced by 15 per cent. [1976] 2 Q.B. 286.

Commentary

(1) The negligence of the plaintiff did not contribute to the accident happening, but his failure to take precautions increased the risk of harm.

(2) In this case the plaintiff had made a conscious decision not to wear the seat belt because of the risk of becoming trapped in an accident. However, in *Condon v Condon* [1978] R.T.R. 483 a plaintiff who claimed to suffer from a seat-belt phobia was held not to be contributorily negligent for failing to do so.

Key Principle

There is a powerful public interest that there should be no enquiry into fine degrees of contributory negligence so that the vast majority of cases can be settled according to the well-understood formula in *Froom v Butcher*.

STANTON V COLLINSON 2010

The 16-year-old claimant had been sharing the front passenger seat with another passenger in a car being driven by the defendant. The driver lost control of the car which resulted in a crash in which the claimant suffered severe brain damage. Neither of the passengers had been wearing a seat belt at the time of the accident. Evidence showed that the claimant's head injury would probably have been less severe if he had been wearing a seat belt but a complete prevention of "serious head injury" would have been unlikely, even if a seat belt had been worn. The judge refused to award contributory negligence on the ground that the defendant had failed to prove that a seat belt, if worn, would have reduced the claimant's injuries sufficiently. The defendant appealed against the finding of no contributory negligence and argued that claimant's level of contributory negligence was greater than that of a passenger who merely omitted to put on a seat belt. He also questioned whether the reduction for contributory negligence in these circumstances should be greater than the 15 per cent set out by Lord Denning and whether the court ought to revisit the decision in *Froom v Butcher* and increase the levels of contributory negligence attributable to failure to wear a seat belt in light of developments over the intervening 30 years.

Held

The Court of Appeal upheld the finding of the trial judge that medical evidence was required to resolve the uncertainties in this case and that the defendant had not proved that the failure to wear a seat belt made a "substantial difference" to the claimant's injuries. A sense of proportionality had to be exercised and even if the seat belt would or might have made a lesser difference to the injury as distinct from "a considerable difference" the **Law Reform (Contributory Negligence) Act 1945** s.1 required the court to investigate the extent of the difference. In stating that the Act required that the reduction be such as appeared to the court to be just and equitable the approach set out in *Froom v Butcher* was endorsed by the Court.

THINK POINT

Contributory negligence was argued in *Smith v Finch* [2009] EWHC 53 (QB) in a case involving a cyclist who sustained serious head injuries in a road accident caused by the defendant. Although there is no legal requirement to wear a cycling helmet, the Court made an analysis of *Froom v Butcher* and came to the conclusion that the judgment and observations of Lord Denning M.R. should apply to the wearing of helmets by cyclists. However, in *Smith v Finch*, contributory negligence failed because the defendant was unable to show that an approved safety helmet would have prevented the claimant's serious head injuries or made them less severe.

Key Principle

The principle of contributory negligence is that a person has responsibility for his actions and it is just and equitable that the reduction in damages should take account of the relative blameworthiness of the claimant's conduct.

BADGER V MINISTRY OF DEFENCE 2006

The asbestos fibres to which claimant's husband had been exposed during his employment as a boiler maker with the MoD were causative of the lung cancer that killed him. The MoD admitted liability in negligence for his death at the age of 63. However, the deceased had smoked for the majority of his life, which was also causative of his cancer. Despite warnings about the risk of damage to his health caused by smoking, he did not stop. The MoD claimed that damages should be reduced by 25 per cent on account of the deceased's contributory negligence.

Held

When the deceased began smoking the connection between smoking and serious ill health was not widely accepted so he could not be criticised for starting to smoke. However, when health warnings were put on cigarette packets, it was reasonably foreseeable by a reasonably prudent man that if he smoked he risked damaging his health. In assessing damages, the deceased's continued smoking constituted contributory negligence and the appropriate reduction in damages attributable was 20 per cent. [2005] EWHC 2941 (QB); [2006] 3 All E.R. 173.

Key Principle

Accepting a lift from a driver whom the plaintiff knows has consumed large quantities of alcohol may amount to contributory negligence.

OWENS V BRIMMELL 1977

The plaintiff and the defendant went on a pub-crawl together and each consumed about eight or nine pints of beer. On the journey home the defendant negligently drove into a lamp post.

Held

The plaintiff was 20 per cent contributorily negligent in getting into the car with a driver whom he knew to be drunk, even if at the time he himself was too drunk to know how drunk the driver was. [1977] Q.B. 859.

Key Principle

The injury sustained must be within the scope of the risk created by the claimant's negligence.

> **JONES V LIVOX QUARRIES LTD 1952**
> The plaintiff, disregarding his employer's safety instructions, was riding on the towbar of a traxcavator when another employee negligently drove into the back of the vehicle and caused him injury. The plaintiff argued that his contributory negligence should not count against him because the obvious danger arising from riding on the towbar was being thrown off, not being run into from behind and crushed by another vehicle.

Held

❖ (CA) The risk of being run into from behind was also one to which the plaintiff had exposed himself and his damages were reduced accordingly. [1952] 2 Q.B. 608.

Commentary

Lord Denning said that the plaintiff's carelessness would have been irrelevant if, instead of being hit by another vehicle, he had been struck in the eye by a shot fired by a negligent sportsman.

Key Principle

In the case of children, age is a circumstance which must be considered in deciding if there has been contributory negligence.

> **YACHUK V OLIVER BLAIS CO LTD 1949**
> The defendants supplied a nine-year-old boy with a pint of petrol. He had falsely stated that his mother wanted the petrol for her car. When he used the fuel to make a burning torch for the purposes of a game he suffered severe injury.

Held

The defendants were liable in negligence for supplying petrol to so young a boy. He had not been guilty of contributory negligence for he neither knew nor could be expected to know of the danger. [1949] A.C. 386.

Commentary

(1) In *Gough v Thorne* [1966] 3 All E.R. 398, the plaintiff, a 13-year-old girl, was waiting to cross the road. She was beckoned to proceed by the driver of a lorry and as she did so she was struck by the defendant who was driving too fast. The fact that she had relied entirely on the driver's signal to cross the road did not constitute contributory negligence. According to Lord Denning: "A very young child cannot be guilty of contributory negligence."

(2) Where an employee is suing an employer the courts are reluctant to make a finding of contributory negligence. In *Caswell v Powell Duffryn Associated Collieries* [1940] A.C. 152, it was held that regard must be had to the dulling of the sense of danger through familiarity, repetition, noise, confusion, fatigue and preoccupation with work.

Key Principle

Where a defendant's negligence creates an emergency the court is reluctant to find contributory negligence on the part of a plaintiff who makes a wrong decision in the agony of the moment.

> JONES V BOYCE 1816
>
> The plaintiff was a passenger on the defendant's coach and, fearing that it was about to overturn, he jumped off. The coach did not overturn and had he stayed where he was the plaintiff would have been safe.

Held

He was not guilty of contributory negligence because he had acted reasonably in the circumstances. (1816) 1 Stark 493.

VOLENTI NON FIT INJURIA

Key Principle

The defendant will not be liable if the plaintiff voluntarily assumed to take the risk involved, but knowledge of the danger does not necessarily imply consent.

Smith v Charles Baker & Sons 1891

The plaintiff was employed drilling holes in a rock cutting over which a crane often swung heavy stones while he was working. He was aware that there was a risk of the stones falling and he had complained to his employer about the dangerous practice. When he was injured by a falling stone he brought an action against his employers, who pleaded *volenti non fit injuria*.

Held

❖ (HL) *Volenti* was rejected; even though the plaintiff had knowledge of the danger and continued to work, he had not voluntarily undertaken the risk. [1891] A.C. 325.

Commentary

See also *Ratcliff v McConnell* (1998) (see p.204) where, knowing of the risk involved, the plaintiff was held to have willingly accepted the risk as his.

THINK POINT

The defence will rarely be successful in an action by an employee against an employer. However, it was accepted by the House of Lords in *Imperial Chemical Industries Ltd (ICI) v Shatwell* [1965] A.C. 656. The plaintiff, in defiance of his employer's orders and statutory safety regulations, went to test some detonators without taking the required safety precautions. During the testing an explosion occurred and the plaintiff was injured. His employer was not liable because the plaintiff was held to have consented to and fully appreciated the risk of injury.

Key Principle

In circumstances where the plaintiff accepts a lift from an obviously inebriated driver the plea of *volenti* depends on the degree of intoxication.

Morris v Murray 1991

After a bout of heavy drinking Murray suggested to Morris that they go for a spin in his light aircraft. Soon after take-off the aircraft crashed killing Murray and severely injuring Morris who brought an action against the deceased's estate.

Held ....

❖ (CA) The defence succeeded on the ground that the pilot's drunkenness was so extreme and obvious that the plaintiff was *volens* to the risk. [1991] 2 Q.B. 6.

Commentary ....

In *Dann v Hamilton* [1939] 1 K.B. 509, the defendant had driven the plaintiff and her mother to see the Coronation decorations. They visited several public houses and it became obvious that the defendant's ability to drive was impaired. But the plea of *volenti* was rejected and the plaintiff was found not to have consented to or absolved the defendant from subsequent negligence on his part. Asquith J. held that *volenti* did not apply to this situation, unless the drunkeness was so extreme and so glaring that accepting a lift was equivalent to "... walking on the edge of an unfenced cliff". (*Volenti* is excluded by s.149 of the Road Traffic Act 1988, see *Pitts v Hunt*, below.)

Key Principle ....

The doctrine of the assumption of risk does not apply to a rescuer when the emergency was created by the defendant's negligence.

> BAKER V HOPKINS 1959
> The defendant employer had adopted a dangerous system of working by lowering a petrol engine down into the inside of a well. The engine discharged poisonous emissions and two of the workmen were over-come by the fumes. The plaintiff, a doctor, had volunteered to go down the well to rescue the workmen. He too was overcome by the fumes and was killed.

Held ....

❖ (CA) *Volenti* was inapplicable because the plaintiff's actions as a rescuer were not truly voluntary. This decision can also be explained on policy grounds as it is against the public interest to deter rescue. [1959] 3 All E.R. 225.

Commentary ....

If there is no genuine emergency the plaintiff might be *volens*. In *Cutler v United Dairies Ltd* [1933] 2 K.B. 197 the plaintiff was *volens* because there was nobody in danger when he tried to calm a horse which had bolted into a field.

EX TURPI CAUSA NON ORITUR ACTIO

Key Principle ....

The courts will not assist a plaintiff who has been guilty of illegal conduct.

> PITTS V HUNT 1990
>
> On their way back from a disco at which they had both consumed large amounts of alcohol, the plaintiff encouraged the defendant to drive his motorbike in a reckless and dangerous fashion. The defendant was killed and the plaintiff, who was a pillion passenger, was badly injured.

Held ....

❖ (CA) The defendant's own criminal and disgraceful conduct gave rise to a successful defence of the *ex turpi causa*. The court concluded that the defence of *volenti non fit injuria*, which was also raised, is excluded under the **Road Traffic Act 1988** in circumstances where insurance is compulsory (as it is with motor insurance). [1991] 1 Q.B. 24.

Key Principle ....

Acceptance by the court that an accused's mental responsibility is substantially impaired at the time of commission of a serious criminal act does not remove the accused's liability for that act. The defence of *ex turpi causa* is applied in these circumstances to prevent the court being made an instrument to enforce obligations alleged to arise out of the claimant's own criminal act.

> CLUNIS V CAMDEN AND ISLINGTON HEALTH AUTHORITY 1998
>
> The plaintiff, who had a history of mental illness, killed a stranger in a violent attack. Before he killed the victim the plaintiff had been discharged into the care of the defendant health authority. He pleaded guilty to manslaughter on the grounds of diminished responsibility for the killing but claimed that the health authority was negligent in failing to treat him with reasonable care and skill. [1998] 3 All E.R. 180.

Held ....

❖ (CA) The maxim *ex turpo causa non oritur action* applied. A plaintiff who had been convicted of a serious offence could not, on the ground of public policy, sue a health authority in negligence in failing to treat him properly, thereby preventing him from committing the offence.

Commentary

In *Vellino v Chief Constable of Greater Manchester Police* [2001] EWCA Civ 1249, when the police arrived to enforce an arrest warrant on the claimant for failure to appear in court, he attempted to escape from their custody by jumping from a window of his second floor flat. As a result of the fall, he suffered brain damage and tetraplegia and claimed negligence on the part of the arresting officers, alleging that they had stood idly by and let him jump. The Court of Appeal held that the maxim *ex turpi causa non oritur action* made the claim untenable because the defendant had to rely on his own criminal conduct in escaping lawful custody to found his claim.

THINK POINT

In *Gray v Thames Trains Ltd* [2009] W.L.R. (D) 195 as the result of a serious rail crash caused by the defendant's negligence, the claimant suffered severe psychological depression which led him to kill a man. At the criminal trial for this offence his plea of guilty to manslaughter on the ground of diminished responsibility was accepted and he was ordered to be detained in a mental hospital under the **Mental Health Act 1983**. His claim in damages for loss of earnings after he committed the manslaughter was allowed by the Court of Appeal which held it was not defeated by *ex turpi causa* because the damages were not inextricably bound up with or linked to his criminal conduct. Thames Trains Ltd appealed against this decision arguing that a claimant cannot recover compensation for loss which has been suffered in consequence of his own criminal act. In allowing the appeal the House of Lords ruled that Gray's conviction for manslaughter precluded a claim for loss of earnings during his detention by reason of the public policy expressed in the doctrine of *ex turpi causa*. Lord Hoffman said the maxim *ex turpi causa non oritur actio* expresses not so much a principle as a policy; that policy is not based upon a single justification but on a group of reasons, which vary in different situations: "The wider and simpler version was that you could not recover for damage which was the consequence of your own criminal act. In its narrower form, it was that you could not recover for damage which was the consequence of a sentence imposed upon you for a criminal act."

Employers' Liability at Common Law

. . . .

8

INTRODUCTION

The liability of an employer to an employee has two aspects. The first, liability for harm caused by employees in the course of their employment, vicarious liability, is dealt with in Ch.2 but it should be noted here that vicarious liability concerns an employer's liability for harm caused *by* his employees. The second form of liability which is the subject of this Chapter is an employer's personal liability *to* employees in respect of harm suffered at work. In *Priestly v Fowler* (1837) 3 M. & W. 1 it was decided that an employer would not be vicariously liable for harm inflicted on workers by fellow employees. This was known as the doctrine of "common employment" and the theory was that the contract of employment contained an implied term that an employee agreed to accept the risks incidental to the employment, including the risk of negligence of fellow employees. Where a risk had been created by the employer the defence of *volenti non fit injuria*, which was a complete defence until the Law Reform Contributory Negligence Act 1945, could usually be established by the employer. These two defences, together with the defence of contributory negligence, were known as the "unholy trinity" and, combined, they prevented virtually any action in tort by employees.

As judicial attitudes began to change the law developed techniques to mitigate the harshness of the rule. In *Smith v Charles Baker & Sons* (1891) (see p.135) the House of Lords made it difficult for employers to establish the defence of *volenti*. In *Wilsons & Clyde Coal v English* (1938) (below) it was held that an employer owed a personal and non-delegable duty to an employee and where the employer was in breach of this duty the defence of common employment could not be relied on. The employer's duty is a general duty to take reasonable care for the *physical* safety of the employee and advances in medical and scientific knowledge about the effects of asbestos and repetitive strain injury have lead to an expansion of an employer's liability to safeguard employees against these types of harm.

An employer's liability for *psychiatric* harm as the result of occupational stress is also a developing area of liability. An employer who becomes aware that stress at work is having an adverse effect on the mental health of an employee is under a duty to take positive steps to prevent the harm.

However, an employer's liability does not extend to protecting the employee's economic welfare. In *Reid v Rush & Tompkins Group Plc* [1989] 3 All E.R. 228, it was held that an employer had no duty to arrange accident insurance for a person working abroad or to warn the employee of the need to take out such insurance.

Key Principle

The employer's obligation for the employee's safety is fulfilled by due care and skill. But it is not fulfilled by delegation to employees, even though selected with due care and skill.

WILSONS & CLYDE COAL CO LTD V ENGLISH 1938

The plaintiff miner was injured at the defendant's coal mine. He was travelling through the pit at the end of a day shift and was crushed when the haulage plant was set in motion. The haulage equipment should have been stopped during travelling time. The defendant employers claimed that they had discharged their duty of providing a safe system of work by appointing a competent and qualified manager.

Held

❖ (HL) The employers were liable. They could not avoid their duty to provide a reasonably safe system of working by delegation to a competent employee. [1938] A.C. 57.

Commentary

The employer's duty, which was stated to be "the provision of a competent staff of men, adequate material and a proper system and effective supervision", is commonly analysed in four elements. The following cases are grouped to reflect this approach.

COMPETENT STAFF

Key Principle

The employer owes a duty to employees to select competent employees and to give them proper instructions and supervision.

GENERAL CLEANING CONTRACTORS V CHRISTMAS 1953

A window cleaner was sent to clean the windows of a club. He was instructed by his employers in the sill method of cleaning windows and, while he was holding on to a window-sash for support, the window came down on his fingers causing him to fall to the ground.

Held ....

❖ (HL) The employers were liable, the plaintiff should have been given proper instruction and told to test the sashes. [1953] A.C. 180.

SAFE PLACE OF WORK

Key Principle ....

The employer must provide a safe place of work, but this duty is discharged if the employer takes reasonable steps to see that the premises are safe.

LATIMER V AEC LTD 1953

The defendants' large factory was flooded after a heavy rainfall and the water mixed with an oily liquid which usually collected in channels in the floor. When the mixture drained away it left the floor very slippery. Sawdust was spread over most, but not all, of the surface. A workman was injured when he slipped on the untreated part of the floor. The trial judge had found the defendants liable on the ground that they had not closed down the factory.

Held ....

❖ (HL) Allowing the appeal, it was held that the defendants were not liable; they had acted as a reasonable employer would have acted. The danger was not such as to impose on the employer an obligation to close down the factory. [1953] 2 All E.R. 499.

PROPER PLANT AND EQUIPMENT

Key Principle

At common law an employer was not liable for the defects in the manufacture of a tool which could not have been discovered with reasonable inspection.

> DAVIE V NEW MERTON BOARD MILLS 1959
> The plaintiff employee was blinded when a particle of metal chipped off the tool with which he was working. The tool had been negligently manufactured but outwardly it appeared to be in good condition.

Held

The employer had bought the tool from a reputable manufacturer and had therefore discharged his duty to the employee. [1959] A.C. 604.

Commentary

The effect of this decision was to leave the injured employee without compensation where the manufacturer or supplier could not be found or who was bankrupt. The decision has been reversed by the Employers' Liability (Defective Equipment) Act 1969 which makes the employer liable where an employee is injured in the course of employment by defective equipment.

Key Principle

The Employers' Liability (Defective Equipment) Act 1969 covers defective plant of every sort with which the employee is compelled to work.

> COLTMAN V BIBBY TANKERS 1988
> This case arose out of the sinking of *The Derbyshire* with the loss of all hands off the coast of Japan in 1980. The plaintiffs, personal representatives of a crew member, alleged that, due to the manufacturer's negligence, the ship was defectively constructed. They claimed that these were defects in equipment and argued that the ship was "equipment" within s.1 of the Employers' Liability (Defective Equipment) Act 1969.

Held

The meaning of the word "equipment" can include ships or vessels for the purposes of the Act. [1988] A.C. 276.

Commentary

Equipment is given a broad interpretation and in *Knowles v Liverpool City Council* [1993] 1 W.L.R. 1428 was found to include a flagstone being laid by a council workman.

SAFE SYSTEM OF WORK

Key Principle

The duty will normally apply in a system of working which is regular or routine and includes: the physical lay-out of the job; the sequence in which the work is to be carried out; the provision in appropriate cases of warnings and notices; and the issue of special instructions.

> SPEED V THOMAS SWIFT AND CO LTD 1943
> The plaintiff was loading a ship from a barge, an operation which was normally carried out while the ship's rails were left in position. Sections of the rail had been damaged and the resulting circumstances made it unsafe on the occasion in question to load the ship. As a result the plaintiff was injured.

Held

The employers were liable because in the circumstances they had not laid out a safe system of work. [1943] K.B. 557.

Commentary

The general practice of a particular trade will be relevant in deciding whether or not the duty has been breached, but in *General Cleaning Contractors v Christmas* (1953) (see p.140) the House of Lords said that where a practice of ignoring an obvious danger has evolved it is not reasonable to expect an individual workman to devise precautions.

THINK POINT

What is reasonable depends on the circumstances. In *Hopps v Mott MacDonald Ltd* [2009] EWHC 1881 (QB) a consultant electrical engineer was injured by an explosive device as he was working in and around Basrah. He claimed that his employer should have carried out a risk assessment to assess the suitability of the proposed transport arrangements and should only have allowed him to travel in an armoured vehicle. In determining whether particular steps, such as confinement to the airport until armoured vehicles were available for transport, should have been taken, the court took account of the risks to which the claimant and others were exposed. It was held that the risks the claimant faced could not, if he was to carry out his job, be eliminated and it was not unreasonable for the claimant to have been carried around Basrah in an unarmoured vehicle. In this case the **Compensation Act 2006** (s.1) was applied on the ground that a finding of liability on the employer would prevent the desirable activity of reconstructing the infrastructure of Iraq being undertaken.

Key Principle

The concept of a safe system of work includes an employer's duty to protect against psychiatric harm in circumstances where such harm is foreseeable as the result of occupational stress.

> WALKER V NORTHUMBERLAND COUNTY COUNCIL 1995
> The plaintiff, an area social services officer, having suffered two mental breakdowns was dismissed on grounds of ill health. He alleged that his ill health was caused by the stress of his work and claimed damages from his employers.

Held

The first nervous breakdown was unforeseeable but when the plaintiff returned to work after this nervous breakdown the risk to his mental health was reasonably foreseeable. The employer was liable for failing to take extra steps to protect him against the risk of foreseeable psychiatric harm. [1995] I.R.L.R. 35.

Key Principle

There are no intrinsically stressful occupations and unless an employer knows of some particular problem or vulnerability of an employee he is usually entitled to assume that employees can withstand the normal pressures of a job.

> HATTON V SUTHERLAND (2002)
> Here, four conjoined appeals were made against the trial judges' findings that the employers concerned were liable for psychiatric injury as the result of stress at work (three of the cases involved public sector employers).

Held ....

Three of four appeals were allowed. The Court of Appeal stressed that the ordinary principles of employers' liability applied; an employer will only be liable if he had reason to believe that the damaging stress was foreseeable and had failed to take reasonable steps to prevent it. There are no special control mechanisms (as per *Alcock*) applying to claims for psychiatric injury arising from the stress of the work; the issue is simply whether the employer has breached his duty not to injure the health of his employees. [2002] EWCA Civ 76.

Commentary ....

(1) The indications of the employee's vulnerability to psychiatric injury caused by occupational of stress must be plain enough for any reasonable employer to realise that steps should be taken to assist the employee. According to Hale L.J.:

> "His duty is to take reasonable care. What is reasonable depends, as we all know, upon the foreseeability of harm, the magnitude of the risk of that harm occurring, the gravity of the harm which may take place, the cost and practicability of pre-venting it, and the justifications for running the risk ...".

(2) Hale L.J. stressed that in every case it is necessary to ask not only what the employer *could* but what the employer *should* have done. Also, whether the claim involves either a public or a private sector employer, its resources and the size and scope of the employer's operation will be relevant to this question.

Key Principle ....

An employer's duty of care is owed to workers as individuals and, since capacity to stress varies between employees, an employer must heed warnings from those who are less able. The overall test is that of the conduct of the reasonable and prudent employer, taking positive thought for the safety of his employees in the light of what he knew or ought to have known.

BARBER V SOMERSET 2004

Barber, a conscientious school teacher and one of the unsuccessful claimants in *Hatton*, appealed to the House of Lords. He had spoken about his work overload with one of the senior management team and was subsequently on certified sickness absence suffering from stress and depression. On his return to work he told his managers that he was not coping with his workload. No steps were taken to assist him and as a consequence of the pressure he developed a psychiatric illness and had to stop working.

Held

Barber's appeal against the Court of Appeal's finding, that it was not foreseeable if he continued with his existing workload he was liable to develop a psychiatric illness, was allowed. The House of Lords unanimously approved of the general guidance in respect of psychiatric harm caused by stress at work set out in *Hatton v Sutherland* (above). [2004] UKHL 13.

Commentary

(1) In terms of the steps the employer should take to prevent harm their Lordships approved the 16 guiding propositions and statement by Hale L.J. in *Hatton*.

(2) In *Hartman v South Essex Mental Health and Community Care NHS Trust* [2005] EWCA Civ 6 the employer was not liable because it was not reasonably foreseeable that the employee would suffer psychiatric injury. Hartman's vulnerability to suffer from stress was provided in a confidential medical questionnaire submitted to the occupational health department. Applying the *Hatton* principles the Court of Appeal held that under these circumstances the employer could not be fixed with knowledge of her vulnerability.

THINK POINT

In *Daw v Intel Corporation* (UK) Ltd 2007 the Court of Appeal held that reference to counselling services in *Barber* did not make such services a panacea by which employers could discharge their duty of care in all cases. Here the employee repeatedly told her managers that she had to work excessive hours to complete her work and it was held that the only way of dealing with her problems would have been for management to reduce her workload. The consequences of these management failings were not avoided by the provision of counsellors.

Where an employer knows or can foresee that an employee might suffer physical or psychiatric harm through the acts of fellow employees the employer owes a duty to protect its employees from such harm.

> WATERS V COMMISSIONER OF POLICE OF THE METROPOLIS 2000
> A female police officer made a complaint of sexual assault against a fellow officer. After she made this complaint she was subjected to a campaign of victimisation by other police officers and suffered psychiatric injury as a result. She claimed that her employer had carelessly failed to prevent this happening.

Held ....

In allowing her appeal against the striking out of the claim, the House of Lords held that she had an arguable case. It was reasonably foreseeable that following the nature of the complaint made by the officer she might suffer mistreatment. An employer owes a duty to take reasonable care to protect its employees from harm, including workplace bullying and psychiatric harm, during employment. [2000] 1 W.L.R. 1607.

Key Principle ....

Employers must warn employees of any inherent dangers in the work which they are required to do.

> PAPE V CUMBRIA COUNTY COUNCIL 1992
> The plaintiff was a part-time cleaner employed by the defendants. She was required to use various detergents and chemical cleaning products in the course of her work. Although the defendants had provided gloves they did not warn her of the danger of contracting dermatitis or instruct her to wear the gloves. When the plaintiff developed dermatitis she sued the employers.

Held ....

The employers were liable; they had failed to provide a safe system of work in not warning the plaintiff of the dangers of contracting dermatitis if the gloves were not worn. [1992] I.C.R. 132.

EMPLOYER'S INDEMNITY

Key Principle

An employer who has been held vicariously liable for an employee's negligence is entitled to seek an indemnity from the employee to recover any damages paid.

> ### LISTER V ROMFORD ICE & COLD STORAGE CO 1957
> Lister was employed as a lorry driver. In the course of his employment he was driving negligently when he injured his father, a fellow employee. The employers were vicariously liable and the father's damages were paid by the employers' insurers. Exercising their right of subrogation the insurers then brought an action against the son for an indemnity.

Held

❖ (HL) The son was liable to indemnify the employers, and hence the insurers. [1957] A.C. 555.

Commentary

It must be noted that the employer is liable as well as the employee. As joint tort-feasors they are each fully liable to the plaintiff.

THINK POINT

Because of the problems predicted for industrial relations following this decision the employers' liability insurers entered into a "gentleman's agreement" not to take advantage of this principle unless there was evidence of collusion or misconduct.

Product Liability

. . . .
INTRODUCTION

In addition to rights under the common law, with which the cases in this Chapter are concerned, there is an additional form of liability for defective products. The Consumer Protection Act 1987 imposes strict liability for defective products which cause personal injury and damage to private property. The most notable feature of the Act is that it removes the need for those injured by a defective product to establish fault on the part of the producer. Originally the Act did not apply to injuries caused by unprocessed agricultural products but this agricultural exception has now been removed in respect of goods put into the market after December 2002.

Central to liability under the Act is the requirement that the harm is caused by a "defect" in the product but the question of what makes a product defective takes account of what "persons generally are entitled to expect" in relation to a product. All the circumstances in the case are considered in determining what constitutes a "defect" and many of the factors taken into account in common law negligence are relevant to the question. In *Tesco Stores v Pollard* [2006] EWCA Civ 393 the defendant was not liable under the Act when a small child suffered injury after swallowing detergent from a bottle which was supposed to have a child resistant cap. The Court of Appeal held that the product was not defective within the meaning of the Act because the resistance required to open the cap was significantly more than a child could be expected to apply and the cap therefore provided the level of protection that persons generally would be entitled to expect.

The consequences of taking account of all the surrounding circumstances when determining whether the product is defective and the availability of state of the art defence, together with the application of the defence of contributory negligence have been criticised for diminishing the concept of strict liability under the **Consumer Protection Act 1987.**

It is important to note that the Act has not replaced the common law. The focus of the Act is to protect against products which cause *harm* to the consumer but it only applies to "producers", so where an injury is caused by a defectively repaired product the claimant will need to rely on the common law. The main restrictions on the scope of the Act relate to recovery for property damage so where a defective product causes damage to goods used for commercial purposes or where the special limitation periods under the Act have expired, a common law action in negligence will be available to the claimant.

Key Principle

Even in the absence of a contract a manufacturer can be liable to the ultimate consumer where a product has caused physical damage.

> ### DONOGHUE V STEVENSON 1932
> As a consequence of drinking ginger beer from an opaque bottle which allegedly included the remains of a decomposed snail, the plaintiff became ill. Because the drink had been bought for her by a friend, there was no contractual duty between the plaintiff and the manufacturer of the ginger beer.

Held

❖ (HL) The court rejected the privity defence and found the manufacturers liable. [1932] A.C. 562.

Commentary

(1) The element of this decision which provided the foundations for a general duty of care in negligence is known as the wide ratio. But the case actually concerned liability for defective products which caused harm and this specific duty expressed by Lord Atkin is known as the narrow ratio:

> "... a manufacturer of products, which he sells in such a form as to show that he intends them to reach the ultimate consumer in the form in which they left him with no reasonable possibility of intermediate examination and with the knowledge that the absence of reasonable care in the preparation or putting up of the products will result in an injury to the consumer's life or property, owes a duty to the consumer to take reasonable care."

In the cases below each of the elements of the narrow ratio will be considered in turn.

(2) Generally speaking, there is no tort action where a product is merely defective and has not caused any physical damage. The law of contract provides the basis of protection for products which are defective in quality, though not dangerous.

Key Principle

A manufacturer has been given a wide interpretation by the courts and extended beyond the maker of a product. Mere distributors or suppliers and repairers of goods may incur liability.

> STENNETT V HANCOCK AND PETERS 1939
> The plaintiff pedestrian was injured when he was struck by a flange which had come off one of the wheels of the first defendant's lorry. The wheel had earlier been repaired by the second defendants and the cause of the accident was found to be the careless reassembly of the wheel by one of the second defendant's employees.

Held

The claim against the first defendant failed but the second defendant (the repairer) was held liable under the principle of *Donoghue v Stevenson*. [1939] 2 All E.R. 578.

THINK POINT

The principle in *Donoghue v Stevenson* has been extended to:
  (i) suppliers: liability can arise in circumstances where a supplier would normally be expected to check for safety before selling the goods. In *Andrews v Hopkinson* [1957] 1 Q.B. 229, a second-hand car dealer was held liable because defective steering on an 18-year-old car could easily have been discovered by a competent mechanic;
  (ii) distributors: in *Watson v Buckley, Osborne, Garrett & Co* [1940] 1 All E.R. 174, the distributors who failed to test a hair dye for themselves before they advertised it as harmless were held to be negligent.

Key Principle

The definition of a product has been extended beyond food and drink to include all manufactured products capable of causing damage.

> GRANT V AUSTRALIAN KNITTING MILLS LTD 1936
> The plaintiff contracted dermatitis through wearing woollen underpants which had been manufactured by the defendants. The disease was caused by invisible excess sulphites which had been negligently left in

the underwear during the manufacturing process. The defendant contended that *Donoghue v Stevenson* could be distinguished on the ground that the ginger beer was to be consumed internally whereas the underpants were to be worn externally.

Held

❖ (PC) The defendants were liable. No distinction can be logically drawn between a noxious thing taken internally and a noxious thing applied externally. [1936] A.C. 85.

Commentary

In *Haseldine v CA Daw & Son Ltd* [1941] 2 K.B. 343, the definition of a product was extended to include a lift.

Key Principle

The ultimate consumer is construed very widely to include any user of the product and persons less obviously at risk may be within the scope of the manufacturer's duty.

> BARNETT V H & J PACKER & CO 1940
> The plaintiff, a shop-keeper, was injured by a piece of metal protruding from a sweet. He sued the defendant manufacturers.

Held

The plaintiff was a "consumer" and as the manufacturer of the product the defendant was liable. [1940] 3 All E.R. 575.

Commentary

The expansion of the class of plaintiffs is illustrated by *Stennett v Hancock and Peters* (1939) above where a pedestrian was held to be within the rule in *Donoghue v Stevenson*.

Key Principle

No reasonable possibility of intermediate examination has been widely interpreted by the courts. A mere opportunity for intermediate examination will not exonerate the defendant; there must be a reasonable probability of intermediate inspection.

GRIFFITHS V ARCH ENGINEERING CO 1968

The plaintiff was injured by a portable grinding tool which he borrowed from the first defendants but which was actually owned by the second defendants. It was lent by the first defendants without further inspection and without knowledge that it had been made dangerous by an employee of the second defendants.

Held

The first defendants were liable because they had an opportunity to examine the tool and failed to do so. The second defendants were equally liable because they had no reason to suppose that such an examination would be carried out. [1968] 3 All E.R. 217.

Commentary

A manufacturer who has no reason to believe that an intermediate inspection will take place, whether by a third party or the consumer, will be liable. The product need not reach the ultimate consumer in a sealed package for the duty to arise; in *Grant v Australian Knitting Mills* (1936) (above) the Privy Council stated that for the rule to apply, "the customer must use the article exactly as it left the maker, that is in all material features, and use it as it was intended to be used".

Key Principle

The plaintiff will generally discharge the burden of proof by showing the existence of the defect and that on the balance of probabilities it arose in the course of manufacture.

MASON V WILLIAMS & WILLIAMS LTD 1955

While using a cold chisel which was too hard for its purpose the plaintiff suffered an eye injury and had to have his eye removed. The chisel had been supplied by the first defendants, the employers, and manufactured by the second defendants. There was no suggestion that the plaintiff had been at fault in using the chisel, and it had only been taken out of the stores a few weeks beforehand.

Held

Since the plaintiff had established that nothing had happened to the chisel after it had left the defendant manufacturer's factory which could have caused the excessive hardness, their negligence was established. [1955] 1 W.L.R. 549.

Commentary

In *Carroll v Fearon*, *The Times*, January 26, 1998, a serious accident occurred when a car went out of control and crashed into an oncoming vehicle. The cause of the accident was a sudden and complete thread strip of a rear tyre. The Court of Appeal found that there was overwhelming evidence of a defective manufacturing process and held that there was no requirement to identify any particular individual as being responsible for the defect, nor any need for the particular aspect of negligence to be specified.

Key Principle

In order to establish liability there must be sufficient evidence that the defect existed in the product when it left the manufacturer.

EVANS V TRIPLEX SAFETY GLASS CO LTD 1936

The plaintiff bought a Vauxhall car fitted with a windscreen made of "Triplex Toughened Safety Glass". A year later when he was driving the car, with his wife and son as passengers, the windscreen suddenly and for no apparent reason cracked and disintegrated. The occupants of the car were injured and brought an action against the manufacturers of the windscreen.

Held

The defendants were not liable. The windscreen might have been interfered with and the defect introduced by any one of a range of alternative causes other than a defect in manufacture. Relevant factors were the lapse of time between the purchase of the windscreen and the accident and the possibility that the glass may have been strained when screwed into its frame. [1936] 1 All E.R. 283.

Key Principle

A warning of danger, provided it is adequate in the circumstances, may absolve the defendant.

KUBACH V HOLLANDS 1937

A manufacturer sold a chemical to the second defendants (retailers) and an accompanying invoice expressly stated, inter alia, that the chemical must be "examined and tested by user before use". The retailer failed to observe the manufacturer's instructions to test the product before labelling it and sold it to a science teacher. The chemical was used in a school experiment and it exploded, injuring a schoolgirl and her father.

Held

The retailer was liable but the manufacturers were not. They had given an adequate warning and the retailer had ignored it. [1937] 3 All E.R. 907.

Key Principle

Knowledge of the risk will be irrelevant if there were no practical steps that the plaintiff could take to avoid the danger.

DENNY V SUPPLIES AND TRANSPORT CO 1950

The plaintiff, in the course of his employment, was injured while he was unloading a barge of badly stowed timber. The plaintiff had complained to the wharf superintendent that the barge was badly loaded. Even though he realised that danger was imminent, it was shown that there is no safe way of unloading badly-stowed timber.

Held

❖ (CA) The defendants were liable. The plaintiff had "no practical alternative to the course of conduct adopted." [1950] 2 K.B. 374.

Commentary

This case can be distinguished from *Farr v Butters Bros* [1932] 2 K.B. 606 where there was no evidence of any legal or economic obligation on the plaintiff. The defendant, crane manufacturers, sent out a crane in parts to be assembled by the buyers. An experienced foreman realised the crane was defective but nevertheless ignored the danger and assembled it. The defendants were not liable when he was killed while working the crane on the grounds that the foreman had deliberately incurred the risk.

Key Principle

Liability for defective products is limited to personal injuries and physical damage to property other than the product itself.

ASWAN ENGINEERING ESTABLISHMENT CO V LUPDINE LTD 1987

The plaintiffs, a construction company, bought a quantity of water-proofing compound called Lupguard from the first defendants. The Lupguard was packed in heavy duty plastic pails manufactured by the second defendants. The pails containing the Lupguard were shipped to

Kuwait where they were stacked on the quayside. Because of the high temperatures to which they were exposed the pails collapsed and much of the Lupguard was lost. The action failed in contract because the pails were of merchantable quality and there was no liability in tort because the damage was outside the range of what was reasonably foreseeable. One issue was whether the product had merely damaged itself or whether the Lupguard was "other property" separate from the pails.

Held

❖ (CA) Lloyd L.J. with whom Fox L.J. agreed expressed the provisional view that the contents of the pails was "other property". Nicholls L.J. accepted that, in strict legal analysis, the Lupguard and the pails were different property. However, he was unhappy with the idea that the manufacturer of a container could be liable under *Donoghue v Stevenson* for loss of the contents due to a defect in the container. [1987] 1 All E.R. 135.

THINK POINT

In *D & F Estates Ltd v Church Commissioners* [1989] A.C. 177 Lord Bridge had advanced the "complex theory structure". In a complex structure or complex chattels one part of a structure or chattel might, when it caused damage to another part of the structure or chattel, be regarded in tort as having caused damage to "other property" for the application of the *Donoghue v Stevenson* principles. But in *Murphy v Brentwood District Council* (1990) (see p.40), where the foundations of a house subsided causing cracks in the walls, the House of Lords made it clear that the cracks in the walls constituted damage to the very property in question; it was not a case of the defective foundations causing damage to "other property".

THE CONSUMER PROTECTION ACT 1987

As outlined at the start of this Chapter, the **Consumer Protection Act 1987** provides a further possible basis of claim. The Act creates strict liability on the producer of a product which is defective and causes personal injury and, in certain circumstances, property damage. The most notable feature of the Act is that the plaintiff does not have to show fault on the part of the producer but the Act does provide a number of defences to the producer, the most important and controversial of which is the development risks defence. The Act does not cover: damage to the product itself; damage to property which is not ordinarily intended for private use; there is no liability for damage to business property; and damage where the amount of the loss is less than £275. The exclusion of liability is prohibited under the Act and in all cases there is a 10-year limitation period for bringing an action.

Commentators have argued that the Consumer Protection Act has failed to make any significant change to English law and that there is very little difference between the standard of care under the Act and common law negligence.

THINK POINT

The Act was interpreted in *A v National Blood Authority* [2001] 3 All E.R. 289, where the court held that factors which would have been relevant in a negligence action were completely irrelevant when applying a strict liability principle. Here the claimants had been infected with Hepatitis C through blood transfusions which had used blood products obtained from infected donors. Although the defendants argued that the product was as safe as might be expected and that the defect in the particular transfusion could not have been detected, they were held to be liable under the **Consumer Protection Act**. This decision would suggest that liability under the statute is considerably stricter than the common law. This case also clarified that human blood and blood products for transfusion are "products" within the meaning of the Act.

In *Ide v ATB Sales Ltd* [2008] EWCA Civ 424, following an accident in which the left-hand end of the handlebar of his mountain bike had snapped off the claimant was found lying unconscious with serious head injuries. The claimant had no recollection of the accident and there were no witnesses and on this ground the defendant argued that the claimant had failed to discharge the burden of proving that there was a defect in the bike that had caused his injury. The bike had been imported into the UK by the defendants so the claim was based upon the provisions of the **Consumer Protection Act 1987**. The Court of Appeal held that since the claim was under the Act it was not strictly necessary make any finding as to the *specific* cause of the defect and the claimant was entitled to succeed.

Pure information is thought not to be covered by the Act because a "product" must be in some tangible form, but the producer may be liable in respect of information contained in deficient printed instructions or warnings which accompany a product and thereby make it unsafe.

Defamation, Privacy and Human Rights

. . . .

10

INTRODUCTION

Other torts discussed in this casebook are mainly concerned with the protection of personal safety or protection against some other form of physical interference. However, the tort of defamation is different because it is concerned with protecting the claimant against harm caused by words. Defamation is also different because the legal procedures involved in taking or defending an action are more complicated than other torts and it is the only tort in which trial by jury is widely used. The role of the judge is to direct the jury on the legal meaning of a defamatory statement but the question as to whether the words in question are in fact defamatory is for the jury to decide. Although the aim of defamation is to provide protection to reputation, when considering this protection it should be remembered that the competing right to freedom of expression is also protected by law. Where a conflict between these competing rights arises, the courts must strike a balance between the protection of reputation and freedom of speech. Traditionally, the common law protected freedom of expression through the defences to defamation and for this reason it should be noted that an understanding of the defences to defamation is as important as understanding the elements of liability.

Free speech is given further protection under the **European Convention on Human Rights and Fundamental Freedoms**. Article 10(1) provides that everyone has the right to freedom of expression and gives individuals the right to hold opinions and receive and impart information and ideas without interference by public authorities. However, the Convention acknowledges the potential conflict between freedom of expression and the protection of reputation and in order to strike a balance between freedom of expression and protection of reputation, art.10(2) places certain restrictions on the exercise of freedom of expression. *O'Shea v MGN Ltd* [2001] E.M.L.R. 40 provides an example of the approach taken by the English courts towards balancing these rights. The issue here was whether the imposition of strict liability for unintentional defamation by the publication of a "lookalike" photograph of a woman was an infringement of the right to freedom of expression under the **Human Rights Act 1998**. The claimant alleged that the photograph, which appeared in an internet website offering pornographic services, was the "spit and image of her" and she sought to rely on principle of strict liability in defamation (liability for unintentional defamation) which was established by the House of Lords in *Hulton v Jones* (1910), (p.166 below). In *O'Shea* it was held that although the publication would have fallen under the common law principle of strict liability for unintentional defamation, to hold the defendant strictly liable in this case would amount to an unjustifiable interference with the right to freedom of expression. The Court said that strict liability in circumstances such as these would impose an impossible burden on a publisher if he were required to check if the true picture of someone resembled someone else. This would amount to an unjustifiable interference with the right to freedom of expression disproportionate to the aim of protecting the reputations of "lookalikes". Further, strict liability could not be justified under art.10(2) as necessary in a democratic society because no claim had been made in respect of a "lookalike" picture in over a century.

It should be noted that the protection of reputation provided by the law of defamation only extends to *un*true statements; where harm is caused by words or images which are true there is no remedy in defamation. However, in the context of the protection of human rights, the emerging law of privacy (discussed below) may provide protection to claimants in these situations.

LIBEL—SLANDER

Key Principle
Libel is a defamatory statement which is conveyed in a permanent form.

> MONSON V TUSSAUDS 1894
> The plaintiff had been tried for murder in Scotland and had argued successfully that the victim was killed by the accidental discharge of his own gun. The jury returned a verdict of not proven. Shortly after the trial, the defendants placed a model of the plaintiff and his gun in their exhibition of wax figures in a room which gave access to the Chamber of Horrors. The plaintiff applied for an interlocutory injunction to restrain the display of the wax figure until the trial of a libel action.

Held
The injunction was not granted but the action was properly framed in libel. Lopes L.J. stated that:

> "... Libels are generally in writing or printing, but this is not necessary; the defamatory matter may be conveyed in some other permanent form. For instance, a statute, a caricature, an

effigy, chalk marks on a wall, signs or pictures may constitute a libel." [1894] 1 Q.B. 671.

Commentary

Libel, defamatory material in a permanent form, should be distinguished from slander which takes a transient form; for example, spoken words, gestures, or mimicry.

THINK POINT

Libel is actionable per se but to succeed in an action for slander, damage must be proved. However, there are four exceptional cases where slander is actionable per se:

(i) imputation of crime. In *Webb v Beavan* (1883) 11 Q.B.D. 606 the statement "I know enough to put you in goal" was actionable per se;

(ii) words imputing that a person is suffering from a contagious disease, as in *Bloodworth v Gray* (1844) 7 Man.& G. 334: "He has got that damned pox [meaning venereal disease] from going to that woman on the Derby Road";

(iii) under the **Slander of Women Act 1891**, words imputing unchastity or adultery in any woman or girl. In *Youssoupoff v Metro-Goldwyn-Mayer Pictures Ltd* (1934) 50 T.L.R. 581 a company was liable when a film about Rasputin suggested that the plaintiff had been seduced by him. It was held that a statement that a woman has been raped can affect her reputation;

(iv) words calculated to disparage the plaintiff in any office, profession, trade or calling. In *Jones v Jones* [1916] 2 A.C. 481 an accusation that a schoolmaster had committed adultery with one of the school cleaners was not actionable per se (though an imputation of impropriety with a pupil might be).

PLAINTIFFS

Key Principle

A local authority or an organ of central government may not sue for defamation.

DERBYSHIRE CC V TIMES NEWSPAPERS LTD 1993
The defendant had published articles questioning the propriety of dealings in the plaintiff council's pension fund. The preliminary point arose as to whether the plaintiff council could maintain an action for libel.

Held

❖ (HL) A local authority cannot maintain an action for libel on the ground that the threat of a civil action for defamation would have an inhibiting effect on freedom of speech and it was contrary to public interest that the organs of government, whether central or local, should have a right to sue for libel. [1993] A.C. 534.

Commentary

(1) Individual councillors or officials may bring proceedings. Lord Keith stated:

> "If the reputation of any of these is wrongly impaired by the publication any of these can himself bring proceedings for defamation."

(2) Only living persons can sue or defend an action in defamation. However, in *Metropolitan Saloon Omnibus Co v Hawkins* (1859) 4 H. & N. 87 insolvency was imputed and it was held that where the statement affects its business or property a trading corporation has a right to sue for defamation. But in *Electrical, Electronic, Telecommunication & Plumbing Union v Times Newspapers* [1980] Q.B. 585 it was held that trade unions, not being corporate bodies, lack the legal personality to sue.

A DEFAMATORY STATEMENT

Key Principle

Defamation is the publication of material which tends to lower the plaintiff in the estimation of right-thinking members of society generally.

SIM V STRETCH 1936
When Edith Saville, a maid who had left the plaintiff's employment, went to work for the defendant he sent a telegram to the plaintiff saying:

"Edith has resumed service with us today. Please send her possessions and the money you borrowed also her wages to Old Barton. Sim."

The plaintiff alleged that the telegram meant that he was in pecuniary difficulties and had to borrow money from his housemaid.

Held

❖ (HL) The words in question were not reasonably capable of a defamatory meaning. [1936] 2 All E.R. 1237.

Commentary

In *Parmiter v Coupland* (1840) 6 M. & W. 105, Parke B. held a defamatory statement to be one "which is calculated to injure the reputation of another, by exposing him to hatred, contempt or ridicule." In *Youssoupoff* (see p.161) Slesser L.J. expressed a defamatory statement to be one which tends to cause people to shun or avoid the plaintiff.

Key Principle

In defamation the test of what "right-thinking members of society" think appears to be determined by what they should think rather than what in fact they do think.

BYRNE V DEANE 1937

A golf club had some gambling machines unlawfully kept in the club house. These were removed by police after somebody had informed of their illegal presence. Soon after this a verse appeared on the notice board of the club which ended with the lines: "But he who gave the game away, may he byrnne in hell and rue the day." The plaintiff brought an action for libel alleging that by these words the defendants meant, and were understood to mean, that he was guilty of underhand disloyalty to his fellow members.

Held

❖ (CA) The plaintiff's claim failed. It could not be defamatory to "allege of a man ... that he has reported certain acts, wrongful in law, to the police ...". [1937] 1 K.B. 818.

Commentary

In *Hartt v Newspaper Publishing Plc*, *Independent*, December 8, 1989, the Court of Appeal said the right-thinking person is not unduly suspicious but can read between the lines and engage in a certain amount of loose thinking, but is not avid for scandal, and will not select one bad meaning where other non-defamatory meanings are available.

THINK POINT

In *Gillick v BBC*, *The Times*, October 20, 1995, it was held that words spoken in the course of a live television programme on the provision of contraceptive advice to young girls were capable of adversely affecting the plaintiff in the estimation of reasonable persons. In deciding whether the words were capable of bearing a defamatory meaning, they should be given the natural meaning which would be conveyed to an ordinary and reasonable hypothetical viewer watching the programme once, who was neither naïve nor unduly suspicious.

Key Principle

The statement must be understood by others to have a defamatory meaning.

CASSIDY V DAILY MIRROR NEWSPAPERS LTD 1929

The defendants published a photograph of Mr Cassidy with a woman, below which was carried an announcement of their engagement. The information on which the defendants based their statement came from Mr Cassidy alone and they had made no effort to verify it from any other source. Mr Cassidy was already married although he lived apart from his wife. However, he did occasionally stay with his wife at her flat. She brought an action in libel claiming that readers who knew her as Mr Cassidy's wife would assume that she had been lying about whether she was married to him.

Held

❖ (CA) The defendants were liable. The story would be understood by others to refer to the plaintiff and the newspaper's complete ignorance of the circumstances could not prevent the statement from having a defamatory meaning. [1929] 2 K.B. 331.

INNUENDO

Key Principle

The plaintiff must rely on an innuendo where the words are not defamatory in their natural and ordinary meaning but may be defamatory when combined with extrinsic facts known to others about the situation.

> TOLLEY V JS FRY & SONS LTD 1931
> The defendants published an advertisement in which the plaintiff, a famous amateur golfer, was shown with a bar of Fry's chocolate in his back pocket and words which were understood to be his endorsement of the defendant's brand of chocolate. The defendants had not asked his permission to do this and the plaintiff alleged an innuendo that he had agreed to the advertisement for gain and had thus compromised his reputation as an amateur.

Held

(CA) The advertisement was capable of bearing a defamatory meaning. [1931] A.C. 333.

Commentary

(1) It is immaterial whether or not the defendant knows of the external facts which transform an innocent statement into a defamatory one, as in *Cassidy v Daily Mirror* (see above) where the innuendo was that Mr Cassidy was not the plaintiff's husband but lived with her in immoral cohabitation.

(2) This type of innuendo, where the words are combined with extrinsic facts, is known as a "true" innuendo. It should be distinguished from a "false" innuendo where the defamatory implication is drawn from the words themselves, such as, for example, in *Allsop v Church of England Newspapers Ltd* [1972] 2 Q.B. 161, where the defendant newspaper described a well-known broadcaster as "bent". The court said that in these circumstances the plaintiff must specify the slang meaning of the word relied on.

THE WORDS MUST REFER TO THE PLAINTIFF

Key Principle

The defendant's comment must be shown to refer to the plaintiff, but it need not be a specific reference. The test is to ask would ordinary sensible observers believe what the plaintiff referred to.

MORGAN v ODHAMS PRESS LTD 1971

The newspaper, the *Sun*, alleged that a girl had been kidnapped by a dog-doping gang because she was threatening to inform the police of their activities. At the relevant time the girl had been staying at the plaintiff's flat and the plaintiff produced six witnesses who swore that they understood from the article that he was connected with the gang.

Held

❖ (HL) The story was capable of a defamatory meaning. There was no rule that the article should contain some kind of key or pointer to indicate the plaintiff; the question was whether readers who knew of the circumstances would reasonably have understood the article as referring to the plaintiff. [1971] 1 W.L.R. 1239.

Key Principle

For liability to be imposed it is irrelevant that the defendant did not intend to refer to the plaintiff.

HULTON & CO v JONES 1910

The defendants published a humorous account of a motor festival at Dieppe which implied that a fictitious character "Armetus Jones", a churchwarden at Peckham, was behaving in a discreditable way with a woman in France. The plaintiff, a barrister who was not a churchwarden nor did he live in Peckham or visit the festival in Dieppe, sued for libel. Friends of his swore they believed that the article referred to him.

Held

(HL) The defendants were liable. What mattered was how the words would be understood by others, not what they meant in the minds of the writer and the publisher. [1910] A.C. 20.

Commentary

(1) In *Newstead v London Express Newspapers Ltd* [1940] 1 K.B. 377, the defendants were liable when the statement was true of one person and honestly intended for him but which could reasonably be attributed to the plaintiff. The statement that: "Harold Newstead, thirty-year old Camberwell man" had been convicted of bigamy was true of a barman of that name but not of the plaintiff, Harold Newstead, an unmarried hairdresser from Camberwell aged about 30.

(2) These cases are now provided with the defence of "unintentional defamation" under s.4 of the Defamation Act 1952.

(3) The Defamation Act 1996 (ss.2—4) has substantially changed the rules regulating unintentional defamation. The requirement of non-negligent innocence has been removed. The burden is on the plaintiff to show that the defendant had no reason to believe the statement referred to the plaintiff or that it was false and defamatory. The 1996 Act also permits a person who has published a statement alleged to be defamatory to make an offer of amends.

THINK POINT

Section 1 of the 1996 Act extends the principle of innocent defamation to operators of communications systems (such as the internet) where a defamatory statement is published electronically. An ISP is not considered to be the "publisher" of the defamatory statement in these circumstances but is treated as a secondary publisher (distributor) and may be able to rely on the defence of innocent dissemination.

Key Principle

As a general rule, where a statement is directed to a class of persons no individual belonging to that class is entitled to sue unless:
  (i)   the class is so small that the statement must refer to each person in it; or
  (ii) the words point to a particular plaintiff.

KNUPPFER V LONDON EXPRESS NEWSPAPERS LTD 1944
The defendants published an article about a political party called Young Russia which linked them with fascism. The party was an international organisation with a British branch consisting of 24 members. The plaintiff alleged that as the person responsible for the politics of the party the libel personally affected him.

Held

❖ (HL) That plaintiff's action failed. A general rule was laid down that where a class of persons is defamed it must be proved that the defamatory statement was capable of referring to the plaintiff and was in fact understood to do so. [1944] A.C. 116.

The *Knuppfer* principles were applied in respect of an allegation that a family business was going "bust" in *Aspro Travel Ltd v Owners Abroad Group* [1996] 2 W.L.R. 132. The Court of Appeal held since it was a family business the words might be understood to refer to the company and to them as individual directors of the company.

PUBLICATION

Key Principle
There is publication where the statement is made known to a third party. This rule applies where the defendant knew or ought to have foreseen that the statement would come to the attention of a third party.

> **HUTH V HUTH 1915**
> The defendant sent a letter in an unsealed envelope to the plaintiff which she alleged to be defamatory. The letter was opened and read by her inquisitive butler in an admitted breach of his duty. The plaintiff argued that since there was a presumption that postmen read post-cards, even though they have no business doing so, the same presumption ought to apply to unsealed envelopes.

Held
❖ (CA) There was no publication even though the envelope was unsealed; it was not part of the butler's duty to open the letter and his conduct was not a direct consequence of sending it. [1915] 3 K.B. 32.

Key Principle
There can be negligent publication if the reading of a letter is a natural and probable consequence of what the defendant did.

> **THEAKER V RICHARDSON 1962**
> The defendant wrote a defamatory letter to the plaintiff, a married woman and a fellow member of the local district council. The letter was placed in a sealed envelope similar to those used for election addresses and sent to the plaintiff. Her husband opened the letter thinking it was an election address.

Held
❖ (CA) There was publication. A natural and probable consequence of the defendant's writing and delivery of the letter was that it would be opened and read by her husband. [1962] 1 W.L.R. 151.

Commentary

In *Wennhak v Morgan* (1888) 20 Q.B.D. 635, it was held that making a statement to one's own spouse is not publication.

Key Principle

Every repetition of a defamatory statement is a fresh publication and creates a fresh cause of action against each successive publisher all the way down the chain of publication. However, those who are concerned with mere mechanical distribution of such matter, for example, newsagents, libraries and booksellers may have a defence of "innocent publication."

> VIZETELLY V MUDIE'S SELECT LIBRARY 1900
>
> The defendants, proprietors of a circulating library, allowed people to use a book which, unknown to them, contained a libel on the plaintiff. In a publication taken by the defendants the publishers had circulated a notice requesting the return of copies of the offending book.

Held

❖ (CA) The defendants had failed to establish their "innocence" and were found liable. They had no procedure for checking whether their books contained libels and they had overlooked a publisher's request for the return of the particular book. [1900] 2 Q.B. 170.

Commentary

The rule set out by Romer L.J. provides that mere mechanical distributors of such matter would have a defence if they could show that:

(i) they were innocent of any knowledge of the libel in the work disseminated by them;

(ii) there was no reason for them to be aware that the work contained a libel;

(iii) when the work was disseminated by them it was not by any negligence on their part that they did not know it contained a libel.

THINK POINT

In *Slipper v British Broadcasting Corporation* [1990] 1 All E. R. 165 the plaintiff, a senior police officer, claimed that he was defamed in a film about his unsuccessful attempts to secure the extradition of one of the Great Train Robbers and that the BBC had caused widespread

DEFAMATION, PRIVACY AND HUMAN RIGHTS

repetition of the libel through reviews in the television columns of newspapers. The Court of Appeal held that in appropriate cases the original publisher may be liable where a third party repeats the sting of the libel.

Key Principle

Publication by omission (failing to remove the defamatory statement) as in *Byrne v Deane (*above) applies where an internet service provider who has been informed of a libel on its internet server, fails to remove it. The ISP will be unable to show that they had exercised reasonable care in relation to the publication in question.

GODFREY V DEMON INTERNET 1999

Statements defamatory of the claimant which were posted by an unknown person on an internet newsgroup hosted on the defendant's server. The claimant notified the defendant about the defamatory material which could be accessed on its server but the defendant did not remove the material from the Internet for about two weeks. The defendants claimed that they were not responsible for postings by users on their internet sites.

Held

Although the defendants successfully showed that they were not the author, editor or publisher of the defamatory statement within the meaning of the Defamation Act 1996, they could not show that they had taken reasonable care in relation to its publication and the defence of innocent dissemination under s.1(b) of the Act was therefore unavailable to them. [1999] 4 All E.R. 342.

THINK POINT

Search engine liability for defamation under UK law was considered in *Metropolitan International Schools Ltd v Designtechnica Corporation, Google UK and Google Inc* [2009] EWHC 1765 (QB). The question was whether Google should be regarded as a "publisher" of the words complained of (whether before or after Google had been notified of their defamatory comments) or whether it was a mere facilitator. Google was held not to be liable for publication of the statements because it had no control over the search terms entered by users of the search engine or of the material which is placed on the web by its users. This case confirms that mere facilitators, like telephone carriers, are generally not liable for defamatory content.

SELECTED DEFENCES TO DEFAMATION

JUSTIFICATION (OR TRUTH)

Key Principle
The burden of proof is on the defendant to show that the statement was true, rather than on the plaintiff to prove that it was false. But it is not necessary to prove the literal truth of every word if the facts of the defamatory statement are true in substance.

> ALEXANDER V NORTH EASTERN RAILWAY CO 1865
> The plaintiff was charged for travelling on a train from Leeds for which his ticket was not valid and for refusing to pay the proper fare. He was convicted and sentenced to 14 days' imprisonment in default of payment of the fine and costs. The defendant published a statement which said that the plaintiff was sentenced to three weeks' imprisonment.

Held
Justification succeeded because the statement was not sufficiently inaccurate to defeat the defence. The defendant only has to prove "the sting of the libel". (1865) 6 B. & S. 340.

Commentary
(1) What constitutes a minor inaccuracy is ultimately a matter of interpretation of the facts in each case. In *Wakley v Cooke and Healy* (1849) 4 Exch. 511, the defendant called the plaintiff a "libellous journalist" and showed evidence that he had once been successfully sued for libel. The defence failed because in the context the words meant that the plaintiff habitually libelled people.

(2) The **Defamation Act 1952** s.5 provides that where two or more distinct charges are made against the plaintiff the defence will not fail by reason only that the truth of every charge is not proved. The Civil Evidence Act 1968 s.13 provides that proof of a previous conviction is conclusive evidence that a person committed the crime. Where allegations are based on criminal

convictions which have become "spent", the Rehabilitation of Offenders Act 1974 s.8 provides that justification may be used as a defence except in cases where the publication has been made with malice.

Key Principle

The defendant may widen the meaning of the words relied on by the plaintiff to show that they impute a more general wrong-doing than that imputed in a particular instance.

> WILLIAMS V REASON 1988
>
> The allegation was that the plaintiff, an amateur rugby player, had written a book for money and had thereby compromised his amateur status as a Rugby Union player.

Held

In pleading justification the defendant was allowed to introduce evidence showing the plaintiff to have received "boot money" from a manufacturer of sports equipment. The sting of the libel was "Shamateurism" and not merely the writing of the book. [1988] 1 All E.R. 262.

Commentary

The defendant may only justify a meaning which the words are reasonably capable of bearing. In *Bookbinder v Tebbit* [1989] 1 All E.R. 1169, a local politician was specifically accused of squandering public money by over-printing stationery with words supporting nuclear-free zones. The words, in the context in which they were used, were not capable of meaning a large-scale squandering of public money and the Court of Appeal refused to allow evidence showing a wide range of alleged instances of irresponsibility with public money.

FAIR COMMENT

Key Principle

Fair comment protects honest expressions of opinion based on true facts made in good faith on matters of public interest.

> LONDON ARTISTS LTD V LITTLER 1969
>
> The four top performers in a play terminated their contracts through their agents, the plaintiffs. The defendant producer was convinced that

there was a plot to stop the play. He wrote and published a letter suggesting that the plaintiffs and the actors had taken part in a plot to end a successful production. The trial judge held the plea of fair comment to fail because the matter was not one of public interest.

Held

❖ (CA) Although the appeal was dismissed on a different ground (see p.175), public interest was interpreted widely. Lord Denning said:

> "Whenever a matter is such as to affect people at large, so that they may be legitimately interested in, or concerned at, what is going on; or what may happen to them or to others; then it is a matter of public interest on which everyone is entitled to make fair comment."

The defence is available, for example, for comments made on matters of government, public figures, literature and art. [1969] 2 Q.B. 375.

COMMENT AND FACT

Key Principle

Words relied on in the defence of fair comment must constitute expressions of opinion and not assertions of verifiable fact. Where the words amount to statements of fact the defence of justification is available and the defendant must prove that the words were factually true. However, where the words were expressions of opinion, no matter how paraphrased or expressed, the defendant is entitled to rely on the defence of fair comment.

British Chiropractic Association v Dr Singh 2010

The British Chiropractic Association (BCA) claimed that comments made by a science writer in the the *Guardian* on April 19, 2008 were defamatory in asserting that the association knowingly supported bogus treatments. The judge held that to a reasonable reader the words would mean that the association claimed that the treatments were effective in helping to treat the stated ailments, although it knew that there was absolutely no evidence to support this claim. The words therefore amounted to assertions of verifiable fact, not expressions of opinion. The BCA did not bring the claim against the the *Guardian* but sued the science writer instead. He appealed against the finding that the words were a statement of fact.

Held

Where the evidence of the efficacy of the treatments depended heavily on context, and whether such evidence amounted to proof, is what scientific opinion was there to debate. A view that there was no worthwhile or reliable evidence for the efficacy of the treatments expressed in the course of this debate was as much a value judgment as a contrary viewpoint and it therefore fell within the scope of fair comment. The Court of Appeal held the statements about the lack of worthwhile evidence to support the efficacy of the treatments were not an assertion of fact but a statement of opinion, protected by the defence of fair comment. [2010] EWCA Civ 350.

Comment

The impression that the BCA was attempting to silence one of its critics gave rise to concerns that libel laws in England would adversely affect the right to express scientific views and curtail public debate of these issues. However, in allowing the appeal the Court of Appeal stated that words should not be used which obscure the true meaning of a defence to defamation:

> "Recent legislation in a number of common law jurisdictions—New Zealand, Australia, and the Republic of Ireland—now describes the defence of fair comment as 'honest opinion'. It is not open to us to alter or add to or indeed for that matter reduce the essential elements of this defence, but to describe the defence for what it is would lend greater emphasis to its importance as an essential ingredient of the right to free expression. Fair comment may have come to 'decay with ... imprecision'. 'Honest opinion' better reflects the realities."

THINK POINT

The **Defamation Bill 2010**, introduced by Lord Lester aims to amend the law of defamation and encourage the free exchange of ideas and information, while providing an effective and proportionate remedy to anyone whose reputation is unfairly damaged. He said of the Bill: "It creates a framework of principles rather than a rigid and inflexible code, and it seeks a fair balance between reputation and public information on matters of public interest."

Key Principle ....

The statement must be a comment based on true facts but it is not necessary that all the facts upon which the comment is based should be specified in the alleged libel.

> KEMSLEY V FOOT 1952
> The defendants attacked a newspaper by publishing an article headed: "Lower than Kemsley". Kemsley, a newspaper proprietor not connected with the newspaper sued the defendants, alleging that the article's heading imputed that his name was a byword for false and foul journalism.

Held ....

❖ (HL) The defence of fair comment was available. The words implied certain conduct and commented on that conduct and it was sufficiently clear that the relevant facts were the conduct of the Kemsley Press. [1952] A.C. 345.

Commentary ....

(1) The facts upon which the comments are based must be true—in *London Artists Ltd v Littler* (see p.172) the comment was in the public interest but the defence failed: the defendant could not prove the correctness of the underlying fact that there had been a plot between the plaintiff theatre owners and the actors. One of the questions which arose was whether the allegation of a plot was a statement of fact or comment. The court concluded that it was a fact. But what is fact and what is opinion is not always clear. In *Dakhyl v Labouchere* [1908] 2 K.B. 325, the plaintiff described himself as a "specialist for the treatment of deafness, ear, nose and throat diseases". The House of Lords held that the defendant's statement which described him as "a quack of the rankest species" might be comment rather than fact and he was entitled to raise the defence of fair comment.

(2) By the **Defamation Act 1952** s.6 the defence of fair comment will not fail merely because the truth of every allegation of fact is not proved.

Key Principle ....

In deciding whether the statement is one of fact or comment the court must confine itself to the subject matter of the publication and cannot have regard to the wider context of the material.

TELNIKOFF V MATUSEVITCH 1991
The defendant had written an angry and critical letter to the *Daily Telegraph* refuting an article written by the plaintiff. The key issue was whether, in determining which parts of the letter constituted allegations of fact and which were merely comment, the letter could be read alongside the offending article.

Held
❖ (HL) The court was confined to considering the letter itself. Readers of the letter would not necessarily have read the original article and the publication in question must be judged on its own merits. [1992] 2 A.C. 343.

FAIRNESS OF THE COMMENT

Key Principle
The defence of fair comment can be defeated by proving that a statement was made with malice which, in this instance, means evil motive, spite or ill will.

THOMAS V BRADBURY, AGNEW & CO LTD 1906
A book reviewer for *Punch* had written a critical review of the plaintiff's book to which they pleaded fair comment. The reviewer's personal hostility against the plaintiff's books was evident not only from the review itself but also by his behaviour in the witness box and elsewhere.

Held
❖ (CA) The defendant's malice negatived a plea of fairness. [1906] 2 K.B. 627.

THINK POINT

To be fair the defendant must have honestly believed the opinion expressed. In *Slim v Daily Telegraph* [1968] 2 Q.B. 157, the court stated it to be irrelevant that a reasonable person would not hold such an opinion. Lord Denning said:

"... the right of fair comment is one of the essential elements which go to make up our freedom of speech. We must ever maintain this right intact. It must not be whittled down by legal refinements."

ABSOLUTE PRIVILEGE

The following defences to defamation arise not from the content of the defamatory statement but from the circumstances of its publication or the identity of the publisher. These are privilege defences. Absolute privilege is not affected by proof of malice and a person defamed on an occasion of absolute privilege has no legal redress no matter how untrue or malicious a statement may be. Absolute privilege protects: statements in respect of anything said in parliamentary proceedings; judicial proceedings; communications made in the course of official duty by one officer of state to another; and fair and accurate newspaper and broadcast reports of judicial proceedings in the United Kingdom.

DANIELS V GRIFFITHS 1997
The plaintiff was serving a life sentence imposed in 1993 for rape. He claimed that the defendant had defamed him by telling police that there had never been any form of relationship between them. The defendant also claimed that she was concerned for her safety should the plaintiff be released because he was fixated by her. It was submitted that publication of this statement to the police for the purposes of providing information to the Parole Board should be protected by absolute privilege on ground of public policy.

Held
❖ (CA) To extend the immunity attached to court proceedings to communications to the Parole Board would be unwarranted, since its proceedings were not part of the proceedings of a court of law.

Commentary
In *Waple v Surrey County Council*, *The Times*, December 29, 1997, the Court of Appeal stated that in actions for libel the courts should be slow to extend the rule about absolute privilege granted to statements made in connection with judicial or quasi-judicial proceedings.

QUALIFIED PRIVILEGE

Qualified privilege operates only to protect statements which are made without malice and it is for the judge to determine whether the occasion was privileged and whether the communication was made with reference to the privileged occasion.

Key Principle

An occasion is privileged if the statement is made in pursuance of a legal, social or moral duty only if the person to whom the statement is made also has an interest or duty to receive the information.

WATT V LONGSDON 1930

The defendant, a company director, received a letter from the foreign manager of the organisation. The letter alleged that the plaintiff, who was managing director of the company abroad, was immoral and dishonest. The defendant informed the company chairman of his suspicion that the plaintiff was misbehaving with women. He also communicated the statements, which were false, to the plaintiff's wife.

Held

(CA) The communication to the chairman was privileged because both publisher and receiver had a common interest in the affairs of the company. The publication to the plaintiff's wife was not privileged because the defendant had no social or moral duty to inform her about unsubstantiated allegations even though she might have an interest in hearing them. [1930] 1 K.B. 130.

Key Principle

If the defendant honestly believed the statement to be true, qualified privilege will not be lost even if the belief is arrived at from unreasoning prejudice or was irrational.

HORROCKS V LOWE 1975

The plaintiff, a Conservative Party councillor in Bolton, complained that at a council meeting the defendant, a leading Labour Party opposition member, made defamatory remarks about him. The trial judge held that the occasion was privileged but that the defendant, being in the grip of gross and unreasonable prejudice, was guilty of malice.

Held

❖ (HL) However prejudiced or irrational, the plaintiff's belief in the truth of what he said on that privileged occasion entitled him to succeed in his defence of privilege. [1975] A.C. 135.

Commentary

> ### THINK POINT
>
> In *Spring v Guardian Assurance* (1994) (see p.93) the Court of Appeal finding that a duty of care in negligence would undermine the defence of qualified privilege (which can only be defeated on proof of malice) was overruled by the House of Lords. The majority held that the preservation of the law of defamation would not be sufficient to deny the plaintiff a remedy. It may therefore be possible to frame an action in negligent misstatement if the defamatory statement causes actual loss.

Key Principle

Notwithstanding the arguments about the importance of freedom of the press and the right to freedom of expression contained in art.10 of the **European Convention on Human Rights**, "political information" was not to be adopted as a new category of qualified privilege.

REYNOLDS V TIMES NEWSPAPERS LTD 2001
The former Taoiseach (Prime Minister) of the Republic of Ireland, Albert Reynolds, brought an action against the defendant newspaper concerning an article which he claimed contained defamatory statements about his handling of a political crisis and political events leading up to his resignation from office. Although Mr Reynolds succeeded at first instance, the jury awarded no damages and he sought a retrial because of errors in the judge's summing-up. *The Times* cross-appealed against the judge's ruling that the publication was not protected by qualified privilege, basing their argument for a wide qualified privilege for "political speech" on the right of freedom of expression in art.10 of the **European Convention on Human Rights**. On *The Times*' cross-appeal, the Court of Appeal held that the defence of qualified privilege was not available in respect of "political information": the existing tests for the defence were still to be applied, including the "circumstantial test" as

to whether the nature, status and source of the material published, and the circumstances of the publication, were such that, in the public interest, the publication should be protected by privilege in the absence of malice.

Held

The special defence argument was rejected by the House of Lords. Their Lordships were unanimous in the view that the common law should not develop "political information" as a new category of the qualified privilege defence. It would be unsound in principle to distinguish political discussion from discussion of other matters of public concern. The established common law approach to qualified privilege (the test of whether there was a duty to disseminate the information and an interest in receiving it) continues to apply, and there is no separate and additional circumstantial test. In determining the issue, Lord Nicholls identified 10 factors to be taken into account in making a detailed factual inquiry into the circumstances of each case. Applying this test in the present case meant that the defendants could not rely on qualified privilege. In particular, the fact that the article had failed to mention Mr Reynolds' own explanation of his conduct to the Irish Parliament was taken into account. [2001] 2 A.C. 127.

Commentary

(1) It was held that the established common law approach allowed the court flexibility to give appropriate weight to the importance of freedom of expression by the media on all matters of public concern. This decision also emphasised the importance of freedom of expression and the importance of art.10. Their Lordships held that interference with freedom of speech should be confined to what was necessary in the circumstances of the case: the court should be slow to conclude that a publication was not in the public interest and doubts should be resolved in favour of publication.

Key Principle

The "public interest" aspect of *Reynolds'* privilege should not be applied too cautiously.

JAMEEL V WALL STREET JOURNAL EUROPE 2006

An article suggesting that the claimants' bank accounts were involved in funding terrorism was found to be defamatory. The defence of qualified privilege was rejected by the judge at first instance because, although there was a public interest in the prevention of terrorism generally, there was no need to publish the names of those allegedly being monitored or to publish the story without waiting for the claimant to respond to it. The Court of Appeal upheld this decision and said that when considering *Reynolds'* privilege in respect of the publication of a potentially defamatory article it was necessary to decide whether the publishers acted as responsible journalists. In demonstrating responsible journalism the test was more stringent than that the public should be interested in receiving the information; the subject matter of the publication had to be such that it was in the public interest that it should be published.

Held

This was rejected by the House of Lords which overturned the Court of Appeal's finding of liability. In clarifying the *Reynolds* principle their Lordships said that the public interest aspect of *Reynolds'* privilege was being applied too cautiously by the lower courts. Journalists are under a professional duty to report on matters of public interest and the public has an interest in receiving such information. Where a publication is in the public interest, the duty and interest are taken to exist and, in the context of editorial judgment, the question then is whether responsible steps had been taken to gather and publish the information [2006] UKHL 44.

Key Principle

The denial of legal aid to enable impecunious persons to properly defend a defamation action may amount a violation of art.6, s.1 (right to a fair hearing) under the **European Convention of Human Rights.**

Commentary

In *Flood v Times Newspapers Ltd* [2010] EWCA Civ 804 newspaper allegations about a police officer under investigation for corruption were not covered by the Reynolds defence because the steps taken by the journalists to verify the information were inadequate and did not meet the requirements of responsible journalism.

STEEL & MORRIS V UNITED KINGDOM 2005

The applicants, two London Greenpeace campaigners concerned about environmental and social issues, began an anti-McDonald's campaign the mid-1980s. As part of that campaign they produced and distributed a six-page leaflet entitled "What's wrong with McDonald's?". They were sued by McDonald's for libel allegedly caused by statements published in the leaflet relating to destruction of the rainforest, responsibility for Third World starvation, cruelty to animals and exploitation of children.

The applicants denied publication and argued that the material was already in the public domain and they also denied that the words complained of had the meanings attributed to them by McDonald's. They contended, in the alternative, that the words were substantially true or else were fair comment on matters of fact. Throughout the trial, which lasted for 313 court days and was the longest trial in English legal history, the applicants represented themselves, with only some help from volunteer lawyers whereas McDonald's were represented by experts in the law of libel. Although Mr Morris was unemployed and Ms Steel was either unemployed or on a low wage during the period surrounding the trial, they had been refused legal aid to defend the action.

In a further case which lasted 28 days, they appealed against a finding in favour of McDonald's. The majority of their submissions as to general grounds of law and unfairness were rejected by Court of Appeal but the amount of damages awarded to McDonald's by the trial judge was reduced. The applicants then appealed to the European Court of Human Rights on the ground that the trial proceedings in the action taken by McDonald's against them were unfair because the denial of legal aid by the UK Government had deprived them of the opportunity to present their case effectively. They claimed that the denial of legal aid was a breach of art.6, s.1 of the **European Convention of Human Rights.**

Held

The European Court of Human Rights held that in an action of such complexity neither the help given by the volunteer lawyers nor the extensive judicial assistance provided during the hearing was any substitute representation by expert lawyers. The denial of legal aid deprived the applicants of the opportunity to present their case and contributed to an unacceptable inequality of arms with McDonald's and was, therefore, a violation of art.6.1. [2005] E.M.L.R. 15.

Commentary

The question as to whether the provision of legal aid is necessary for a fair trial is to be determined on the basis of the particular facts and circumstances of each case. The relevant factors would include the importance of what was at stake for the applicant in the proceedings and the complexity of the relevant law and procedure.

The court found that art.10 (freedom of expression) had also been violated. The UK Government had contended that, as the applicants were not journalists, they should not attract the high level of protection afforded to the press under art.10. The defamation proceedings and their outcome, however, were held to constitute a disproportionate interference with the applicants' rights to freedom of expression.

PRIVACY AND HUMAN RIGHTS

As seen above, the aim of law of defamation is to provide compensation for those whose reputations are harmed by *un*true statements and to enable those threatened with loss of reputation to obtain an interim injunction to prevent the publication of a potentially defamatory statement. However, where a statement contains true facts, no matter how much a person wants to them to remain private, the law of defamation offers no protection. A general right of privacy has traditionally not been recognised in English common law but since the enactment of the **Human Rights Act 1998**, which incorporates the **European Convention on Human Rights** (ECHR) into English law, privacy is now an emerging area of law. Consequently, when considering situations where an individual claims a legal right to the protection of personal or private information from misuse or unauthorised disclosure, the courts are required to have regard to the ECHR. However, although art.8 of the ECHR provides an explicit right to respect for a private life for the first time in English law, this must be balanced with art.10 which protects the right to freedom of expression. One of the difficulties with the law in this area is that privacy is a difficult concept to clearly define and the distinction between what constitutes public information and when information is private is blurred. The concern of the courts is that if privacy is defined too widely it could lead to an undesirable restriction on the freedom on the press to report and comment on matters of public importance. One definition of privacy was provided by American Judge Cooley, in 1888 as: *"the right to be left alone"*. The Calcutt Committee, *Report on Privacy and Related Matters* (1990) (Cm 1102) reported: *"nowhere have we found a wholly acceptable statutory definition of privacy."* The following working definition of privacy was adopted by the Report: *The right of the individual to be protected against intrusion into his personal life or affairs, or those of his family, by direct physical means or by publication of information.*

Key Principle

Privacy is a value underlying the common law doctrine of breach of confidence, but this is not in itself a principle of law: there is no tort of invasion of privacy in English law. (Breach of confidence is a cause of action arising from the breach of a duty to keep confidence arising from a confidential situation, transaction or relationship.)

WAINWRIGHT V HOME OFFICE (2003)

The claimant was visiting her son in prison. As part of a security measure within the prison, she and another son were taken to separate rooms and strip searched by prison officers. She claimed that the strip searches amounted to invasion of privacy and a breach of art.8 of the ECHR (see also p.8).

Held

There House of Lords confirmed that there is no tort of invasion of privacy and doubted that the European Court of Human Rights jurisprudence required a principle of privacy to comply with art.8. [2003] UKHL 53

Commentary

In *Von Hannover v Germany* [2004] ECHR 294 the ECHR subsequently confirmed that a positive obligation in respect of privacy rights is imposed by art.8.

Key principle

A pre-existing obligation of confidence will give rise to a reasonable expectation of privacy and, unless the information holds some important public interest value, the right to private and family life under art.8 will not be outweighed by the art.10 right to freedom of expression.

MCKENNITT V ASH (2006)

McKennitt, a well-known folk musician claimed that a substantial part of the book written by Ash, her former close friend, revealed personal and private details about her that she was entitled to keep private. In the course of their friendship Ash had acquired confidential information about McKennitt's personal and sexual relationships, her personal feelings and in particular in relation to her deceased fiance and the circumstances of his death. The trial judge made a ruling to prevent the further publication and found that Ash realised that substantial parts of the book would fall within the scope of a reasonable expectation of privacy or a duty of confidence. Ash appealed against this decision on the ground that the matters the judge found to be confidential were not merely McKennitt's experiences, but her's as well, and contended that this gave her a property in the information. She further claimed freedom of speech on the ground that she was entitled to tell her own story and that included her various experiences with McKennitt.

Held

The Court of Appeal considered whether the information in question was private in the sense that it was, in principle, protected by the right to privacy under art.8 and whether the passages containing details of McKennitt's personal and sexual relationships would fall within the scope of a reasonable expectation of privacy. In upholding McKennitt's right to prevent publication of significant parts of the book on the ground that details of her personal and sexual relationships were intrusive and distressing, the court placed great weight on there being a pre-existing obligation of confidence. Ash's claim that her art.10 right to freedom of expression outweighed McKennitt's right to private and family life under art.8 was rejected. [2006] EWCA Civ 1714

Commentary

The weight given by the courts to preserving the public interest in employees respecting obligations of confidence that they have assumed is further illustrated by the decision in *HRH Prince of Wales v Associated Newspapers* [2006] EWCA Civ 1776. HRH contended that a private leaked travel journal about his 1997 visit to Hong Kong which set out his private and personal thoughts, constituted confidential information. The defendant argued that the information in the journal was not confidential as it was of a political nature and related to the HRH's public life in office, in which there was powerful public interest. The court considered *McKennitt v Ash* and examined the balance between protecting confidential information and copyright on the one hand and the extent of press freedom on the other, particularly where the information relates to a well known person. HRH's right to keep the information in the journal private was upheld: all staff who may have encountered the journal were subject to confidentiality undertakings and therefore HRH did have an expectation of privacy in respect of the journal.

THINK POINT

Douglas v Hello! Ltd [2005] EWCA Civ 595 concerned the publication of a celebrity couple's unauthorised wedding photographs by *Hello!* Magazine. The couple who had already entered into an exclusive agreement with *OK* magazine for publication of the photographs claimed against *Hello!* Magazine for breach of confidence on the ground that the wedding was a valuable trade asset. Although there was no existing law of privacy under which the claimants were entitled to relief, the photographic representations of the event were held to have the necessary quality of confidence and deserved protection as a trade secret.

Key Principle

Protection of privacy in England is based not on a distinct tort of infringement of privacy but principally on an action for breach of confidence which takes account of both art.8 (right to respect to private and family life) and art.10 (right to freedom of expression) of the ECHR.

CAMPBELL V MGN LTD (2004)

Naomi Campbell, a celebrity model sought damages for breach of confidence and compensation for MGN's publication of a newspaper article with details about her treatment for drug addiction at Narcotics Anonymous (NA) accompanied by covertly taken photographs of her leaving a NA meeting. Campbell claimed that the publication of this private information amounted to an interference with her right to respect for private life and that there was no overriding public interest in publication. However, MGN said that Campbell had misled the public in a previous statement asserting that she did not take drugs and argued that their publication of the fact that she had taken drugs and was seeking treatment was necessary to set the record straight.

Held

The House of Lords conceded that, given her previous statements, the publication of the fact that Campbell had taken drugs and was receiving treatment was necessary to set the record straight. However, the publication of additional information relating to the fact that she was receiving treatment at NA, details of that treatment and a photograph of her leaving the clinic was an unjustified intrusion into her private life. In balancing the competing interests under the **Human Rights Act 1998** Campbell's art.8 right to privacy outweighed MGN's competing interest in freedom of expression under art.10. [2004] UKHL 22.

The particular facts in this case are important. The Court attached significant weight to the photograph which accompanied the article and found its inclusion in the publication added greatly to the intrusion. The fact that a report in a newspaper about treatment for drug addiction could do great harm to a person was also relevant: Baroness Hale noted that recovering drug addicts are bound to be in a fragile state.

Key Principle

The law affords protection to information where there is a reasonable expectation of privacy and this protection extends to cover circumstances where there was no pre-existing relationship giving rise to an enforceable duty of confidence.

MOSLEY V NEWS GROUP NEWSPAPERS 2008

The claimant Max Mosley (a prominent figure in the world of motor racing) brought an action against News Group Newspapers (NGN) for breach of confidence and the unauthorised disclosure of information in respect of sado-masochistic and sexual activities with which he was involved. Mosley claimed the material and images NGN published in newspapers and on their website was inherently private in nature and infringed his rights of privacy under art.8 ECHR. He contended that there had also been a pre-existing relationship of confidentiality between the participants in the activities who had all known each other for some time and had participated on the understanding that they would be private and that none of them would reveal what had taken place. NGN argued that Mosley, as a public figure, had no reasonable expectation of privacy in relation to the information or, alternatively, that Mosley's right to privacy under art.8 was outweighed by a greater public interest in the disclosure and NGN's right to freedom of expression under art.10 should be allowed to prevail.

Held

Mosley had a reasonable expectation of privacy in relation to sexual activities carried on between consenting adults on private property. In the circumstances the clandestine recording of the sexual activity on private property violated the rights protected by art.8 and serious reasons had to exist before interferences with it could be justified. The Court found that the degree of intrusion into Mosley's privacy (which had been done on a massive scale) was not proportionate to the public interest supposed to be served in publishing the information. [2008] EWHC 1777 (QB).

THINK POINT

The Court noted that although such behaviour was viewed by some people with distaste and moral disapproval, in the light of modern rights-based jurisprudence, NGN had not provided any justification for the intrusion on Mosley's personal privacy. [2008] EWHC 1777 (QB).

Occupiers' Liability

11

INTRODUCTION

The liability of occupiers towards persons injured on their premises is governed by two statutes. The Occupiers' Liability Act 1957 is concerned with liability to lawful visitors and provides that all lawful entrants are owed the same "common duty of care". The 1957 Act did not deal with trespassers, therefore a subsequent statute, the Occupiers' Liability Act 1984 was enacted to govern the duty of an occupier to persons other than visitors (e.g. trespassers). The standard of care imposed by the statutes is very similar to Lord Atkin's neighbour principle in *Donoghue v Stevenson* (1932) in common law negligence.

OCCUPIERS' LIABILITY ACT 1957

Section 2(1) provides:

> "An occupier of premises owes the same duty, the 'common duty of care', to all his visitors, except in so far as he is free to and does extend, restrict, modify or exclude his duty to any visitor or visitors by agreement or otherwise."

OCCUPIER

Key Principle
The 1957 Act does not define "occupier" but provides that the rules of the common law shall apply. An occupier is one who has sufficient control over the premises so as to be under a duty of care towards lawful entrants: there can be more than one occupier of the same premises at any one time.

> WHEAT V LACON (E) & CO LTD 1966
> The defendant brewing company were owners of a pub which was run by a manager. They granted him a license to use the top floor of the premises for his private accommodation. His wife took in paying guests

and one evening as it was getting dark a guest fell down the back staircase in the private portion of the premises and was killed. The handrail on the stairs was too short and did not stretch to the bottom of the staircase and someone had removed the light bulb from the top of the stairs.

Held

❖ (HL) There may be two or more occupiers at any one time. Although the grant of a license to occupy had been made to the manager the defendants remained occupiers and under a duty of care. On the facts of the case the duty to the deceased had not been broken and the defendants were not liable. [1966] A.C. 522.

Key Principle

It is possible to become an occupier without taking actual physical possession of the premises.

HARRIS V BIRKENHEAD CORP 1976

A compulsory purchase order was made on a house and the local authority served notices of entry on the tenant and the owner. The tenant left the house and before the local authority moved in to have the property boarded up a child got in and was injured. The local authority argued that before it could be an occupier there had to be an actual or symbolic taking possession on its behalf.

Held

❖ (CA) The argument was rejected. Because it had the legal right to control the state of the property the local authority had become an occupier when the tenant vacated the premises. [1976] 1 W.L.R. 279.

THINK POINT

For the purposes of the Act, s.1(3) occupiers' duties apply not only to land and buildings—"premises" means any fixed or movable structure. In *Wheeler v Copas* [1981] 3 All E.R. 405, a ladder was held to come within the definition.

LAWFUL VISITOR

The Act brings together the previous categories of invitee and licensee into one category of visitor. Under s.1(2) of the Act the common duty of care is owed to all lawful visitors and includes invitees, licensees and those who have a contractual right to enter. Where a person enters under a contract a term will be implied into the contract that the visitor is owed the common duty of care (s.5(1)). Persons who enter under a right conferred by law, whether or not they have the occupiers' express permission, enter as visitors (s.2(6)). In *Robson v Hallett* [1967] 2 Q.B. 939, it was held that police officers entering without a warrant may take advantage of the generally implied license to approach a front door via the garden path. The occupier owes a duty to all lawful visitors but the Act provides that the duty may be limited or restricted. An occupier may set limits on the visitor's permission as to time spent on the premises or permit the visitor to be on the premises only for certain purposes. A visitor who has permission only to enter a certain part of the premises has no permission to go to another part. In *The Calgarth* [1927] P. 93 at 110, Scrutton L.J. said:

> "When you invite a person into your house to use the staircase,
> you do not invite him to slide down the banisters, you invite him
> to use the staircase in the ordinary way in which it is used."

It remains important to distinguish visitors from other entrants because the duties of an occupier to other entrants is governed not by the 1957 Act but by the later 1984 Act.

Key Principle

A person who claims to have entered a premises under an implied permission must prove that an implied license has been granted.

LOWERY V WALKER 1911
For 35 years members of the public had used a short cut across the defendant's field to a railway station. Although he had attempted to prevent this he had never taken any serious action to do so because most of the people involved were customers for his milk. The plaintiff was savaged by a dangerous horse which had been put into the field by the defendant.

Held

❖ (HL) The plaintiff had an implied license and was not a trespasser. [1911] A.C. 10.

Key Principle

Permission may not be implied merely because the occupier knows of the entrant's presence or has failed to take the necessary steps to prevent entry.

EDWARDS V RAILWAY EXECUTIVE 1952

Children had been accustomed to climbing through a fence dividing a recreation ground from a railway. The Railway Executive knew this and had taken steps to deter entry by repairing the fence whenever damage had been observed. The plaintiff child had got through the fence and was injured by a passing train.

Held

❖ (HL) The plaintiff was a trespasser and not an implied visitor. Lord Goddard observed that "repeated trespass of itself confers no licence." [1952] A.C. 737.

Commentary

The occupier may set limits on the visitor's permission as to time, place or purpose of visit. A person who has permission only to enter a certain part of the premises has no permission to go to another part.

COMMON DUTY OF CARE

Section 2(2) of the Act provides that:

> "The common duty of care is a duty to take such care as in all the circumstances of the case is reasonable to see that the visitor will be reasonably safe in using the premises for the purposes for which he is invited or permitted by the occupier to be there."

The standard of care expected under s.2(2) is the same as that in an ordinary action in negligence. In *Wheat v Lacon* (see p.189) Lord Denning said: "This duty is simply a particular instance of the general duty of care which each man owes his 'neighbour'".

The following cases will illustrate the operation of certain aspects of the duty of care as specified in s.2(3) of the Act. Meanwhile, it should be noted that under the Act it is the visitor that must be reasonably safe and not necessarily the premises.

CHILDREN

Key Principle ···

Section 2(3)(a) provides that "an occupier must be prepared for children to be less careful than adults."

> ### GLASGOW CORP V TAYLOR 1922
> A seven-year-old child died from eating poisonous berries which he had picked from a shrub in a public park. The berries looked like cherries or large blackcurrants. It was alleged that the local authority knew of the poisonous nature of the berries but the shrub was not fenced nor was any warning of the danger given.

Held ···

❖ (HL) The defendants were liable. The tempting-looking berries constituted an "allurement" to children. [1922] 1 A.C. 44.

Commentary ···

In *Latham v Johnson & Nephew* [1913] 1 K.B. 398 the court said that there is a duty not to lead children into temptation. But an object, such as a pile of stones against a wall, could not possibly constitute a trap and will not amount to an allurement.

THINK POINT

In *Jolley v Sutton LBC* [1998] 3 All E.R. 559, a derelict boat had constituted an allurement and a trap but these were not the causes of the accident. The immediate cause was that the plaintiff, a 14-year-old boy, and a friend decided to repair the boat and jacked it up with a car jack. The Court of Appeal had ruled that, even making full allowance for the unpredictability of children's behaviour, it was not reasonably foreseeable that the boys would work under a propped up boat; it was too remote because it occurred in an unforeseeable manner. Allowing an appeal, the House of Lords approached the question of what risk was foreseeable in much wider terms and said that the trial judge had been correct to consider the reasonable forseeability of the wider risk that children would meddle with a dilapidated boat and be at risk of physical injury.

Key Principle ....

Although an occupier must be prepared for children to be less careful than adults, the extent of the occupier's liability is a question of fact and degree and depends on the particular circumstances of the case.

> KEOWN V COVENTRY HEALTHCARE NHS TRUST 2006
>
> When the claimant was 11 years old he had been climbing the under-side of the defendant's fire escape when he fell to the ground and was injured. The trial judge acknowledged that the claimant had not only appreciated that there was a risk of falling but also that what he was doing was dangerous and that he should not have been climbing the fire escape. However, he found that the fire escape, which could be climbed from the outside, constituted an inducement to children habitually playing in the grounds of the hospital.

Held ....

Allowing the defendant's appeal, the Court of Appeal said that it would not be right to ignore a child's choice to indulge in a dangerous activity in every case merely because he was a child. In this case it could not be said that the risk arose not out of the state of the premises but out of what the claimant chose to do. [2006] EWCA Civ 39.

Commentary ....

According to Lewison J.:

> "In the present case there was nothing inherently dangerous about the fire escape. There was no physical defect in it: no element of disrepair or structural deficiency. Nor was there any hidden danger. The only danger arose from the activity of Mr Keown in choosing to climb up the outside, knowing it was dangerous to do so."

Key Principle ....

In some circumstances occupiers are entitled to assume that parents will exercise reasonable care for their children's safety.

> PHIPPS V ROCHESTER CORP 1955
>
> A boy aged five and his sister aged seven walked across a large open space which was being developed by the defendants. It was known to the defendants that people crossed their land but they apparently took

no action. A long deep trench, which would have been obvious to an adult, had been dug in the middle of the open space. The plaintiff fell in and broke his leg.

Held

The defendants were not liable. Devlin J. placed the responsibility for small children primarily on their parents and concluded that both the parents and the occupier must act reasonably. [1955] 1 Q.B. 450.

Commentary

In *Simkiss v Rhondda Borough Council* [1983] 81 L.G.R. 460 this reasoning was followed and the plaintiff failed. A seven-year-old girl fell off a steep slope which was situated opposite the block of flats where she lived. Her father stated in evidence that he had not considered the slope to be dangerous and the Court of Appeal concluded that if the child's father did not consider the area dangerous, the defendants could not be asked to achieve a higher standard of care.

THINK POINT

In *Bourne Leisure Ltd T/A British Holidays v Marsden* [2009] EWCA Civ 671 the question was whether a holiday site owner was liable for the drowning of a child in a pond, by failing to highlight the dangers and bring the pond's location or existence of an access pathway to the parent's attention. Bourne Leisure appealed against the trial judge's finding that by failing to give warnings of that nature to the parents they were in breach of their common duty of care. In allowing Bourne Leisure's appeal, the Court of Appeal held that although an occupier ought reasonably to anticipate that small children might escape the attention of parents and wander into places of danger, it does not follow that the occupier is under a duty to take precautions against such dangers. In this case the problem with attaching blame in cases involving young children was noted by Lord Justice Moses who said that accidents may and do happen to young children without anyone being at fault.

COMMON CALLING

Key Principle

Section 2(3)(b) of the 1957 Act provides that an occupier may expect that a person, in the exercise of his calling, will appreciate and guard against special risks ordinarily incident to it.

> ### ROLES V NATHAN 1963
>
> Two chimney sweeps were called to clean an old coke-burning boiler which smoked badly. They were warned by an expert that the sweep-hole and inspection chamber should be sealed before the boiler was lit. They disregarded the warning and died when they were overcome with the fumes.

Held

❖ (CA) The occupier was not liable. His duty had been discharged by warning the sweeps of the particular risks, and also, he could reasonably expect a specialist to appreciate and guard against the dangers arising from the very defect that he had been called to deal with. [1963] 1 W.L.R. 1117.

Commentary

Lord Denning said:

> "If it had been a different danger, as for instance if the stairs leading to the cellar gave way, the occupier might no doubt be responsible."

Key Principle

Skills possessed by the entrant will not automatically absolve the occupier of all liability under s.2(3)(b).

> ### SALMON V SEAFEARER RESTAURANTS 1983
>
> A fireman entered a fish-and-chip shop to extinguish a fire. There was an escape of gas followed by an explosion in which the fireman was injured. The defendant argued that an occupier's duty to a fireman attending a fire at his premises was limited to protecting him from special or exceptional risks over and above ordinary risks which are a necessary part of his job.

Held

The court rejected this argument. Woolf J. took the view that although an occupier could expect a fireman attending a fire at his premises to be skilled in protecting himself against the risks of fire, an occupier could not be exempt from risks which would threaten a fireman who was exercising the normal skills of his profession. [1983] 3 All E.R. 729.

THINK POINT

The House of Lords expressly approved this approach in *Ogwo v Taylor* [1988] A.G. 431 where a fireman had entered the roof space of the defendant's house to control a fire. Although he was exercising reasonable care in using a hose he suffered severe burns from scalding steam. The defendant contended that no liability arose from an injury caused by the ordinary risks involved in fire-fighting. This contention was rejected but, if the fireman took a foolhardy and unnecessary risk in fighting the fire, his own conduct might break the chain of causation.

WARNING OF DANGER

Under s.2(4)(a) a warning of the danger may discharge the duty of care. But the Act specifically states that a warning notice is not enough unless in all the circumstances it enables the visitor to be reasonably safe. In *Rae v Mars (UK) Ltd* [1990] 3 E.G. 80 it was held that where an unusual danger exists the visitor should not only be warned, but a barrier or added notice should be placed to show the immediacy of the danger.

LIABILITY FOR INDEPENDENT CONTRACTORS

Key Principle

Under s.2(4)(b) an occupier will not be liable for damage caused to a visitor due to the faulty execution of work by an independent contractor provided:

(i)   that it was reasonable to entrust the work to an independent contractor;

(ii) the occupier had taken reasonable care to see that the contractor was competent; and

(iii) the occupier had taken reasonable care to see that the work was properly done. The more technical the work the more reasonable it will be to entrust it to an independent contractor.

HASELDINE v CA DAW & SON LTD 1941

The plaintiff was injured when the lift in a block of flats fell to the bottom of its shaft. The accident happened as a result of the negligence of a firm of independent contractors who the defendant had employed to repair the lift.

Held

The defendant was not liable. He had discharged his duty by employing a competent firm of engineers to make periodical inspections of the lift. Having no technical skills meant that he could not be expected to check that the work had been satisfactorily done. [1941] 2 K.B. 343.

Commentary

This case was distinguished in *Woodward v The Mayor of Hastings* [1945] K.B. 174, where a child at school slipped on an icy step and was injured. The step had been left in a dangerous condition by a cleaner, and even assuming that the cleaner was an independent contractor, the defendants were liable since there was no technical knowledge required to check the cleaning of a step. According to Du Parcq L.J.:

> "The craft of the charwoman may have its mysteries, but there is no esoteric quality in the nature of the work which the cleaning of a snow-covered step demands."

Key Principle

It is fair, just and reasonable to impose liability on an occupier who allows an extra-hazardous activity to take place on its land without taking ordinary precautions to ensure that the independent contractor has public liability insurance and a proper safety plan.

BOTTOMLEY v TODMORDEN CRICKET CLUB 2003

As part of a fundraising event, the defendant club had allowed independent contractors to carry out a pyrotechnic display on its land. It appealed against a decision which held it liable for the personal injuries of the claimant (a voluntary and unpaid assistant of the independent contractors) who suffered severe burns and other injuries during the display.

Held ....

The Court of Appeal, rejecting the appeal, held that although the case was not about a risk caused by the state of the premises under the **Occupiers' Liability Act 1957**, the defendant occupier, along with the contractors (who had no public liability insurance), was liable in common law negligence. [2003] EWCA Civ 1575.

THINK POINT

It should be noted that in the absence of special circumstances, there is no free-standing duty on an employer to satisfy himself that an independent contractor has public liability insurance cover. In *Naylor v Payling* [2004] EWCA 560, the claimant suffered severe injuries while being forcibly ejected from a nightclub by a door attendant employed by the independent contractor responsible for security at the nightclub. The independent contractor had no public liability insurance and the claimant sued the defendant nightclub owner for failing to ensure that his independent contractor was insured. The Court of Appeal held the job of doorman not to fall within the type of hazardous activity considered in *Bottomley*. Selecting a door attendant accredited as part of a scheme operated by the local authority to carry out the very task which was to be performed by the independent contractor could not be said to be negligent. Save in special circumstances, there was no free standing duty to take reasonable steps to ensure that the independent contractor was insured.

Key Principle ....

Occupiers will not normally be expected to supervise the contractor's activities to ensure that they operate a safe system of work for the employees. Competent contractors can be presumed to have safe systems.

FERGUSON V WELSH 1987

A tender awarded by a district council for the demolition of a building stipulated that the work must not be sub-contracted without the council's consent. The plaintiff was the employee of a sub-contractor who had been carrying out the work without the council's consent. He suffered serious injury as a result of the sub-contractor's unsafe system of work. When it was discovered that neither the main contractor nor

TORT

the sub-contractor were covered by insurance, he sued the local authority as occupiers of the premises.

Held

❖ (HL) The district council was not liable. It would not ordinarily be reasonable to expect an occupier, having engaged a contractor whom he has reasonable grounds for regarding as competent, to supervise the contractor's activities in order to ensure that he was discharging his duties to his employees to observe a safe system of work. [1987] 3 All E.R. 777.

Key Principle

In certain circumstances an occupier may be liable for negligently failing to prevent deliberate injury done by one visitor to another.

CUNNINGHAM V READING FOOTBALL CLUB 1991
Police officers on duty at a football match were injured by hooligans who broke off loose pieces of the concrete from the football ground and hurled them at the police.

Held

The wrong-doing of the visitors was foreseeable and the club was liable. The concrete could easily be prised up and a similar incident had happened four months previously. *The Times*, March 22, 1991.

ACCEPTANCE OF RISK

Key Principle

Section 2(5) provides that the common duty of care does not impose on an occupier any obligation in respect of risks willingly accepted as his by the visitor.

SIMMS V LEIGH RUGBY FOOTBALL CLUB LTD 1969
A Rugby League player was thrown against a wall in the course of a tackle and as a result suffered injury to his leg.

Held

The defendants were not liable. The plaintiff, a professional rugby player, had accepted the risk of playing on a rugby ground that complied with the byelaws of the Rugby League. [1969] 2 All E.R. 923.

Commentary ....

(1) This is a specific application of the general defence of *volenti non fit injuria* (see p.134).

(2) In *Bunker v Charles Brand & Sons Ltd* [1969] 2 Q.B. 480 it was stated that s.2(5) had to be read in conjunction with s.2(4)—the effect of this is that knowledge of the danger is not sufficient to establish *volenti* unless it was enough to enable the visitor to be reasonably safe.

(3) See also *Ratcliff v McConnell* (1998) (see p.204).

EXCLUSION OF LIABILITY

Key Principle ....
The liability of occupiers (s.2(1), above) can be excluded "by agreement or otherwise" but the ability of business occupiers to exclude liability has been severely restricted by the **Unfair Contract Terms Act 1977**. However, private occupiers, within certain limits, still have freedom to exclude liability.

> ASHDOWN V SAMUEL WILLIAMS & SONS LTD 1957
> The second defendants occupied industrial premises surrounded by land owned by the first defendants. Access to the defendant's land was by two roads, one of which was safe. The other road, a short cut, could be used at the user's risk and notices to that effect had been posted on the land. The plaintiff was taking a short cut when she was injured by the negligent shunting of railway trucks.

Held ....
❖ (CA) The defendants, who had taken all reasonable steps to bring to the plaintiff's attention the conditions attached to their permission to enter, were not liable. [1957] 1 Q.B. 409.

Commentary ....
Even though this was a pre-**Occupiers' Liability Act 1957** decision it is still good law. In *White v Blackmore* [1972] 2 Q.B. 651 a majority in the Court of Appeal concluded that it was an effective defence. The plaintiff's husband was killed at a jalopy race when a car's wheel became entangled in the safety ropes and he was catapulted 20 feet through the air. A notice had been posted at the entrance to the course, and at other points about the field, absolving the defendants of all liability arising from accidents. The deceased was held to have entered subject to these conditions.

CONTRIBUTORY NEGLIGENCE

The **Law Reform Contributory Negligence Act 1945** applies to an action for a breach of the common duty of care. Where the visitor's failure to use reasonable care for his/her own safety is a cause of the harm suffered the amount of damages will be reduced in the same manner as in an ordinary negligence action.

LIABILITY TO ENTRANTS OTHER THAN "VISITORS"

THE OCCUPIERS' LIABILITY ACT 1984

The 1984 Act s.1(1)(a) is concerned with the duty of an occupier to "persons other than his visitors." The Act applies to three categories of entrants:
  (i)   trespassers;
  (ii) persons who enter land in the exercise of rights conferred by the National Parks and Access to the Countryside Act 1949; and
  (iii) persons lawfully exercising a private right of way.

THINK POINT

In practice the most important category of entrant to which the Act applies is trespassers. For the purposes of s.1(3) of the 1984 Act a duty will arise if three requirements are met. First, the occupier must be aware of the danger or have reasonable grounds to believe that it exists. Second, the occupier must know or have reasonable grounds to believe that the entrant is either in the vicinity or may come into the vicinity of the danger concerned. Finally, the risk is one against which, in all the circumstances of the case, the occupier may reasonably be expected to offer the non-visitor some protection. The duty, when it arises, is defined by s.1(4) as the duty to take such care as is reasonable in all the circumstances of the case to see that the non-visitor does not suffer injury on the premises by reason of the danger concerned.

Key Principle

The mere fact that a defendant had taken measures to stop entry on to land containing some danger does not necessarily mean that the "reasonable grounds to believe" element in s.1(3)(b) has been satisfied.

> **WHITE V ST ALBANS DISTRICT CITY AND DISTRICT COUNCIL 1990**
> The plaintiff, a trespasser, was taking a short cut across the defendants' fenced-off property when he fell into a trench and was injured.

Held

❖ (CA) The defendants were not liable. The fact that an occupier had taken precautions to stop people getting on to land where there was a danger does not necessarily mean that he had reason to believe that someone was likely to come into the vicinity of the danger for the purposes of s.1(3)(b). *The Times*, March 12, 1990.

Key Principle

The statutory duty owed by occupiers to non-visitors under the 1984 Act, which replaces the common law "duty of common humanity" owed to trespassers, is similar to the obligation at common law.

> **BRITISH RAILWAYS BOARD V HERRINGTON 1972**
> The plaintiff, aged six, was badly burned when he was trespassing on the defendants' land. The child had obtained access to the land through a gap in a chain link fence. The gap was used as a short cut by members of the public and the fence had been trodden down. The defendants knew that in the past children had been seen on the line, but they took no action.

Held

❖ (HL) Although the plaintiff was a trespasser he could recover in negligence. A trespasser is owed a lower duty of care, but nevertheless an occupier does owe a duty to act humanely. [1972] A.C. 877.

Key Principle

An occupier may owe a duty to a trespasser who is engaged in committing a crime at the time of the injury.

> **REVILL V NEWBERRY 1996**
> In order to guard his allotment shed the defendant was sleeping in it armed with a loaded shotgun. The plaintiff, a 21-year-old man, who had

already committed crimes of damage to property and theft that night, tried to break into the defendant's shed. The defendant, who shot the plaintiff through a hole in the door of the shed, was sued for the resulting personal injuries.

Held

❖ (CA) The defendant was liable, he had used greater force than was reasonably necessary in defence of himself or his property. [1996] 1 All E.R. 291.

Commentary

(1) The defendant's liability for negligence, in firing the gun through the door when he was unable to see whether there was anyone on the other side, was not dependant on his status as an occupier. The plaintiff's injury, which related to the defendant's activity on the premises rather than the state of the premises itself, was governed by the common law and the 1984 Act did not apply.

(2) The defence of illegality of the plaintiff's conduct was not allowed but his damages were reduced by two-thirds for contributory negligence.

DEFENCES

Any duty in respect of risk may, by taking reasonable care in all the circumstances, be discharged by a warning (s.1(5)). The defence of *volenti non fit injuria* is preserved by the 1984 Act; no duty is owed by virtue of s.1(6) to any person in respect of risks willingly accepted as his by that person. The 1984 Act is silent on whether the duty owed to trespassers can be excluded.

Key Principle

Volenti non fit injuria has to be considered in determining if a duty of care exists. If the trespasser willingly accepts the risk there is no duty owed by the occupier.

RATCLIFF v McConnell 1998
The plaintiff, a 19-year-old student, having drunk about four pints, agreed to go swimming with two friends. At about 2.30 am they climbed over the gate of a college open-air swimming pool and, although conscious of the word "Warning", the plaintiff did not read the notice by the gate. He got undressed and took a running dive into the pool either at the point where the shallow end started or at the slope from

the deep to the shallow end. He hit the top of his head on the bottom, suffering tetraplegic injuries.

Held

The Court of Appeal held that the occupiers owed no duty under s.1 of the **Occupiers' Liability Act 1984**. Knowing that the pool was closed for the winter, that it was dangerous to dive into water of unknown depth and that the water level of the pool was low, the plaintiff had willingly accepted the risk as his within the meaning of s.1(6). [1999] 1 W.L.R. 670.

Key Principle

Where the risk is obvious, an occupier is under no liability under s.1(3) Occupiers' Liability Act 1984 for a claimant's injuries.

TOMLINSON V CONGLETON BOROUGH COUNCIL 2004

On a hot day, the 18-year-old claimant went to a popular park with some friends. Ignoring the warning signs around a shallow lake, he dived into the water from a standing position. The stretch of water into which he dived was shallow and he struck his head and suffered appalling personal injury. The claimant accepted that on entering the water he ceased to be a visitor and became a trespasser but he claimed that the council was in its breach of duty to persons other than visitors under s.1(3) **Occupiers' Liability Act 1984**. The defendants were aware of the danger and the claimant argued that the warning notices and other precautionary measures taken by the council were shown to be ineffective and did not discharge the council's duty under s.1(3). The trial judge dismissed his claim but the Court of Appeal held that on account of: the attraction of the lake to swimmers; the frequency of exposure to danger; and the relatively inexpensive and simple deterrents available to reduce the risk of persons entering the lake, the council's duty had not been discharged by its notices, oral warnings and the safety leaflets issued by its employees.

Held

The House of Lords allowed the council's appeal and held that no duty of care was owed. There was no risk to the claimant from the state of premises or from anything done or omitted to be done on them. The risk of striking the lake bottom from diving into shallow water was perfectly obvious and not a risk against which the defendant might reasonably have been expected to offer the claimant some protection under s.1(3) of the Act. Judicial concern about the effect of liability preventing desirable activities being undertaken can be seen in the comments of Lord Scott and Lord Hoffman:

Lord Scott:

"And why should the council be discouraged by the law of tort from providing facilities for young men and young women to enjoy themselves in this way? Of course there is some risk of accidents arising out of the joie-de-vivre of the young. But that is no reason for imposing a grey and dull safety regime on everyone."

Lord Hoffmann:

"Mr Tomlinson was a person of full capacity who voluntarily and without any pressure or inducement engaged in an activity which had inherent risk. The risk was that he might not execute his dive properly and so sustain injury. Likewise, a person who goes mountaineering incurs the risk that he might stumble or mis-judge where to put his weight. In neither case can the risk be attributed to the state of the premises. The risk of striking the bottom of the lake by diving into shallow water was perfectly obvious and it was his own misjudgement which had caused his injury. ... A duty to protect against obvious risks or self-inflicted harm exists only in cases in which there is no genuine and informed choice, as in the case of employees, or some lack of capacity, such as the inability of children to recognise danger (*British Railways Board v Herrington* [1972] A.C. 877) or the despair of prisoners which may lead them to inflict injuries on themselves (*Reeves v Commissioner of Police* [2000] 1 AC 360)."

Commentary

Mann v Northern Electric Distribution Ltd [2010] EWCA Civ 141 involved a trespasser aged 15 who was electrocuted when he climbed into an electricity substation and suffered devastating injuries. The question was whether the unauthorised access was reasonably foreseeable and whether the security precautions taken by the occupier were sufficient to keep the reasonable trespasser out. In a decision consistent with case precedent limiting the imposition of liability on occupiers where claimants have acted carelessly, the Court of Appeal found that the occupier had discharged the burden of showing that it had done what was reasonably practicable to prevent unauthorised access.

Trustees of the Portsmouth Youth Activities Committee v Poppleton [2008] EWCA Civ 646 is a further example of case precedent limiting the imposition of liability on occupiers where claimants have acted carelessly and supports the idea of personal responsibility. Here, the claimant suffered serious injuries as the result of an accident which occurred as he was engaged in simulated rock climbing at the defendant's indoor climbing premises. He claimed for damages on the grounds that the defendant had failed to provide sufficient supervision and was in breach of its duty of care to him by failing to warn him of the nature of the risks involved. The Court of Appeal, applying *Tomlinson*, held that there was an inherent risk in the activity that the claimant voluntarily undertook and the law did not require the defendant to prevent him from engaging in that activity. Judicial concern expressed in *Tomlinson* about the effect of imposing liability preventing desirable activities from taking place can be seen in the comments of May L.J:

> "If the law required training or supervision in this case, it would equally be required for a multitude of other commonplace leisure activities which nevertheless carry with them a degree of obvious inherent risk—as for instance bathing in the sea."

Nuisance

12

INTRODUCTION

The tort of nuisance protects against "indirect" interference with the claimant's use and enjoyment of land, such as excessive noise and the emission of smells or noxious fumes. Direct interferences, such as unlawfully walking across a neighbour's land or dumping rubbish in his garden, are dealt with by the law of trespass to land. Private nuisance, which is not the same tort as public nuisance, is commonly defined as an unreasonable interference with the use or enjoyment of land. In *Crown River Cruises Ltd v Kimbolton Fireworks Ltd* [1996] 2 Lloyd's Rep. 533, following a fireworks display held by the defendants, the plaintiffs claimed in negligence, nuisance and under the principle in *Rylands v Fletcher* for damage caused to their floating barge and a passenger vessel moored alongside it on the River Thames. Kimbolton Fireworks argued that that the essence of nuisance was an interference with the use or enjoyment of land, not a floating barge. In rejecting this the court held that a permanently moored barge, occupied under a mooring licence, could give rise to the possibility of an action in private in nuisance.

Although the same state of affairs may constitute both private and public nuisance, it must be noted that the rules relating to them are not identical. The central issue in the whole law of nuisance is the question of reasonableness and what constitutes unreasonable interference. In nuisance the law does not concentrate so much on the reasonableness of the defendant's conduct but rather on the unreasonableness of the interference; it seeks to strike a balance between the rights of occupiers to use their property as they choose and the rights of their neighbours not to have their use of land interfered with. In *Sedleigh-Denfield v O'Callagan* (below) Lord Wright said a useful test is what is reasonable according to the ordinary usage of mankind living in a particular society. As the following cases will illustrate, the approach taken by the courts to the protection of such interests is one of compromise, a "rule of give and take, live and let live": *Bamford v Turnley* (1862) 3 B. & S. 66.

PRIVATE NUISANCE

TYPES OF ACTIONABLE INTERFERENCE

Key Principle

The overflow of water on to the land of another constitutes physical damage and is actionable in nuisance.

> SEDLEIGH-DENFIELD V O'CALLAGAN 1940
> Without the defendants' permission, and therefore technically trespassing, Middlesex County Council laid a pipe in a ditch on their land. The workmen involved did not place a grid near the mouth of the pipe to prevent leaves and debris blocking it. The defendants were aware of the trespass and the ditch was cleaned out twice a year on their behalf. Some years later, after a heavy rainstorm the pipe became blocked and caused flooding on the plaintiff's adjoining land.

Held

❖ (HL) The defendants were liable for the nuisance because they were aware of its presence. They ought to have appreciated the risk of flooding and taken reasonable steps to abate it. [1940] A.C. 880.

Commentary

(1) In *Leakey v National Trust* [1980] Q.B. 485 a land slip was held to constitute a nuisance.

(2) In *Hunter v London Docklands Development Corp* [1997] A.C. 655, it was held that a deposit of dust is capable of giving rise to an action in nuisance.

Key Principle

Damage caused by roots of trees which encroach into adjacent land constitutes a nuisance.

> DAVEY V HARROW CORP 1958
> Roots of trees which were growing on the defendant corporation's property had penetrated the land of the plaintiff's adjoining property. This encroachment caused extensive damage to the plaintiff's house.

Held

❖ (CA) The plaintiff was entitled to succeed. Lord Goddard said: "... if trees encroach, whether by branches or roots, and cause damage, an action for nuisance will lie ...". No distinction is to be drawn between trees which may have been self-sown and trees which were deliberately planted on land. [1958] 1 Q.B. 60.

Key Principle

The emanation of smells which interfere with the plaintiff's comfort or convenience can amount to a nuisance.

> BONE V SEALE 1975
> Nauseating smells had emanated from a village pig-farm for a period of 12 years. The plaintiffs did not suffer ill health but they were disgusted by the smells.

Held

❖ (CA) The plaintiffs succeeded. An injunction was granted and damages awarded to compensate for the loss of amenity in the enjoyment of their property. [1975] 1 All E.R. 787.

Commentary

(1) In *Tetley v Chitty* (see p.223) noise coming from a go-cart track which could be heard in the plaintiffs' houses was held to be a nuisance.

(2) In *Laws v Florinplace* [1981] 1 All E.R. 659 a sex shop in a residential street was held to constitute an unreasonable interference with enjoyment of property.

UNREASONABLE INTERFERENCE—LOCALITY

Key Principle

In assessing whether the interference amounts to an actionable nuisance the nature of the locality is taken into account. However, in cases where the interference causes physical damage to property this rule does not apply.

> ST HELEN'S SMELTING CO V TIPPING 1865
> The plaintiff purchased a very valuable estate which was within a mile and a half of a large smelting works. Fumes from a copper smelter damaged trees and crops on the plaintiff's land. The defendant contended that the whole neighbourhood was devoted to similar

manufacturing purposes and that the smelting should be allowed to carry on with impunity.

Held

❖ (HL) The defendants were liable. The court drew a distinction between nuisances causing property damage and those causing personal discomfort. Lord Westbury highlighted that the locality rule applies only to cases of personal discomfort and does not apply where there is physical damage to the plaintiff's property. Property damage must not be inflicted wherever the defendant is carrying on the activity. (1865) 11 H.L. Cas. 642.

Commentary

Interference which would not be permissible in one area may be in another. In *Sturges v Bridgman* (1879) (see p.202) Thesiger L.J. said: ". .what would be a nuisance in Belgrave Square would not necessarily be so in Bermondsey."

THINK POINT

Not every interference with enjoyment of property will amount to a nuisance. Personal discomfort is measured by reference to the standards of an ordinary person who might occupy the plaintiff's property. To be actionable the inconvenience ought to be more than fanciful—it must be:

"... an inconvenience materially interfering with the ordinary comfort physically of human existence, not merely according to elegant or dainty modes and habits of living, but according to plain and sober and simple notions among the English people."

Per Knight-Bruce V.C. in *Walter v Selfe* (1851) 4 De G. & Sim. 315.

Key Principle

The granting of planning permission to facilitate an activity on a site already used for that purpose does not carry with it an immunity in nuisance in respect of implementation of that planning permission.

WHEELER V JJ SAUNDERS LTD 1995
The defendants had obtained planning permission for two pig-weaning houses to facilitate the intensification of pig farming on a site already

used for that purpose. In response to the plaintiff's claim in nuisance the defendants contended that, since they had obtained planning permission, any smell emanating from the pigs kept in the weaning houses could not amount to a nuisance.

Held

❖ (CA) The defendants were liable. Staughton L.J. said:

> "It would be in my opinion be a misuse of language to describe what has happened in the present case as a change in the character of the neighbourhood. It is a change of use of a very small piece of land, a little over 350 square metres according to the dimensions on the plan, for the benefit of the applicant and to the detriment of the objectors in the quiet enjoyment of their house. It is not a strategic planning decision affected by considerations of public interest. Unless one is prepared to accept that any planning decision authorises any nuisance which must inevitably come from it, the argument that the nuisance was authorised by planning permission in this case must fail." [1996] Ch. 19 at 35.

Commentary

(1) This view was endorsed in *Hunter v Docklands Development Corp* (1996) (not an issue on appeal to HL, see p.210). The Court of Appeal rejected the submission that the powers and duties conferred on planning authorities were such that, in granting planning permissions, they were conferring an immunity in nuisance on works pursuant to the permissions.

(2) However, planning permission can, in some circumstances, act as a defence. If planning permission is granted for a large-scale development that may change the character of the locality, the question of whether an interference arising from the activity on the land amounts to a nuisance will be decided with reference to its present use (with the development) and not the previous nature of the locality. In *Gillingham Borough Council v Medway (Chatham) Dock Co Ltd* [1993] Q.B. 343 planning permission to develop a commercial dock was held to have changed the character of the neighbourhood and the local residents were therefore unable to claim in nuisance for the disturbance it created.

In *Watson v Croft Promo-Sport Ltd* [2009] EWCA Civ 15 the principle in *Wheeler v JJ Saunders Ltd* was applied by the Court of Appeal where owners of a home located close to a motor racing circuit were awarded damages for the diminution in value of their property and loss of amenity. Applying the principle in *Wheeler v JJ Saunders* the Court of Appeal rejected the argument put forward by the operator of the motor circuit that although the racing did cause noise and some discomfort, there was no actionable nuisance because the nature and character of the locality had been changed by the planning permission.

DURATION

Key Principle

In determining the reasonableness of the interference, the duration of the alleged nuisance will be taken into account.

> HARRISON V SOUTHWARK AND VAUXHALL WATER CO 1891
> The defendants, in the exercise of their statutory powers, sank a shaft into land adjoining the plaintiff's house. In the course of carrying out the work a certain amount of noise and vibration was created. The plaintiff brought an action in nuisance in respect of this interference.

Held

As the disturbance was only temporary and for a lawful object it was not an actionable nuisance. Vaughan Williams J. said that a man who pulls down his house for the purpose of building a new one no doubt causes considerable inconvenience to his next door neighbour but he is not liable in nuisance, "... if he uses all reasonable skill and care to avoid annoyance to his neighbour." [1891] 2 Ch. 409.

Commentary

If the temporary interference is substantial it may amount to a nuisance. In *De Keysers Royal Hotel Ltd v Spicer Bros Ltd* (1914) 30 T.L.R. 257, pile driving at night during temporary building works was held to be a nuisance.

NUISANCE

Key Principle

The existence of a nuisance is usually associated with a continuing "state of affairs" but an isolated event can give rise to an action.

> BRITISH CELANESE V HUNT CAPACITORS 1969
> The defendants stored strips of foil used for making electric components on their premises. Some of the strips were blown by the wind on to an electricity power station and caused the power supply to be cut off. The plaintiffs were manufacturers of synthetic yarn which solidified when their machinery came to a halt as a result of the power cut.

Held

A one-off event can create an actionable nuisance and the defendants were liable. [1969] 2 All E.R. 1252.

Commentary

The one-off event in question arose from a continuing "state of affairs" (storing the strips of metal) for which the defendants were responsible. In *SCM v Whittall* [1970] 1 W.L.R. 1017 Thesiger J. said that:

> "while there is no doubt that a single isolated escape may cause the damage that entitles a plaintiff to sue for nuisance, yet it must be proved that the nuisance arose from the condition of the defendant's land or premises or property or activities thereon that constituted a nuisance."

SENSITIVITY

Key Principle

In considering what is reasonable the law does not take account of abnormal sensitivity in either persons or property.

> ROBINSON V KILVERT 1889
> The defendant's manufacture of paper boxes in the cellar of a building required hot and dry air and they heated the cellar accordingly. This raised the temperature on the floor above which resulted in damage to the plaintiff's stock of brown paper.

Held

The heat would not have harmed normal paper and therefore the defendant was not liable. (1889) 41 Ch.D. 88.

Commentary

If normal paper would have been harmed the defendant would have been liable. In *McKinnon Industries v Walker* [1951] 3 D.L.R. 557 the plaintiff's business of growing orchids was unusually sensitive. However, the noxious fumes from the defendant's factory would have damaged non-sensitive plants and the plaintiff was able to recover the full extent of the loss, including the damage to the sensitive orchids.

Key Principle

If the interference is due to the sensitivity of the plaintiff and is one which would not disturb ordinary healthy people, there is no redress.

> HEATH V MAYOR OF BRIGHTON 1908
>
> The plaintiff, a minister of religion, sought an injunction against the operators of a slightly noisy electricity generator. The noise, although annoying the plaintiff, did not prevent him from preaching or conducting his services and it would not have disturbed ordinary healthy people.

Held

The injunction was not granted because the noise was not such as to distract the attention of ordinary healthy persons attending the church. (1908) 98 L.T. 718.

Key Principle

Sensitivity to television reception was held (in 1965) not to be actionable in nuisance because the activity was sensitive and interference with the recreational amenity of television viewing was not a substantial interference.

> BRIDLINGTON RELAY CO V YORKSHIRE ELECTRICITY BOARD 1965
>
> The plaintiffs operated a television relay service to provide their customers with a television signal by cable which was better than they could otherwise receive. The defendant's electricity cable interfered with the reception and affected the plaintiff's business.

Held

The plaintiff failed, according to Buckley J., because he had an unusually vulnerable business which, if it were to prosper, required an exceptional degree of immunity from interference. In addition, interference with radio and television reception was found not to be a substantial enough interference to give rise to an action in nuisance. [1965] Ch. 436.

THINK POINT

This decision would probably not be followed today. In *Nor-Video Services v Ontario Hydro* (1978) 84 D.L.R. (3rd) 221, on similar facts the Canadian courts refused to follow it and held television reception to be a protectable interest.

Key Principle

In certain circumstances, an action for interference with television reception might be protected. However, "more is required than the mere presence of a neighbouring building to give rise to an actionable private nuisance."

HUNTER V DOCKLANDS DEVELOPMENT CORP 1997
The plaintiff and hundreds of others claimed damages for nuisance from Canary Wharf Ltd for interference, over a period of years, with reception of television broadcasts at their homes in east London. The interference was caused by the existence of the Canary Wharf Tower which is 250 metres high and over 50 metres square with stainless steel cladding and metalised windows.

Held

❖ (HL) The erection or presence of a building in the line of sight between a television transmitter and other properties was not actionable as an interference with the use and enjoyment of land. [1997] 2 W.L.R. 684.

Commentary

In *Nor-Video Services v Ontario Hydro* and *Bridlington Relay Ltd v Yorkshire Electricity Board* [1965] Ch. 436 the cause of the interference with the television reception was an electrical power point operation. In the present case, it was the presence of the building and not any activity in the building which interfered with the television signal.

SOCIAL UTILITY OF THE DEFENDANT'S CONDUCT

Key Principle

In balancing the conflicting interests of neighbours the utility of the defendant's conduct is a factor, albeit a small factor, that is taken into account.

> MILLER V JACKSON 1977
> In 1972 the plaintiff bought a house. It was built in such a place that it was inevitable that cricket balls from a cricket ground nearby would be hit into the garden. Cricket had been played on the ground since 1905 but the plaintiff contended that since the houses were built it had become a substantial interference and claimed in negligence and in nuisance.

Held

❖ (CA) The playing of cricket was held to constitute an unreasonable interference with the plaintiff's enjoyment of land and was therefore a nuisance. [1977] Q.B. 966.

Commentary

(1) Because of the pleasure derived from cricket and its social utility in keeping village communities together, Lord Denning argued that cricket playing could not be a nuisance for those living near to the ground into whose property cricket balls would be hit. However, the majority considered that the social utility of cricket could not justify a substantial interference in the plaintiff's enjoyment of their land.

(2) Note that in this case no injunction was granted to restrain the cricket. The court took the view that the utility of the club outweighed the plaintiff's interest. (See Defences, p.224.)

(3) In *Adams v Ursell* [1913] 1 Ch. 269 the utility of a fish-and-chip shop to local poor inhabitants could not justify its presence in a fashionable street.

MALICE

Key Principle

Conduct which is motivated by malice may convert what would otherwise have been a reasonable act into an actionable nuisance.

CHRISTIE V DAVIE 1893

The plaintiff, a music teacher, lived in a semi-detached house. The defendant, who lived next door, was annoyed by the music lessons and in retaliation he banged on the party wall, beat trays, whistled and shrieked.

Held

An injunction was granted but North J. indicated that he would have taken a different view of the situation if the defendant's acts had been "innocent". [1893] 1 Ch. 316.

Key Principle

The presence of malice in the defendant's conduct in the use of their own land may tip the balance towards finding the user unreasonable.

HOLLYWOOD SILVER FOX FARM LTD V EMMETT 1936

The defendant's premises adjoined the plaintiff's silver fox farm. The vixens of these animals are very nervous during breeding-time and are likely to devour their young if disturbed. In attempting to prevent the foxes from breeding the defendant discharged guns on his own land as near as possible to the boundary of the plaintiff's land in order to scare the foxes.

Held

Macnaghten J. considered the intention of the defendant to be relevant in nuisance and an injunction and damages were awarded. [1936] 2 K.B. 468.

WHO CAN SUE?

Key Principle

The traditional view has been that only those who have a legal interest in the land affected can sue in private nuisance.

MALONE V LASKEY 1907

Vibrations on the defendant's property caused the collapse of a cistern in the adjoining premises. The plaintiff, the wife of the occupier of the adjoining premises, suffered injury as a result.

Held

She had no claim in private nuisance because she had no proprietary or possessory interest in the land. [1907] 2 K.B. 141.

Commentary ....

(1) In *Khorasandjian v Bush* [1993] 3 All E.R. 669 (see p.7), the Court of Appeal held that the plaintiff, who lived with her mother and had no proprietary interest in the property, was entitled to an injunction to restrain a private nuisance in the form of telephone harassment. Dillon L.J. said:

> "To my mind, it is ridiculous if in this present age the law is that the making of deliberately harassing and pestering telephone calls to a person is only actionable in the civil courts if the recipient of the calls happens to have the freehold or a leasehold proprietary interest in the premises in which he or she has received the calls."

(2) However, in *Hunter v Docklands Development Corp* (1997) (p.216) the House of Lords overruled this decision and put beyond doubt the principle that a propriety interest in land is required to found an action in private nuisance. In reiterating this principle in *Dobson v Thames Water Utilities Ltd* [2009] EWCA Civ 28 the Court of Appeal rejected a claim for damages for arising from the emanation of odours and mosquitoes from the defendants' sewage treatment because the claimants had no legal interest in the land affected.

(3) *Delaware Mansions Ltd v Westminster City Council* [2001] UKHL 55 concerned damage under a block of flats by encroachment of the roots of a tree which was growing on the pavement. Westminster, as highways authority, was owner of the tree. It was held that where there is a continuing nuisance of which the defendant knew or ought to have known, reasonable remedial expenditure may be recovered by the owner, even if the damage had already been inflicted prior to the acquisition of his interest in the land.

....
WHO CAN BE LIABLE?

Key Principle ....
The creator of the nuisance may be sued and liability extends beyond those in occupation of land themselves and covers those who create a nuisance while on somebody else's land.

> SOUTHPORT CORP V ESSO PETROLEUM 1956
> The defendant's oil tanker ran aground and there was a danger that she might break up with the probable loss of the ship and the loss of the lives of her crew. In order to prevent this the master decided to lighten

the ship and 400 tons of oil were discharged into the sea. The river estuary was polluted and the plaintiff corporation alleged that the deposit of oil on the foreshore gave rise to three causes of action: trespass, nuisance and negligence.

Held

❖ (HL) A nuisance, which need not emanate from private land, had been committed. [1956] A.C. 218.

Commentary

The defence of necessity succeeded in this case and the defendants were absolved of liability. Where life and limb are at risk any necessary damage to property will be justified.

Key Principle

Occupiers who become aware of the existence of a nuisance arising out of a natural condition on their land are bound to take positive action.

GOLDMAN V HARGRAVE 1967

A redgum tree, 100 feet high, on the defendant's land was struck by lightning and caught fire. The defendant caused the land around the burning tree to be cleared and the tree was then cut down. He did not extinguish the fire after doing this in the belief that the fire would eventually burn itself out. However, it kept smouldering and subsequently the wind increased and the fire spread to the plaintiff's land.

Held

❖ (PC) The occupier was liable for failing to take adequate precautions to extinguish the fire in the face of foreseeable risk. [1967] 1 A.C. 645.

THINK POINT

The Privy Council applied the rule in *Sedleigh-Denfield v O'Callagan* (1940) (see p.209) where the occupiers were held liable for the nuisance created by a trespasser. In that case the occupiers had made use of the pipe laid by the trespasser to drain water from their land and were therefore found to have both adopted and continued the nuisance.

Ownership of land carries with it a duty to take whatever steps are reasonable in all the circumstances to prevent hazards on the land, however they might arise, from causing damage to a neighbour.

> LEAKEY V NATIONAL TRUST 1980
>
> Because of its geological structure, land owned by the defendants was prone to subsidence which caused land slips on to the plaintiff's property. Although they had been warned of the possibility of a substantial earth slip, the defendants refused to do anything about it and merely gave the plaintiff permission to abate the nuisance at his own expense.

Held ....

The Court of Appeal extended the principle in *Goldman* to include nuisances caused by the natural condition of the land itself and found the defendants liable for failing to take appropriate action when they knew of the risk. [1980] Q.B. 485.

Commentary ....

In *Holbeck Hall Hotel v Scarborough Borough Council* [2000] 2 All E.R. 705, the defendant local authority occupied the cliff adjoining the claimant's hotel. Due to natural coastal erosion, the cliff had become unstable and as the result of a catastrophic land slip, the claimant's hotel was damaged by lack of support and had to be demolished. In arguing that the defendants were liable in nuisance the claimant sought to apply *Leakey*; the council argued that *Leakey* was not applicable to the rights of support but was confined to encroachment or escapes from the defendant's land. The Court of Appeal said that a "measured" duty of care to a neighbouring landowner arose out of a danger due to lack of support caused by a land slip in just the same way as it arose out of an escape or encroachment of a noxious thing. The scope of the defendant's duty, however, was to avoid damage to the claimant's land which they ought to have foreseen. They were not liable for a catastrophic collapse which they could only have discovered by further geological investigation.

THE HUMAN RIGHTS ACT 1998

Common law nuisance may potentially constitute an interference with a claimant's rights under art.8 of the **European Convention on Human Rights** (respect for private and family life) and/or Protocol 1, art.1 (protection of

NUISANCE

221

property). Nevertheless, the courts are reluctant to impose liability where a statutory regulatory scheme exists and an action for breach of statutory duty is available where an enforcement order is not complied with.

Marcic v Thames Water Utilities Ltd 2004

For a number of years, sewers provided by Thames Water had caused flooding which discharged both surface water and foul water on to the claimant's garden. Many thousands of other householders were at a similar risk of flooding as a consequence of the discharge from over-burdened sewers in the Thames area. Thames Water claimed that the cost of work required to alleviate the flooding would result in a total expenditure in excess of £1000 million and they sought to rely on lack of resources to justify their decision to take no steps at all to abate the nuisance. They argued that their system of determining priorities to alleviate flooding was a fair way of devolving their limited resources and, applying these priorities, there was no prospect of carrying out the work for the foreseeable future. At first instance the judge held that: (1) he was bound by authority to dismiss the claims founded in *Rylands v Fletcher*, nuisance and negligence; and (2) he concluded that the failure by Thames Water to carry out suitable work to repair the sewer gave no action for a breach of statutory duty under the Water Industry Act 1991 which imposes a duty of the sewerage undertaker to ensure that the area is effectively drained. Nevertheless, he held that the failure of Thames Water to repair the sewer constituted an interference with the claimant's rights under art.8 and Protocol 1, art.1 of the European Convention on Human Rights. The Court of Appeal, however, held that this was not, in fact, a human rights case at all and said that the claimant was entitled to succeed under the common law of nuisance. The court agreed with the trial judge's conclusion that the defendant had acted incompatibly with the claimant's Convention rights.

Held

When the case reached the House of Lords, their Lordships allowed an appeal and rejected liability in common law nuisance. In holding the claim under the **Human Rights Act 1998** to be ill-founded, their Lordships focused on the statutory regulatory scheme and stated that where Parliament had established a regulatory scheme in which an independent regulator sought to balance the competing interests and consider overall priorities, liability would not be imposed. The regulatory scheme in question was compatible with art.8 and Protocol 1, art.1 and there had, therefore, been no infringement of his rights under the European Convention.

Commentary

(1) The decision of the Grand Chamber of the European Court of Human Rights in *Hatton v United Kingdom* (2003) 37 E.H.R.R. 28 makes it clear that the Convention does not accord absolute protection to property or even to residential premises. It requires a fair balance to be struck between the competing interests of the parties involved.

THINK POINT

Before the House of Lords decision in *Marcic*, the Court of Appeal ruling on the human rights infringement was applied in *Dennis v Ministry of Defence* [2003] EWHC 793. In *Dennis*, the flying of RAF Harrier jets caused severe and frightening noise disturbance which resulted in a reduction in the capital value of the claimant's property. This was held to have been an interference with the claimant's human rights for which damages of £950,000 were awarded. Following the substantial damages awarded in *Dennis* the potential liability of Thames Water was clear when the case reached the House of Lords.

Key Principle

The general rule is that a landlord who has leased premises is not liable for nuisances arising from them except where the landlord granted the lease for the purpose which constitutes the nuisance.

Tetley v Chitty 1986

Residents in Rochester complained of noise from a go-cart track which could be heard in their houses. Medway Borough Council had granted planning permission for the go-cart track on its land and had granted a lease to a go-cart club. The local authority, having leased the land, was no longer in occupation of it.

Held

The local authority was liable: excessive noise was a very predictable consequence of the use for which the land had been let. [1986] 1 All E.R. 663.

Commentary

In *Hussain v Lancaster City Council* [1999] 4 All E.R. 149, the council was held not to be liable in respect of a long-term campaign of racial harassment on a shopkeeper by the local authority's tenants: the acts complained of did not involve the use of the tenants' land. Hussain was distinguished in *Lippiatt v South Gloucestershire Council* [1999] 4 All E.R. 149, where the facts were found to be materially different. In this case, the council allowed travellers (who were trespassers) to park their caravans on a piece of its land bordering the claimant's farm. The council could have evicted the travellers from its land but had failed to so and was therefore liable for the travellers' repeated acts of interference.

Key Principle

A landlord who has an obligation to repair or who reserves the right to enter and repair may be liable.

> **WRINGE V COHEN 1940**
> Because of want of repair, a wall to the defendant's premises collapsed and damaged the plaintiff's shop. The house was let to a weekly tenant but the defendant was liable to keep the premises in repair. He did not know that the wall was in a dangerous condition and that it had, as a consequence of this, become a nuisance.

Held

❖ (CA) The defendant was liable and the court stated:

> "If, owing to want of repair, premises on a highway become dangerous and, therefore, a nuisance a passer-by or an adjoining owner suffers damage by their collapse, the occupier, or owner if he has undertaken the duty of repair, is answerable whether he knew or ought to have known of the danger or not." [1940] 1 K.B. 229.

Commentary

See also Public Nuisance (p.228).

SELECTED DEFENCES

TWENTY YEARS' PRESCRIPTION

Key Principle

The continuation of a nuisance for 20 years will, by prescription, legalise a private nuisance (but not a public one). However, it is not sufficient for the defendant to show that the activity has been carried on for 20 years; the interference must have amounted to an actionable nuisance for a period of 20 years.

> **STURGES V BRIDGMAN 1879**
> The defendant's premises adjoined those of the plaintiff, a medical practitioner. For over 20 years the noise and vibrations from the defendant's business as a confectioner had not interfered with the plaintiff's use of the land. The plaintiff then built a consulting room in the garden and complained of the noise. Prescription was pleaded as a defence.

Held

The defence failed because time ran from when the new building was erected and the nuisance had only commenced from that date. (1879) 11 Ch.D. 852.

STATUTORY AUTHORITY

Key Principle

If a statute authorises the defendant's activity the defendant will not be liable for interferences that are an inevitable result of that activity.

> **ALLEN V GULF OIL REFINING 1981**
> A private Act of Parliament authorised Gulf Oil to acquire land by compulsory purchase for the building of an oil refinery in order to facilitate the importation and refinement of crude oil and petroleum products. However, the Act contained no express authority for the use and operation of the refinery once it had been built. After the refinery had been in operation the plaintiff, living in the vicinity, alleged that it caused a nuisance by smell, noise and vibration.

Held

❖ (HL) Gulf Oil were entitled to statutory immunity in respect of any nuisance which they were able to prove was an inevitable result of constructing the refinery which conformed to the intention of Parliament. Lord Diplock commented that:

> "Parliament can hardly be supposed to have intended the refinery to be nothing more than a visual adornment to the landscape in an area of natural beauty". [1981] A.C. 101.

It should be noted that the granting of planning permission by a local authority (under its own statutory powers) does not give immunity to an action of nuisance in respect of that permission. See *Wheeler v JJ Saunders Ltd* [1996] Ch.11.

INEFFECTIVE DEFENCES

Key Principle
It is no defence that the plaintiff came to the nuisance by occupying the land adjoining it.

BLISS V HALL 1838
The plaintiff occupied a property adjoining the premises of the defendant candle-maker. The plaintiff alleged nuisance in the emission of smells and noxious vapours which resulted from the candle-making process. The defendant argued that the business has been carried on in the same premises for three years before the plaintiff came to the adjoining property.

Held
This would not defeat the plaintiff's claim. The justification for the rule is that it would be unreasonable to expect someone not to purchase land because a neighbour was abusing their rights. (1838) 4 Bing. N.C. 183.

Commentary
(1) This rule has recently been confirmed by the Court of Appeal in *Miller v Jackson* (1997) (see p.217) where Lane L.J. stated:

> "It is no answer to a claim in nuisance for the defendant to show that the plaintiff brought the trouble on his own head by building or coming to live in a house so close to the defendant's premises that he would be inevitably be affected by the defendant's activities where no one had been affected previously."

However, note Lord Denning's dissenting view on this point.

(2) It is also no defence that the defendant's activity is a useful one (see *Adams v Ursell* (1913)) nor is it a valid defence to allege and prove that the

nuisance resulted from the combined acts of different persons, even though the actions of each of them would not, taken individually, amount to a nuisance.

REMEDIES

INJUNCTION

Key Principle

An injunction is the primary remedy in an action for nuisance and its objective is to force the defendant to cease the nuisance or limit it to certain times.

> KENNAWAY V THOMPSON 1981
>
> The plaintiff had built a house by a man-made lake and was disturbed by water-skiing and speed-boat racing which the defendant club was beginning to organise. The defendants were held liable for the nuisance created by the noise but they argued that an injunction should not be granted on the ground that there was a public interest in permitting the watersports to continue. The trial judge had taken into account the public's interest in having sports facilities available to it and, exercising his discretion, awarded damages instead of an injunction.

Held

❖ (CA) The plaintiff was granted an injunction and the traditional view was reasserted: that if there is an actionable nuisance the plaintiff should win an injunction. [1981] Q.B. 88.

Commentary

The court was not prepared to give priority to the public interest and the decision in *Miller v Jackson* (see p.217) was criticised. However, the injunction granted to the plaintiff was formulated in terms which did amount to a compromise that was obviously influenced by public interest. Motor-boat racing was permitted to continue on the lake subject to the injunction restricting the number and extent of racing activities in each year and the noise level of boats using the lake at other times.

THINK POINT

An injunction is one of three remedies available to a plaintiff in nuisance: the other two being damages and a limited form of self-help known as "abatement".

PUBLIC NUISANCE

Key Principle

A public nuisance is an act or omission which materially affects the reasonable comfort and convenience of life of a class of Her Majesty's subjects (per Romer L.J.).

> ATT.-GEN. V PYA QUARRIES LTD 1957
> The defendants used a system of blasting which created dust noise and vibrations and also caused stones and splinters to project from their quarry into the neighbourhood. There were two highways and about 30 houses close to the quarry and the defendants contended that there was at most a private and not a public nuisance.

Held

❖ (CA) Any nuisance is "public" which materially affects a class of Her Majesty's subjects. The number of persons to constitute a class of the public is a question of fact in every case. [1957] 2 Q.B. 169.

Commentary

In *Wandsworth LBC v Railtrack Plc* [2001] EWCA Civ 1236, the Court of Appeal, dismissing an appeal by the defendant, Railtrack Plc, held that droppings from feral pigeons roosting under a railway bridge created a hazard over the footpath to pedestrians and constituted a public nuisance.

Key Principle

In order to succeed in an action for public nuisance a plaintiff must suffer "particular damage" over and above the damage sustained by the public generally.

Tate & Lyle Food and Distribution Ltd v GLC 1983

Ferry terminals constructed by the defendants in the River Thames caused excessive silting. This disrupted the plaintiff's business by obstructing access to their jetty and they had to spend large sums on dredging operations. Their claim in private nuisance was dismissed because: (1) the jetty itself was unaffected and (2) they had no private rights of property in the river bed.

Held

❖ (HL) It was their public right to use the river which had been damaged and their claim lay in public nuisance alone. The expenditure incurred by the plaintiffs on dredging constituted particular damage over and above the ordinary inconvenience suffered by the public at large, and was therefore recoverable. [1983] 2 A.C. 509.

Commentary

(1) The rule that a plaintiff who does not have possession or a proprietary interest in land cannot sue in private nuisance has been confirmed by the House of Lords in *Hunter* (1997) (see p.216).

(2) A danger arising from a premises adjoining the highway constitutes a public nuisance: *Wringe v Cohen* (1940) (see p.224).

The Rule in Rylands v Fletcher

13

INTRODUCTION

Although the tort in *Rylands v Fletcher* is closely related to nuisance, it differs from nuisance, in that it does not depend on the defendant being involved in a continuous activity or an ongoing state of affairs. Unlike the tort of trespass to land, *Rylands v Fletcher* does not require a direct and intentional interference. The rule in *Rylands v Fletcher* differs from the tort of negligence because there is no need for the claimant to show the existence of a duty of care or a breach of that duty.

Key Principle

"... the person who for his own purposes brings on his lands and collects and keeps there anything likely to do mischief if it escapes, must keep it in at his peril, and, if he does not do so, is prima facie answerable for all the damage which is the natural consequence of its escape." Per Blackburn J. (1866) L.R. 1 Ex. 265.

> RYLANDS V FLETCHER 1868
> The defendant mill owners employed independent contractors, who were apparently competent, to build a reservoir on their land to provide water for their mill. Beneath the site there were some disused mine shafts and passages which, unknown to the defendants, were connected to the plaintiff's mine. The contractors negligently omitted to block the old shafts and when the reservoir was filled the water burst through them and flooded the plaintiff's mine.

Held

❖ (HL) The House of Lords affirmed the decision of the Court of Exchequer Chamber that the defendants were liable but Lord Cairns rested his decision on the ground that the defendant had made a "non-natural use" of his land. (1868) L.R. 3 H.L. 330.

Commentary

There is overlap between *Rylands v Fletcher* and nuisance but the rule in *Rylands v Fletcher* is concerned with escapes from the land rather than interference with land. In *Transco v Stockport MBC* (2004) (below) the House of Lords was asked to review the application of the *Rylands* principle in modern conditions. Although the law of negligence has been greatly expanded since *Rylands* was decided and a claimant entitled to succeed under the rule would now have a claim in negligence, their Lordships rejected the abolition of the strict liability rule. The rule, stated as being an aspect of private nuisance which had stood for nearly 150 years, should not be discarded.

THINK POINT

The defendant must be in control of the dangerous thing. However, it is not necessary for the defendant to have a proprietary interest in the land from which the dangerous thing escapes. In *Rigby v Chief Constable of Northamptonshire* [1985] 1 W.L.R. 1242, when the police discharged a CS gas canister from the highway, Taylor J. commented that he could:

> "see no difference in principle between allowing a man-eating tiger to escape from your land on to that of another and allowing it to escape from the back of your wagon parked on the highway."

NON-NATURAL USE

Key Principle

Lord Cairns' requirement in *Rylands v Fletcher* of "non-natural use" has been established as part of the rule. The courts have interpreted "natural" to mean something which is ordinary and usual and "non-natural use'" is equated with extraordinary use or activity.

RICKARDS V LOTHIAN 1913

By a malicious act an unknown third party blocked a domestic water system. The water overflowed and caused damage to the plaintiff's premises on the floor below.

Held ....

❖ (PC) There was no liability under *Rylands v Fletcher* because the supply of water via normal domestic installations was a natural use of land. [1913] A.C. 263.

Commentary ....

Lord Moulton defined non-natural use as "some special use bringing with it increased danger to others." In *Read v Lyons* (1947) (see p.235) it was argued that operating a munitions factory in wartime is a natural use of land. Lord Porter said that in deciding the question of non-natural use:

> "all the circumstances of time and practice of mankind must be taken into consideration so that what may be regarded as dangerous or non-natural may vary according to the circumstances."

For example, in *Musgrove v Pandelis* [1919] 2 K.B. 43, it was held that keeping a car in a garage with a full tank of petrol was a non-natural use.

THINK POINT

....

The word "dangerous" is not interpreted literally and there is no requirement that the thing which escapes must be dangerous. Plainly dangerous things such as explosives and gas come within *Rylands v Fletcher* but the rule has also applied to a "chair-o-plane" in a fairground, *Hale v Jennings Bros* [1938] 1 All E.R. 579, and, in *Att.-Gen. v Corke* [1933] Ch. 89, it even applied to gypsies!

....

Key Principle ....

A non-natural use of land will be demonstrated where the defendant's means of storing and manufacturing the substance involves a very real risk that a fire would spread to adjoining premises.

LMS INTERNATIONAL LTD v STYRENE PACKAGING & INSULATION LTD 2005
The defendant manufactured polystyrene. As the product was being cut a spark accidentally caused large quantities of flammable polystyrene blocks to catch fire. The fire spread to the claimant's neighbouring premises.

Held

The use of land was said to be non-natural and the defendants were liable under *Rylands v Fletcher*. The defendant's means of storing and manufacturing the product "involved a very real risk" that a fire would spread to adjoining premises. [2005] EWHC 2065.

Commentary

(1) The court referred to *Mason v Levy Auto Parts of England Ltd* [1967] 2 Q.B. 530 where the defendants were liable when large quantities of combustible materials stored on their land inexplicably caught fire. The kinds of factors which led the judge to find there had been a non-natural use were the kinds of factor which would also have to be considered in an action for negligence.

(2) There seems to be a similarity between the way in which the concept of non-natural use is generally applied by the courts and the idea of unreasonable risk in negligence.

THINK POINT

In *British Celanese v Hunt* (1969) (see p.214) when the plaintiffs alleged that the metal strips had escaped and caused the power failure, the liability did not arise under *Rylands v Fletcher* on the ground that the manufacture of electrical components on an industrial estate was not a non-natural use of land, as that was the very purpose for which the land was designed. But in *Cambridge Water Co v Eastern Counties Leather Plc* (1994) (see p.235) the House of Lords held that storage of substantial quantities of chemicals on industrial premises is an almost classical case of non-natural use, even in an industrial estate.

Key Principle

The provision of a water supply through a service pipe carrying water from the mains to a block of flats on the council's land, is an ordinary use of land under the principles in *Rylands v Fletcher*.

TRANSCO V STOCKPORT MBC 2004

The council was the owner of a tower block of flats and an adjacent embankment. A large water pipe serving the flats leaked and water escaped into the embankment and caused it to collapse. As a result, a high pressure gas main was left exposed and the claimants sought recovery of the substantial costs spent in taking action to prevent the pipe fracturing. The trial judge held the council liable, finding that its use was not an ordinary use of land. The Court of Appeal overturned this ruling and held that the provision of a water supply through a service pipe to a block of flats is an ordinary use of land.

Held

The House of Lords agreed with the Court of Appeal and held that the piping of a water supply, a routine function which could not be seen as creating any special hazard, was an ordinary use of the council's land. [2003] UKHL 61.

Commentary

The conditions to be met before strict liability is imposed for "non-natural" use will not be easily satisfied unless the defendant's use of land is shown to have been extraordinary and unusual and creating a special hazard.

Key Principle

The rule in *Rylands v Fletcher* applies to things which the defendant deliberately accumulates on the land: it does not apply to things which are naturally on the land.

GILES V WALKER 1890

When the occupier ploughed up forest land a large crop of thistles sprang up and the seeds were blown on to the neighbouring land.

Held

The defendant was not liable because the danger was not caused by the defendant's intervention but was the product of natural forces. (1890) 24 Q.B.D. 656.

THINK POINT

Leakey v National Trust there may now be liability in nuisance or negligence in circumstances such as these.

ESCAPE

For the rule to apply there must be an "escape" from the defendant's premises.

> READ V J LYONS & CO LTD 1947
> The plaintiff was employed as an inspector in the defendant's munitions factory. In the course of her employment she was injured by the explosion of a shell that was being manufactured on the premises. There was no allegation of negligence on the part of the employers.

Held

❖ (HL) As there had been no "escape" of the thing that inflicted the injury *Rylands v Fletcher* was inapplicable, and in the absence of negligence the plaintiff's claim failed. [1947] A.C. 156.

Commentary

Note *Transco* (above) where the House of Lords held there had been no "escape" when the water which leaked from the council's service pipe remained on its land.

DAMAGE

Key Principle

Foreseeability of damage of the relevant type should now be regarded as a prerequisite of liability in damages under the rule in *Rylands v Fletcher*.

> CAMBRIDGE WATER CO V EASTERN COUNTIES LEATHER PLC 1994
> The defendants, an old established leather manufacturer, used a chemical solvent PCE in their tanning process. PCE evaporates quickly in the air but is not readily soluble in water. In the course of the process, before a change of method in 1976, continual small spillages had gradually built up a pool of PCE under their premises. The solvent seeped into the soil below and contaminated the aquifer from which the plaintiffs drew their water. At first instance the claim in *Rylands v Fletcher* was dismissed because it was held that there was no non-natural user of the land. The nuisance action failed because at the time the contamination was taking place it was not foreseen that the quantities of the chemical would accumulate or that if it did, there would be any significant damage.

Held

❖ (HL) The claims in negligence and nuisance failed for lack of foreseeability. The action in *Rylands v Fletcher* also failed because the defendants had not known, and could not reasonably have foreseen, that the seepage would cause the pollution. [1994] 2 W.L.R. 53.

Key Principle

Dispute existed about whether a claimant needed to have an interest in land in order to maintain an action under *Rylands v Fletcher* but a non-occupier has succeeded in respect of damage to property.

> HALSEY V ESSO PETROLEUM CO LTD 1961
>
> The defendants operated an oil-distributing depot near to the plaintiff's house in a partly residential area in Fulham. The depot operated day and night and the plaintiff complained of the following:
>
> (i) acid smuts from a boiler in the depot which damaged the plaintiff's washing;
>
> (ii) the same smuts which caused damage to his car standing on the road outside;
>
> (iii) a smell escaping from the depot which was nauseating but caused no damage to health;
>
> (iv) noise from lorries in the depot; and
>
> (v) noise from tankers on the road outside leaving and arriving throughout the day and night.

Held

There was liability under (i) for nuisance and *Rylands v Fletcher* and under (ii) there was liability under *Rylands v Fletcher* and in public nuisance. [1961] 1 W.L.R. 683.

Commentary

(1) There was also liability for (i) and (iv) in private nuisance. Liability was based on private nuisance or in the alternative in public nuisance by virtue of the defendants' use of the highway. The character of the neighbourhood was also relevant to the question of nuisance by smell and by noise. This case provides a useful illustration of the application of public and private nuisance and the rule in *Rylands v Fletcher*.

(2) In *Read v Lyons* (1947) (see p.235) it was said obiter that the plaintiff must be an occupier in order to maintain an action under the rule in *Rylands v Fletcher* and in *Weller & Co v Foot & Mouth Disease Research Institute* [1966] 1 Q.B. 569 it was held that the plaintiffs could not succeed under the rule

because they did not have an interest in land affected by the escape. In *Transco*, the House of Lords has reaffirmed the approach taken in *Cambridge Water* (above) that only those with rights over land may sue under *Rylands v Fletcher*.

THINK POINT

Claims for personal injury under the rule have been admitted in the past. In *Hale v Jennings Bros* (above), where a chair became detached from a "chair-o-plane" in a fairground and a stallholder suffered personal injuries as a result of the "escape" recovery for personal injury was allowed. [1938] 1 All E.R. 579. In *Read v Lyons* (see p.235) doubts were raised about whether the rule in *Rylands v Fletcher* could be used in a claim for personal injury and in *Hunter v London Dock-lands Development Corp* it was held that personal injuries are not, per se, recoverable. In *Transco*, Lord Hoffman expressed the view that damages for personal injuries are not recoverable under *Rylands v Fletcher*.

DEFENCES

Liability under *Rylands v Fletcher* is strict but it is not absolute. There will be no liability where the plaintiff has consented to the accumulation, unless the defendant had been negligent in causing the escape, nor will the defendant be liable where the damage is caused by the plaintiff's own act. Statutory authority is a defence (as in *Allen v Gulf Oil*) and the defence of necessity is also available.

ACT OF A STRANGER

PERRY V KENDRICKS TRANSPORT 1956

The defendants parked a coach in their vehicle park which was bordered by some waste land. The petrol tank had been drained but an unknown person had removed the cap. A boy of about 10 threw a lighted match into the petrol tank which exploded causing the child plaintiff, who was crossing the wasteland at the time, to be badly burned.

Held

❖ (CA) The defendants were not liable as the explosion was caused by the act of a stranger over whom they had no control. [1956] 1 All E.R. 154.

Commentary

This principle applied in *Rickards v Lothian* (1913) (see p.231).

ACT OF GOD

Key Principle

The defendant is not liable where the escape is caused by natural forces in circumstances "which no human foresight can provide against, and of which human prudence is not bound to recognise the possibility."

> NICHOLS V MARSLAND 1876
>
> The defendant had artificial ornamental lakes on his land which were formed by damming up a natural stream. Following a thunderstorm there was an unprecedented rainfall which caused the banks of the ornamental lake to burst and destroy bridges on the plaintiff's land.

Held

The defendant was not liable. There was found to be no negligence because the flooding was caused by an act of God. (1876) 2 Ex. D.I.

Commentary

On very similar facts, in *Greenock Corp v Caledonian Railway* [1917] A.C. 556 the application of this defence was criticised by the House of Lords. The rainfall was found not to be an act of God and the Corporation was held to be under a duty to make sure that owners or occupiers on a lower ground level are as secure against injury as they would have been had nature not been interfered with.

Index